Inequality in America

Dilemmas in American Politics

Series Editor: **Craig A. Rimmerman**, *Hobart and William Smith Colleges*

If the answers to the problems facing US democracy were easy, politicians would solve them, accept credit, and move on. But certain dilemmas have confronted the American political system continuously. They defy solution; they are endemic to the system. Some can best be described as institutional dilemmas: How can the Congress be both a representative body and a national decision-maker? How can the president communicate with more than 250 million citizens effectively? Why do we have a two-party system when many voters are disappointed with the choices presented to them? Others are policy dilemmas: How do we find compromises on issues that defy compromise, such as abortion policy? How do we incorporate racial and ethnic minorities or immigrant groups into American society, allowing them to reap the benefits of this land without losing their identity? How do we fund health care for our poorest or oldest citizens?

Dilemmas such as these are what propel students toward an interest in the study of US government. Each book in the *Dilemmas in American Politics Series* addresses a "real world" problem, raising the issues that are of most concern to students. Each is structured to cover the historical and theoretical aspects of the dilemma but also to explore the dilemma from a practical point of view and to speculate about the future. The books are designed as supplements to introductory courses in American politics or as case studies to be used in upper-level courses. The link among them is the desire to make the real issues confronting the political world come alive in students' eyes.

BOOKS IN THIS SERIES

Inequality in America

Race, Poverty, and Fulfilling Democracy's Promise

SECOND EDITION

Stephen M. Caliendo

North Central College

WESTVIEW PRESS

Westview Press
Hachette Book Group
1290 Avenue of the Americas
New York, NY 10104

www.westviewpress.com

Printed in the United States of America
Second Edition: July 2017

Published by Westview Press, an imprint of Perseus Books, LLC, a subsidiary of Hachette Book Group, Inc.

The publisher is not responsible for websites (or their content) that are not owned by the publisher.

Library of Congress Cataloging-in-Publication Data has been applied for.

ISBNs: 978-0-8133-5053-0 (paperback), 978-0-8133-5071-4 (ebook)

LSC-C

10 9 8 7 6 5 4 3 2 1

For Jillian

Contents

Introduction   1

1 *Representation and the Roots of Inequality*   17

9 *Affirmative Action* **185**

Conclusion: The Space Between Power and Powerlessness **203**

Illustrations

Feature Boxes

Acknowledgments

When I first set out to write a concise story about racial and economic inequality in the United States, both historical and contemporary, I foresaw the challenges that would come with distilling so much information into a relatively short book. As I began the process, it struck me how deeply indebted I am to the scholars, activists, and journalists who supplied me with information (directly and indirectly). Political scientists, sociologists, anthropologists, criminal justice scholars, geographers, nutritionists, physicians, critical theorists, and education scholars have conducted rigorous empirical studies and laid the theoretical foundations that have advanced the state of knowledge in areas related to these issues.

I am also thankful for the extensive social network connections that I have developed over the years. Through my presence on Facebook and Twitter, in particular, as well as interactions through the Facebook page and Twitter feed that I maintain with my collaborator, Dr. Charlton McIlwain at New York University, under the auspices of the Project on Race in Political Communication, I became aware of a number of helpful articles, books, and data sources. Since the first edition was published, the book's Facebook page (http://www.facebook.com/InequalityWestview/) has been a valuable resource for compiling and sharing studies and news stories related to racial, economic, and gender inequality on a daily basis, serving as a live update to the content in this book. I learn much from the posts that are shared to that page, and I hope that you, as a reader, will "like" the page so that items of interest to you continue to populate your feed and stimulate your thinking about these issues.

My work on the first edition was supported by a grant from the North Central College Faculty Professional Development Committee, a portion of which supplied stipends to members of my dedicated team of undergraduate research assistants for that initial offering: Christopher Bilbro, David Depino, Jaclyn French, Emily Goodfellow, Collin Kee, Nicholas Lopez, Ingeborg Moran, Tanvi Potdukhe, Will Robinson, Pooja Sahai, Meghan Steinbeiss, Carley Timmerman, and, in particular, Kendall Bilbro,

Ricky Brown, and Liz Hasseld. Besides conducting research and document retrieval, they each read the manuscript carefully and provided a student's perspective, which I greatly appreciate.

For the second edition, I benefitted from a highly energetic and generous volunteer team of undergraduate research assistants at North Central College. Alexandra Dominguez, Laura Edmunds, Alexander Pabon, Carlitos Rangel, Zöe White, led by senior assistant Josephine Madrawska, all contributed valuable feedback and new content to help make the book current. I have also received input from professors from across the nation who have assigned the book in their courses—political science, English, communication, social work, and interdisciplinary studies among them—or otherwise provided guidance. I wish to extend my gratitude to Dr. Jennifer Jackson, Dr. Gregory Lynch, Professor Tom Cavenagh, and Dr. Richard Guzman at North Central College; Dr. Tomeka Robinson and Dr. Philip Dalton at Hofstra University; Dr. Andra Gillespie at Emory University, and Dr. Nadia Brown, Dr. Rosalee Clawson, and Dr. Keith Shimko at Purdue University. Their influence runs throughout this volume, and the book is stronger as a result. My professional network continues to grow and inspire me. In particular, I am indebted to the National Conference of Black Political Scientists, whose members are honest yet supportive, welcoming, and brilliant. It is impossible for me to approximate how much my interactions with NCOBPS members and attendance at the annual meeting affect my thinking, research, and writing.

I wish to thank my patient and encouraging editor, Ada Fung, for years of guidance and, indeed, friendship. I would also like to thank Michael Clark, project editor, and Iris Bass, copyeditor, for their hard work on this book. I am grateful to *Dilemmas in American Politics* series editor, Dr. Craig Rimmerman, for his constant support over the years. I'd like to thank the reviewers of the first edition, including: Keona K. Ervin (University of Missouri); Dorisa Slaughter (Bluegrass Community College); Vanessa Hunn (Northern Kentucky University); S. Michael Gaddis (Pennsylvania State University); Jennifer J. Savage (Jacksonville State University); Patience Togo Malm (St. Cloud State University); Julie A. Zaloudek (University of Wisconsin-Stout) and others who wished to remain anonymous. Their feedback was extremely helpful to me as I prepared the new edition. I have incorporated much of what they suggested, and the manuscript is stronger as a result. Any inadequacies that remain are my own.

Finally, I remain indebted to my family for their continuing love and devotion. My wife, Jillian, is a constant source of inspiration, pushing my thinking on these issues and challenging me to consider multiple perspectives. My oldest daughter, Amelia, has always been patient and willing to help with her younger twin siblings, Gianni and Stella, even more than usual when I was not present (physically or mentally) as a result of my work. I am truly fortunate to have so many wonderful friends, family members, students, and colleagues in my life. Those blessings have made this book possible.

Introduction

When Mexico sends its people, they're not sending their best. . . . They're sending people that have lots of problems, and they're bringing those problems with us. They're bringing drugs. They're bringing crime. They're rapists. And some, I assume, are good people.[1]

—Donald J. Trump, June 16, 2015

I think implicit bias is a problem for everyone, not just police. I think, unfortunately, too many of us in our great country jump to conclusions about each other.[2]

—Hillary Rodham Clinton, September 26, 2016

[W]hen you're white, you don't know what it's like to be living in a ghetto. You don't know what it's like to be poor. You don't know what it's like to be hassled when you walk down the street or you get dragged out of a car. And I believe that as a nation in the year 2016, we must be firm in making it clear. We will end institutional racism and reform a broken criminal justice system.[3]

—Bernie Sanders, March 6, 2016

THE MEN WHO DESIGNED THE US SYSTEM OF GOVERNMENT IN THE latter part of the eighteenth century present a frustrating paradox to current students of American politics. The Founding Fathers brilliantly devised a structure of government that would last, relatively unchanged, for well over two hundred years (and counting). They were deeply flawed, however, with respect to their inability to reconcile the sweeping promises

1

they articulated in the founding documents with the reality of widespread and brutal inequality that characterized the nation at that time. We celebrate the Founding Fathers by honoring their birthdays, displaying them on our currency, and studying them in our classrooms. But we need to qualify our admiration because their personal lives and public actions did not fully reflect their rhetoric and broader beliefs. In short, American democracy is at once vibrant because of their vision and imperfect because of their blind spots.

If we are interested in improving American democracy—in making "a more perfect union," as then senator Barack Obama said in his popular 2008 speech on race in America[4]—we are wise to redirect our attention from the individuals who designed the system and occupied key positions in it, to the *system* itself—the key assertion of this book. We will seek to understand how individual actors (both ordinary citizens and political elites) operate within a system that has largely constrained attempts to rectify what many recognize as injustices.

Inequality in America comes in multiple forms, though this volume focuses primarily on two: poverty and racism. But as we will see, it is impossible to disentangle other types of inequality from issues related to race and economics. Although I do not specifically address inequality related to sexual orientation or physical ability, for example, these factors (and more) are very real and meaningful challenges that affect millions of Americans on a daily basis. While I recognize the interaction among these forces at certain points and address gender in Chapter 8, I mostly focus on the distinct and interrelated elements of race and poverty and the intricacies of the legacy of inequality that has come to characterize American government and politics in its first two centuries.

Poverty and the Myth of Meritocracy

On the surface, understanding poverty appears simple: some have the financial resources they need, and some do not. If we want to understand how one of the wealthiest nations in the world can also be home to so much poverty, however, we need to examine the assumptions that accompany the realities of statistics about poverty. These assumptions help explain why ordinary Americans (the vast majority of whom are not wealthy) are willing to tolerate the existence of widespread income and wealth inequality, as well as abject poverty.

In August 2011, broadcaster Tavis Smiley and scholar Cornel West launched an eighteen-city "poverty tour" to call attention to these issues. The tour culminated in the publication of a book, *The Rich and the Rest of Us*,[5] in which the authors lay out a vision for understanding poverty in a more complete (and complicated) way. Subtitled "A Poverty Manifesto," their book serves as a call to action. They ask Americans to eschew the "lies about poverty that America can no longer afford" (e.g., that poverty is a character flaw, that minorities receive the bulk of government entitlements, and that poverty is uniquely urban),[6] and they advocate for public policies that are designed to lead to economic justice. Their work is powerful because it taps into Americans' shared core values, such as egalitarianism and justice. But other core values, such as individualism, are harder to reconcile with policies that promote economic redistribution. Together, we will explore the spaces where there is commonality and the areas where there is friction between liberals and conservatives, Democrats and Republicans on issues relating to racial and economic inequality.

Residing at the core of these differences is the notion of meritocracy, the belief that those who have success earned it while those who do not, did not.[7] Few would deny that Americans start out life with an unequal chance of financial success. But understanding how injustice is perpetuated requires an understanding of how inequality at birth often manifests in a lifetime of advantage or disadvantage.

In November 2010, Meghan McCain,[8] a noted blogger and daughter of longtime US senator (and 2008 Republican nominee for president) John McCain, used her space on *The Daily Beast* blog to criticize former Alaska governor (and 2008 Republican vice presidential nominee) Sarah Palin for calling the Bush family "blue bloods" (a reference to their upper-class status). McCain, who considers herself a Republican, charged that such divisiveness within the party was counterproductive. But her response illustrates some core assumptions that most Americans hold about social class in the United States. In her blog entry, McCain ignores institutional factors that constrain poor Americans' chances of becoming blue bloods while enabling the children of wealthy Americans to follow in their parents' footsteps. She writes:

> I actually had to Google what the meaning of "blue bloods" was, although I could surmise that it was some kind of knock against education and coming from a family of some success. Yes, in essence that is what this statement

meant. Families that work hard and achieve a long line of successful people are "blue bloods" and thus, [Palin] implied the opinions of said people are jaded and elitist, even if that family lineage has a long history of public service and leadership within [the] Republican Party.

As McCain admits later in the piece, she reacted to Palin's accusation personally because she grew up with tremendous privilege. Rather than recognizing that her privilege was unearned (it was a function of her parents' success, not her own work), she dismisses Palin's comment as inappropriate because "blue bloods" is a derogatory term for "families that work hard and achieve a long line of successful people." Here McCain invokes the myth of meritocracy; she believes that hard work leads to economic success (often through education), and she incorrectly (and perhaps unintentionally) suggests that each generation starts from scratch in its achievements.[9] It is certainly possible that members of each generation of a privileged family work hard in their own right, but the lack of recognition of the head start that subsequent generations have (compared to those who begin life in poverty) is startling. Further, it reflects our collective socialization that urges us to accept the legitimacy of the American political and economic systems. We are taught to believe that those who are financially successful (as well as those who have access to excellent educational institutions) are fully deserving of that privilege, whereas those who are not must have acted badly at some point and, therefore, deserve their poverty. As we will see, however, such a generalization is unfair and harmful because it obscures systemic factors that contribute to poverty (and wealth) so as to rectify injustice.

This dynamic was very clearly at work in the 2016 presidential campaign, as millions of poor, primarily white, voters from rural areas of the country put their trust in billionaire real estate mogul and reality television star Donald Trump. On the surface, it should seem curious that millions of working-class Americans would throw their support behind a person who has never struggled economically a day in his life. There are no easy explanations, but one element is that Mr. Trump represented for millions of Americans a pushback against the cultural elite. That is, even though he is wealthy, he spoke to workers, has created jobs for workers, and openly criticized political correctness and other aspects of a cosmopolitan America that many find offensive.[10] His opponent, Hillary Clinton, embodied that elite class; though she was raised of modest means in a Chicago suburb, most of her adult life was spent in the public sphere. By the time she ran for president, she epitomized "establishment" politics, and the alternative was alluring. As we will discover in the following pages, social class is more than income or wealth. Although it is rooted in economic stability, class encompasses a set of norms that involve many aspects of everyday life, from clothing to love to the value of education, and even the way we use and appreciate humor.[11] Wealthy as he is, rural, white Americans[12] found in Donald Trump a fellow American who shared their values and understood their struggles. He promised to help reestablish the American middle class, and they were willing to give him a chance.

Despite our national folklore, America does indeed have a class system that affects individuals' ability to achieve the American Dream. While it is not an officially designated system with titles (such as in Great Britain)[13] or a rigid caste system (such as in India),[14] Americans clearly recognize differences based on economic circumstances and customs that serve to organize society. Class structure in the United States is disproportionately (though not solely) based on wealth.[15] For that reason, we will address the concept of poverty as opposed to the broader concept of class. Economic and racial inequality will be our primary focus; we will explore the reasons that they exist and the myriad paths to reduce such inequality.

Irrespective of class designations—most Americans believe themselves to be in the middle class,[16] so such labels may carry little useful meaning—we will see that the data characterizing the distribution of income and wealth in the United States clearly reveal a large gap between the rich and the poor. That gap has been growing rapidly over the past thirty years, and, as we will see in Chapter 2, the number of Americans who reside in the middle is shrinking.

This notion of class differences came into sharp focus late in the summer of 2011 when the Occupy Wall Street (OWS or Occupy) movement was born with the launch of a website (OccupyWallStreet.org[17]) and a social media campaign, calling attention to the historically high and expanding degree of economic inequality in the United States. Protests began in Lower Manhattan on September 17, 2011, and rallies and demonstrations quickly spread to other cities in the United States and around the globe. The Occupy slogan, "We Are the 99 Percent," refers to the dramatic accumulation of wealth by the top 1 percent of Americans (see Chapter 2).

The mantle was carried even more visibly in the 2016 presidential election, as US senator Bernie Sanders of Vermont ran a strong campaign for the Democratic nomination rooted in the call to rectify economic inequality. Both Occupy and the Sanders campaign were successful in calling attention to an issue that was largely ignored by the media (and thus most of the American public) for nearly fifty years. As a result of Occupy, the 2012 presidential candidates were forced to address the issue, and America became positioned for a frank discussion about whether such trends are consistent with our fundamental shared values. Energized by the relative success of the Sanders campaign (he lost the nomination to Hillary Clinton, but not before winning twenty-one states and Puerto Rico[18]), young Americans in particular appear eager to continue the discussion and find unique ways to create meaningful change to bring about greater economic justice.

Given our history, we cannot consider these economic factors without also considering race. Race and poverty are not interchangeable demographic markers in the United States: there are wealthy people of color, and there are poor whites. However, poverty is disproportionately African American and Hispanic/Latino* in America, and issues that uniquely face persons of color are often present irrespective of economic success.

Racial and Economic Inequality
Through the Lens of Political Science

The first half of the twenty-first century marks a critical period in the racial history of the United States. By many projections, persons who identify as white[19] will become a numerical minority in the next few decades.[20] Barack Obama's election to the presidency in 2008 marked a milestone that just a generation earlier many Americans never expected they would see. Yet the racial tension that surfaced in the shadow of that election, including during his reelection campaign in 2012,[21] increased awareness of police brutality against African American men (which spawned the Black Lives Matter movement[22]) and led to Donald Trump's campaign in 2016,[23] serving as a sober reminder that America's deep racial divisions persist.

---

*The terms "Hispanic" and "Latino" are distinct. The former refers to a category of individuals characterized by a common language root, while the latter refers to individuals whose nation of origin is Latin America (which includes languages other than Spanish). Where there is a clear distinction, the terms will be used purposefully in this book. At other times, they are used somewhat interchangeably.

In the days after the 2008 presidential election, the term *postracial* entered the public sphere in a meaningful way. With an image of civil rights legend Jesse Jackson weeping openly in Chicago's Grant Park while the newly elected president gave his acceptance speech as a cultural backdrop, many Americans—white Americans in particular—believed that the history of racial oppression had come to a dramatic close. After all, the most powerful person in the nation was African American. Those who had been skeptical of racism's legacy in the first place believed that the event was simply a bright marker of what they had been saying for decades—racism ended in the 1960s when Jim Crow segregation was abolished legally. On the other hand, those who recognized that racism was more than racial animosity took comfort in the symbolism, if only momentarily.

The belief that America is characterized by a postracial identity dramatically cuts against the lived experiences of generations of persons of color in America. America's poorest and most economically vulnerable citizens are still distinctly black (African American) and brown (Latino and Hispanic). Further, inequality between middle- and upper-class whites and those who hover near the poverty line has increased dramatically in the past generation, suggesting the existence of "two Americas"[24] with little evidence of inequality being reversed in the near future. This book documents that inequality through the lens of political science. We will examine racial and economic inequality with particular attention to how public policy and power dynamics in America are influenced by—and perpetuate—disparities in income and wealth, housing, education, crime, immigration, employment opportunities, and health. The reasons for this inequality are complicated, but answers on the political left and right often center on "common sense" or other simplistic frameworks. Potential solutions, however, require a sophisticated understanding of the systems and institutional constraints that set parameters for the attitudes and behaviors of the mass public and political elites alike. In the following chapters, we will explore this complexity with an eye to the achievement of increased equality.

Striving for more equality is not a value-neutral proposition. Equality is a core value for Americans, but that does not mean we are unified with respect to what it means or how to achieve it. In considering this dynamic, it is helpful to think about the difference between objectivity and neutrality.

Scholars and journalists both strive for objectivity—the conscious effort to be attentive to one's biases when analyzing a situation. But in

many ways, this goal can never be fully realized. Striving toward neutrality, however, particularly with respect to inequality, is undesirable. Few
of us would approach this book with the attitude "Equality—I can take it
or leave it." To the contrary, this subject tends to inflame passions. Many
Americans have risked and indeed have given their lives in the name of
social justice. The friction, as we will see, most often arises when we consider what equality looks like and, if we decide that we have fallen short of
achieving it, how to remedy that failure.

This book, like all books, is not without bias because this author, like
everyone else, is not without bias. The first lesson of politics is to acknowledge that we all have lived experiences and ideas that shape not only who
we are but how we view the world. This unique perspective (or bias) is a
natural part of discussing issues of public concern. Bias is not problematic; ignoring or (worse) refusing to acknowledge bias is both dangerous
and unproductive. The key is to be as reflective and transparent about that
bias as possible and to work toward minimizing the effects of our precon-
ceptions as we seek to learn and grow.

The baseline assumption in this discussion is twofold: (1) there is racial
and economic inequality in America, and (2) inequality is inconsistent
with the tenets of democracy that undergird our nation's founding principles. There are legitimate arguments against these premises. For instance,
some would argue that inequality is not structural or related to race—
that individuals of all races and ethnicities have, can, and do succeed in
America, and that the values of hard work and persistence adequately explain economic discrepancies. By this logic, if poverty is disproportionately of color in America, it must be either biologically rooted or the result
of a culture within African American and Hispanic/Latino communities
that encourages laziness, criminality, drug use, and other destructive behaviors. Those who subscribe to such a perspective have no interest in
resolving inequality through political channels because they do not perceive the problem as being systemic in nature. For them, this book will
be irrelevant. I start from the position that poverty is neither biologically
determined nor a result of cultural or behavioral choices. To the contrary, America's history of structural, persistent, and infectious racism has
served as bedrock for inequality for the past four hundred years.[25]

Both left and right in American politics broadly acknowledge this assertion, and solutions are proposed from across the ideological spectrum.
As will become clear throughout this book, leaders and interest groups

from both liberal/progressive and conservative traditions wish to rectify this historic oppression, though they approach it in very different ways. While neutrality is not a goal in these pages, some degree of partisan and ideological balance is appropriate. Accordingly, efforts toward greater racial and economic equality proposed by individuals from a variety of perspectives are highlighted. Each reader will decide which approaches seem the most feasible or desirable, but meaningful movement toward a more socially just nation will incorporate a wide variety of ideas.

This book contains both liberal and conservative biases—a position that is increasingly difficult to find in our ideologically stratified public discourse. It is liberal in the sense that it recognizes that inequality has existed on a mass scale in the United States throughout its history, is systemic, and contradicts the underlying core values of the nation as a whole. It is conservative in the sense that it issues no explicit call for radical change to address those injustices. Assumptions about the legitimacy of American governmental institutions and norms go largely unaddressed throughout the book. The message is that there are multiple ways to address inequality, and none should be dismissed because it does not coincide with our personal political beliefs. If we are to ever fulfill America's promise, we must do so in an intellectually collaborative way. The examples in this book strive to model that assertion.

Defining Inequality

It is important to consider what *inequality* means in this context. The relationship between race (and ethnicity) and economic inequality forms the core concern of this text. In a capitalist system, some individuals will acquire, accumulate, or otherwise possess more wealth than others. Accordingly, reducing inequality does not entail allotting the same amount of possessions, money, and debt to each individual. Rather, it refers to the dramatic (and increasing) gap between the wealthiest and poorest Americans, and the disproportionate levels of poverty (and its corresponding characteristics, such as incarceration, illiteracy, health disparities, etc.) in communities of color.

By a number of measures (explained in detail in Chapter 2), the gap between those who have been able to earn money and accumulate wealth and those who struggle to make ends meet has increased dramatically. Part of America's political culture, dating back to the nation's founding, involves a belief in rugged individualism. We herald the person who achieves financial success without coming from a wealthy family. While few could find fault in such a sentiment, the other side of that coin features a lack of compassion for impoverished Americans.

To many Americans, poverty is an abstract concept that refers to others. Most do not believe themselves to be poor,[26] even those who might be considered so by objective measures.[27] Racism—another prominent symptom of "othering" in American culture—is a central (though not sole) culprit in the continued existence of inequality, but perhaps not in the way that is often suggested. Scholars who study race reserve the term *racism* for systemic elements that perpetuate white privilege and power. To understand what this means (and how it works), let us consider it alongside the related concepts of bigotry and prejudice.

All three of these terms—*racism, bigotry,* and *prejudice*—relate to psychological elements of Americans' daily lives, but racism also refers to the ways that institutions, culture, and social systems reflect the historic oppression of persons of color in America and perpetuate inequality as a result. As will become clear in the following pages, decisions that were made at the time of the nation's founding, as well as those made since, have contributed to the construction of a complex system that was originally designed purposefully to disadvantage African Americans and Native Americans. Although much of our collective conscious–level attitudes about racial equality have progressed, this system continues to operate in ways that privilege whites and disadvantage persons of color. This is what scholars refer to as systemic racism, institutional racism, structural racism, or simply racism.

In colloquial use, however, *racism* or *racist* is used to refer to overt and often hostile race-based animosity that resides at the level of individual citizens (rather than systems). Scholars refer to this as racial bigotry.[28] Race-based bigotry can move in all directions. Whereas racism has a clear component of systemic power and therefore can only work to advantage whites, individual-level bigotry can include hostility toward persons of a race different from one's own. For example, if an African American supervisor continually berates or disadvantages white employees compared to black employees, we might say that he or she is bigoted. If an Asian American person has disdain for Latinos, that is bigotry (and is likely rooted in racism because of deeply held negative predispositions about Latinos). If a white person is a member of the Ku Klux Klan, he or she is a bigot. In short, what we generally call racist is more precisely defined as racial bigotry.

Bigotry is usually explicit, but prejudice often is not. It can be embarrassing to realize that we have biases related to race, ethnicity, gender, or anything else, but most of us can recall a time when such prejudices surfaced. Paul Haggis's Academy Award–winning film *Crash* dramatically demonstrates this construct.[29] When we are stressed, scared, deprived of sleep, or otherwise in a position to have our social filters compromised, these deep-seated associations can surface. Consider the frustration we often experience when we encounter a poor driver. Attributing the tendency to drive poorly to a person's gender or race (or any characteristic that is different from our own) but not in others (when the person looks like us) reveals a subconscious bias, or prejudice.[30]

Another way to think about the difference between prejudice and bigotry is considering how we react to racist jokes. If we tell racist jokes or if we laugh when we hear them, we are bigoted. However, simply understanding why the joke might be considered funny reveals prejudice—even if we consciously resist manifesting that prejudice in our behavior. If a joke about Italian Americans contained a punch line that centered on intoxication, most folks would not get the joke because there is no stereotype about Italians drinking heavily. If, however, the same joke centered on Irish Americans, for whom that stereotype exists, most would recognize its humor (revealing prejudicial beliefs) even if they did not laugh (which would reveal bigotry).

In other words, most of this sort of prejudice lies beyond our consciousness. There is a rich (and growing) body of scholarly literature dedicated to exploring the related concepts of implicit association[31] and symbolic racism.[32] As far back as the 1970s, researchers were conceptualizing and working on ways to measure (through sophisticated survey questions) subconscious prejudicial attitudes. More recently, the Project Implicit researchers at Harvard University[33] have demonstrated that most individuals hold subconscious associations about members of racial and ethnic groups (as well as groups based on other characteristics).[34] Research involving physiological indicators promises to reveal even more about these latent prejudices.[35] Experimenters have been busy measuring brain activity, heart rate, sweat on participants' palms, and a host of other variables to determine how race-based stimuli affect the body, and what those reactions may tell us about deeply held biases.

Racism is related to both implicit and explicit prejudice, and all three relate to the persistence of inequality in America. Few would disagree with the assertion that America was founded on racist principles. The superiority of Europeans over Native Americans and Africans was assumed in the nation's earliest years, and the defining document—the Constitution— explicitly dehumanizes African Americans and excludes Native Americans from considerations of representation.[36] The Fourteenth Amendment reversed the Three-Fifths Compromise relating to African Americans, and subsequent laws and court rulings have reflected (and contributed to) the progressive shift in racial attitudes, but the structures relating to economics and opportunity have shifted much more slowly. This has resulted in a cycle of perception and reality that has been difficult to interrupt. For example, as explained in Chapter 5, incarceration rates for Latinos and African Americans are disproportionately higher than for whites, leading to a perception that members of those groups are predisposed to criminality. The reality, of course, is much more complicated. Incarceration rates do not necessarily reflect actual rates of crimes committed (or even arrests). Further, street crime is related to poverty, which is related to economic opportunity, which is related to educational access, which is related to housing, which is related to income and wealth, which is related to race and ethnicity.

This is why the term *racism* as commonly used today is counterproductive to finding real solutions to racial and economic inequality. Calling someone a racist inevitably leads to a denial (e.g., "I don't use the n-word" or "I have black friends").[37] Because most Americans are not bigoted, and because whites are particularly sensitive to accusations of racism, this exchange leads to a dead end with respect to the role that race continues to play in American political culture. Whites tend to believe that racism is either (1) a thing of the past or (2) something that is a problem for overt bigots. This inability to deal honestly with race and inequality is a significant barrier to the political solutions necessary to move forward.

Hegemony and Intersectionality

The concept of cultural hegemony refers to a largely invisible, overarching set of assumptions that pervade a culture. The power of the concept resides in the notion that while there is an accepted hierarchy that structures a culture, it is so widespread and understood that we generally do not even think about it. This results in a troubling cycle: inequality is perpetuated as a given, and at the same time we are not encouraged to think about it. Sociologists and political scientists who study culture and power work to understand how the hegemonic order continues to structure and reinforce inequality, while activists and educators often seek to make those structures visible, which is seen as the first step toward eroding their effects. This book is a combination of those efforts, seeking to understand hegemony by highlighting its effects. Bear in mind that economic and racial inequality are only two elements of America's cultural hegemonic order.

Intersectionality refers to the complicated ways that forms of discrimination and otherness interact to create advantage and disadvantage in a culture.[38] Stemming from a critical theory approach to understanding the politics of inequality, intersectionality acknowledges the limitations of addressing any type of inequality from one's own perspective without being attentive to how that perspective may not be universal. In other words, white feminists are unlikely to question their own privilege (as whites in a racist system) if they do not have heightened consciousness about how race intersects with gender in a society where both classifications have power associated with them. Similarly, African American men who are working for racial justice may not consider their own privilege in a patriarchal system unless they are mindful of where power intersects. The combination is not always additive or even multiplicative. For instance, it is true that white is the privileged race in the United States, and men are the privileged gender. However, it is not always the case that African American women are more disadvantaged than African American men. In some contexts that may be true, but in others (such as with respect to suspicion of crime), black males may be at a greater disadvantage than both black women and white men. To understand how systemic inequality functions, we must keep these dynamics in mind.

The Politics of Inequality

Some of the most interesting and thoughtful work on inequality is written by sociologists. While their findings and theories are represented throughout these pages, this book attempts to help the reader understand the politics of poverty and racial inequality. We will consider how power, government, and public policy issues interact to at once affect and reflect inequality in America. In a nation that was launched with a document that espouses equality for all (the Declaration of Independence), why are we still struggling with these issues more than two centuries later? Where is there space for agreement about solutions? Can liberals and conservatives in America agree on strategies to reduce inequality? Who is working on these issues?

At the core of this exploration is the concept of representation. As explained in the next chapter, the Framers established a democracy in which public officials are elected to stand in for the will of citizens as decision makers. This arrangement—called a republic—means that simple majority rule does not always prevail. As we will discover, this was quite intentional, as the Framers feared tyranny of the majority as well as tyranny of the minority. One result, however, has been that a small minority of wealthy, mostly white and male Americans have had disproportionate access to power throughout our history. That does not necessarily mean that the rights of the poor, women, people of color, and other minorities will not be respected, but generation after generation of such leadership causes skepticism and even cynicism among citizens who do not see themselves reflected in what sociologist C. Wright Mills called "the power elite."[39] Together we will examine how actors in the political system are constrained by institutional factors within a system that was deliberately designed to produce only small, incremental changes.

As a final caveat, the reader is encouraged to try to minimize the tendency we have to personalize and individualize blame for the injustice that is outlined in the following pages. Not only is it counterproductive to engage in the politics of blame, but it is outside the realm of what social and behavioral science can generally explain. Political scientists are more interested in the *effects* of attitudes, behaviors, and structures rather than the *intent* of actors. While it can be tempting to try to catch someone being racist, for instance, it is more thoughtful and productive to understand that racism afflicts every American, at least (and perhaps most importantly) subconsciously, and to consider the effects of those psychological dynamics on public policy and the effort to bring about more economic and racial equality in the United States.

Structure of the Book

This book focuses on one aspect of American government and politics and encourages the reader to think more deeply about the complexities that have led to contemporary racial and economic inequality in the United States. The Notes contain ample references and can be used as a resource for drilling down more deeply into the rich areas of academic research that are too briefly considered in the following pages. Whenever possible, I provide URLs for access to online information.[40]

The book is primarily structured around the notion of representation. Accordingly, each chapter features "Representing" boxes that highlight a particular individual or organization working toward economic and/or racial justice on behalf of the American people. These boxes are designed to be inspirational and to reveal the variations in ideological grounding among those who are seeking to promote change. Similarly, the "What Can I Do?" boxes offer some suggestions about how young Americans can make a difference in myriad ways. Often students leave a course that centers on inequality with a sense of helplessness. While the reality of widespread and deeply rooted injustice in the United States can be sobering, it need not be debilitating. This brief introduction is intended to offer an entry point into deeper reflection and scholarly examination of these issues so that future generations will see marked improvements in these areas.

1

....

Representation and the Roots of Inequality

THE FRAMERS ESTABLISHED THE UNITED STATES AS A REPUBLIC (as opposed to a direct democracy) not simply because of logistics. They offered theoretically grounded arguments about the benefits of this type of system, which allows citizens to choose representatives to make decisions in government. As we examine the roots and perpetuation of inequality in America, we need to focus on the ways that the system, to differing degrees throughout our history, has allowed relatively few to achieve economic, political, and social success. As political and social equality has increased, how has representative democracy played a part? As economic equality has decreased, to what extent is a failure of the system to blame? In this chapter, we will explore the intersection of the government and interest groups as we begin to unpack the complexities of the ways representation works in the United States.

Defining (In)Equality

The concept of equality is not a modern creation; philosophers dating back to antiquity have wrestled with important questions of rights, personhood, and social power. While space does not permit even a cursory overview of those treatments here, it is important to be clear about how "equality" (and, by extension, "inequality") is treated in these pages.

This book primarily focuses on economic inequality, but it also explores how social and especially political inequality is related to financial disparity. However, it is important to understand that injustice related to race, gender, and sexual orientation is problematic in its own right, not simply because of resultant economic disadvantage. Nonetheless, I emphasize the contemporary and historic relationships among social, political, and economic status. For example, while it is empirically accurate to note that the majority of poor Americans are white, because most Americans are white, that is a statistical artifact; poverty in America is disproportionately of color. That reality should not obscure the challenges that white Americans face on a daily basis while living in poverty, but it complicates the picture in an important way. People of color face obstacles that whites with similar socioeconomic status often do not. These latter types of inequality (social, as it relates to our relationships with one another, and political, as it relates to access to power in terms of representation in government) are also examined in this book.

It is important to distinguish between equality of opportunity and equality of outcome with respect to economics.[1] Few voices in American discourse argue for equality of outcome. Rather, those who are concerned about economic inequality point out that many individuals in the United States are disadvantaged from birth. As a result, the ideal of a meritocratic system is undermined because those who achieve success do so either because they had a head start or in spite of significant barriers. If everyone started off with the same opportunity (and did not face structural impediments along the way), inequality of outcome would be acceptable. Put another way, most Americans agree that personal responsibility and initiative are required to achieve success. The disagreement often arises between those who believe that inequality of outcome is largely related to structural inequality of opportunity and those who believe that it is the result of personal failure. That debate is not fully addressed in this book, though it will become clear that systemic disadvantage constrains opportunities for many Americans and puts pressure on the convenient argument that the poor are struggling economically because of character flaws, laziness, bad choices, or other individual-level characteristics.

On the other hand, the idea of social and political equality is often discussed with respect to outcome—in contemporary society, most agree that fundamental rights need not be earned. As a result, equality of opportunity is the same as equality of outcome: African Americans ought not to be denied the right to vote; Latinos ought not to be prevented from owning homes; women ought not to be kept from certain professions; and so forth. But this issue is also more complicated than it might initially appear.[2] As we will see, the concept of representation is complex. Are we to argue, for example, that for women to have equal political rights, they must comprise an equal (50 percent) number of state legislators or US representatives? Or would equality in this regard mean proportionality (in which case, women would hold slightly more seats than men in Congress)? Or by equal do we mean that the interests women have (to the extent that they can be identified as such) are represented, even if by men, in those political bodies? While these are all worthwhile discussions, they lie beyond the scope of this book. From time to time I will highlight these dilemmas, but for the most part, the reader is invited to make his or her own decisions about what types of equality are most appropriate and under what circumstances. Similarly, readers are encouraged to find ways to address inequality—to the extent that it is considered to be problematic—that are consistent with their own values and beliefs. This book is designed to heighten consciousness by pointing out the places where the realities of twenty-first-century American life are seemingly inconsistent with the core principles outlined by the Framers.

Democracy's Promise: America's Founding Principles

The political reasons that led to the American Revolution are many, and we need to briefly consider some of the most important philosophical principles that guided the Framers as they envisioned a new nation—an experiment in democracy—and drafted a system that they hoped would foster those ideals. In this context James Madison's writing is central. Madison, the "Father of the Constitution," contributed a number of essential elements to that document (see Box 1.1), but his ideas about power dynamics between majority and minority factions provide a unique insight into not only the concerns of the Framers at that time, but also the ways that contemporary American government and culture is equipped to deal with inequality.

In *Federalist 10*,[3] for instance, Madison argues that representative democracy is best suited to deal with what he expected would be an enduring dilemma—how to respect the will of the majority while protecting the rights of the minority. Sometimes called Madison's dilemma, the concern is unique to a system of government where the interests of citizens matter in a meaningful way. In authoritarian regimes, rulers can impose their will on the citizenry, often with perceived legitimacy, with the only consequences coming in the form of a coup d'état. In a democracy, however,

Box 1.1. *Representing:* James Madison

The fourth president of the United States, and one of the most important intellectual leaders of America's founding, is a complex historical figure. Not only did he grow up with tremendous privilege on a tobacco plantation in Virginia, but his family's wealth did not stem from the American myth of hard work and fair play. His father inherited wealth and married into a wealthy family, and his wealth was perpetuated through plantation slave labor.

Yet within that privileged context, Madison (perhaps unintentionally) contributed ideas that would ultimately support the struggle of descendants of slaves and other oppressed communities in the United States. He did not argue for an end to slavery but insisted on a strong central government that would provide a contrast to the states' rights position that Confederate states adopted during the Civil War and then during the Jim Crow era of legalized racial segregation in the American South. His belief in fundamental human rights, many of which are codified in the Bill of Rights—the first ten amendments to the US Constitution—are at odds with the lived reality that he and his contemporaries (including Thomas Jefferson) imposed on slaves, Native American Indians, and white women. Yet the broad principles that are encapsulated by those ideas have driven not only movements for women's suffrage and black civil rights, but also the rights of a wide range of groups and associations that lack power or support, such as the Jehovah's Witnesses, the Ku Klux Klan, communists, LGBTQ Americans, and the criminally accused.

Characterizing Madison's representation as substantive, as described in this section, would be improper because many of the groups who have benefited from his ideas did not exist in his time. But the codification (in law and judicial interpretation) of those principles has resulted in support for minority groups far beyond those that were competing for power and consideration in the eighteenth and early nineteenth centuries. In this way, Madison is important to the struggle for racial and economic equality today even though he did not fight for those causes in his day (and very well may not have been willing to do so if he were alive today).[a]

---

a. "The Enslaved Community," James Madison's Montpellier, http://www.montpelier.org/visit/plan-your-visit/enslaved-community; "James Madison," American-Presidents.com, 2011, http://www.american-presidents.com/james-madison; "James Madison: Life Before the Presidency," Miller Center at the University of Virginia, 2011, http://millercenter.org/president/madison/.

each citizen's "opinions and passions" must be permitted to surface without interference. Otherwise the liberty on which the Revolution was based would be meaningless. However, such differences in opinions have the potential to destroy the republic, which is what Madison referred to as the "violence of faction."

That is simple enough, but we need to examine Madison's distinction between majority and minority faction. As disruptive as faction could be in and of itself, one could argue that a healthy political community should include rigorous discussion and debate. Madison was more concerned about tyranny, which he feared would result if one faction consistently had its way against the other. Minority faction was less of a concern to Madison because of the principle of majority rule. That is, if a small group of citizens or elected officials wished to impose their will on the masses, they would most likely be outvoted by the majority. Majority tyranny presented a greater concern, but Madison argued that the very structure of a republic (in particular, a large republic)—along with the specific safeguards built into the Constitution, he and his coauthors would later argue—would lead to a system that would slow people's passions and protect minority rights.

This problem was relevant in the eighteenth century, and even more so today. The extension (and later protection) of political rights to African Americans and white women, as well as vast waves of immigration, greatly diversified the polity. As a result, there are more "factions," and it appears, at least to the casual observer, that a small minority (the very wealthy) has disproportionate power over the majority. But recall that Madison did not expect this to be a problem. What happened?

Representation: Elected Officials

Representation is a concept that appears to be straightforward, but on closer examination is actually quite complicated. What does it mean to "represent" a person or a group of people or an idea? If a Pittsburgher wears her Steelers jersey on a Sunday afternoon in the fall, she is representing her favorite team, or maybe even her hometown. If a student's institutional affiliation is printed on his nametag at an academic conference, he is representing his college or university. In these ways, representation is symbolic and is not particularly important to the lives of others. On the other hand, if a student is selected to represent her residence hall on the university council, she might make decisions that can influence the lives of others in her dormitory. In that situation, variations in how she chooses to understand the concept of representation can result in very different outcomes. Now let us consider a somewhat ridiculous, yet hopefully memorable, hypothetical scenario to demonstrate two prominent theories of representation.

Prior to elections for residence hall council, the administration expressed concerns about students' low energy level during morning classes. The solution: doughnuts. The university president decided that the best way to invigorate students for morning classes would be to infuse them with sugar by offering free doughnuts in classroom buildings. The only problem is that the university's bakery could not offer a variety of doughnuts in such large quantities. Consequently the hall council would have to choose between cake or jelly-filled doughnuts.

Two candidates threw their hats in the ring. Jessica was a sophomore biochemistry major with a 3.8 GPA. She was in a number of clubs and participated in intramural athletics. Michael was a junior English major with a 3.4 GPA. He was on the swim team and active in campus ministry. During the campaign, Jessica favored cake doughnuts because they were denser and "stuck to your ribs" better. Michael, a fitness nut, noted that since jelly came from fruit, jelly doughnuts would be the better choice. When all the votes are tallied, Michael won by a 12 percent margin. However, before he cast his vote for a doughnut, he conducted a poll in the residence hall to learn what his constituents thought. As it turned out, nearly 60 percent of respondents preferred cake doughnuts.

Michael now has a dilemma of representation. If he perceives himself as a *delegate*,[4] he will vote for cake doughnuts. Even though he knows in his heart that jelly would be better for the students, he believes that his job is to do what they would do if they could be there themselves. If he perceives himself as a *trustee*, however, he will vote for jelly doughnuts—not because he is indifferent to his constituents' wishes, but because he believes that he knows best and feels that the students knew his views on doughnuts when they elected him. Even though they clearly selected him for other reasons, they would not be surprised or disappointed if he voted his conscience. Besides, if they did not like his vote, they could choose to not reelect him next year.

So, which would we prefer? In our silly example, most of us would say that Michael should act as a delegate. He clearly knows what we want, and he has no (or very little valid) additional information at his disposal. This is an example of what social scientists refer to as *directive* or *restrictive governance*.[5] On the other hand, it is relatively easy to imagine the practical limits of such a preference. Many of the decisions that government officials make on a daily basis are not particularly salient (relevant to our lives), and many others are very technical. If a member of Congress would take a poll to find out whether her constituents favored or opposed a reduction in the capital gains tax, there would very likely be a lot of "don't know" answers or "nonattitudes."[6] In such an instance, we might very well prefer that our leaders act as trustees—a scenario that is sometimes referred to as *permissive governance*.

Even this level of complexity, though, does not adequately capture the reality of contemporary politics. Yet another dimension has to do with the degree to which the individuals selected to represent us are equipped to do so. At the federal level, at least, most elected officials are wealthier and better educated than the average citizen.[7] In many ways, then, their personal interests ("opinions and passions," to use Madison's language) can be expected to differ from ours. That does not mean, however, that they must (or will) vote for their own personal interests at the expense of the rest of us. They could choose cake doughnuts because they know that is what we prefer, or they could choose jelly doughnuts because information they have (which we may not) indicates they are better for us. Elected officials who ignore the will of their constituents on a regular basis, at least in theory, will have difficulty at the ballot box in subsequent elections. (As we will see, however, that is not the case with appointed officials.) But that does not ensure that our elected officials will share what are perceived to be important characteristics with their constituents. Can those officials represent their constituents effectively?

Not necessarily. Political scientists differentiate between *symbolic* (or *descriptive*) *representation* and *substantive representation*.[8] The former refers to the degree to which representatives have characteristics (e.g., race, gender, wealth, ideology) that reflect their constituencies, while the latter has to do with whether they vote consistently with constituents' interests, even if they do not look like those whom they represent (see Box 1.2). This distinction is relevant to understanding why millionaires[9] can be elected and subsequently presumed to provide appropriate representation to hundreds of thousands (or, in the case of many US senators, millions) of individuals who struggle economically. It is why the US Senate—which

Box 1.2. *Representing:* David Yasskey

In 2006, US representative Major Owens (D-NY), who is African American, decided to retire from his seat representing a Brooklyn district where the majority of voters (about 60 percent) were African American. Four candidates competed for the Democratic Party nomination in the district (which was almost certain to choose a Democrat in the general election), one of whom, David Yasskey, was white.

The seat had been held by an African American member since the 1960s, but the existence of four candidates led to uncertainty as to whether it would remain black. In the midst of the campaign, Yasskey was referred to as a "colonizer" by Owens and further criticized by some African American leaders as trying to take away one of the seats that had come to symbolize important political gains for African Americans in the Congress. There were suggestions that Yasskey, if elected, would seek to join the Congressional Black Caucus (CBC). In a strategy letter to CBC members, former member of Congress (and one of the CBC's founders) William Clay wrote that "it is critical that the Congressional Black Caucus remains an all-black organization," pushing the discussion about symbolic and substantive representation into the contest. When the counting was over, however, it did not matter. Yasskey finished second (26.2 percent) to Yvette Clarke (31.2 percent), with the other two candidates attracting 22.9 percent and 19.6 percent of the vote.

The results were different in Tennessee that year, however. In a district that has a majority of African Americans and had been held for two generations by African Americans, Democrat Steve Cohen, who is white, won his party's nomination in a fifteen-candidate contest (thirteen of whom were African American) and went on to represent the congressional district that includes Memphis. Cohen did not seek to join the CBC.[a]

---

a. Jackson Baker, "Cohen, Hart, and the Schools," *Memphis Flyer*, July 7, 2011, http://www.memphisflyer.com/memphis/cohen-hart-and-the-schools/Content ?oid=3014581; "Congressional Black Caucus to Remain an All-Black Organization," EmergingMinds.org, September 8, 2006, http://emergingminds.org/Congressional -Black-Caucus-to-Remain-an-All-Black-Organization.html; Michael Cooper, "Councilwoman Wins Primary for House Seat," *New York Times*, September 13, 2006, http://www.nytimes.com/2006/09/13/nyregion/13cong.html; Jonathan P. Hicks, "Rivals in House Race Debate White Candidate's Motives," *New York Times*, August 25, 2006, http://www.nytimes.com/2006/08/25/nyregion/25brooklyn.html; Jonathan P. Hicks, "Each Candidate Claims the Advantage in a Fierce 4-Way Congressional Race in Brooklyn," *New York Times*, September 2, 2006, http://www.nytimes.com/2006/09/02 /nyregion/02brooklyn.html; Shailagh Murray, "Candidacy Fosters a Debate on Race," *Washington Post*, July 6, 2006, A1.1.

currently has three African American members[10]—can be considered to be representative of a diverse populace. And it is why a body like the US Congress, comprised overwhelmingly of men,[11] can be presumed (correctly or incorrectly) to be attentive to the interests of women, who comprise more than half of the nation's population. As long as officials take the "opinions and passions" of their constituents into consideration— even if those do not match their own—they can be substantively representative, even if they are not symbolically representative. However, one could certainly argue that a lack of symbolic representation can be concerning, particularly because there is a widespread and historic absence by members of particular groups in some positions.[12]

Representation: The Courts

So far our discussion has centered on elected officials. But many of the people who represent us in government are appointed. Some of those appointments are limited in their power, but others, such as members of the federal judiciary, are quite powerful. In all cases, though, the concept of representation is similar, though its manifestation can be quite different. While bureaucrats at a number of agencies (Health and Human Services, Housing and Urban Development, etc.) can have direct relevance to issues relating to racial and economic inequality, the judicial branch has arguably been the most important tool for members of historically disadvantaged groups to achieve public policy success. As we will see, the courts have, on occasion, made decisions in favor of minority interests that elected officials would have had a hard time making (for fear of reprisal at the ballot box). In this way, the courts illustrate Madison's belief that the protection of minority rights is an essential element of democracy.

Although Alexander Hamilton famously referred to the judiciary as the "least dangerous" branch of the federal government,[13] the power of judicial review has resulted in a system wherein the last word on a particular issue is often handed down from appeals courts. Because courts can declare laws passed by Congress and signed by the president to be unconstitutional (and thus void), there are often concerns that such activism is undemocratic. That is only true, however, if we define democracy as majority rule. The 535 members of the US Congress and the president of the United States must appeal to the majority (or at least a plurality[14] of their constituents) to win a seat and keep it. This is particularly true with members of Congress, who have no term limits, and specifically members of the House of Representatives, who face election every two years. As a result, it is very difficult for members to routinely take unpopular positions.

Members of the federal judiciary, however, serve life terms (though they can be impeached and removed from office for particularly egregious behavior) and are not elected. This design is a function of the Framers' desire to allow one branch of government to make decisions that are immune from direct public pressure. If we understand democracy to mean respect for majority will and protection of minority rights, it is more appropriate to refer to judicial action that cuts against popular opinion as being countermajoritarian, rather than undemocratic.

The US Supreme Court often abstains from making overtly political decisions if it can avoid it (the Court's action in *Bush v. Gore*,[15] however, is a notable exception to this rule), but every governmental decision affects people and is a reflection of power differences in society. In that way, everything the Court does is political, and even what the Court does *not* do is political. Unlike the legislative and executive branches, members of the judiciary cannot technically set their own agendas; they must wait until a case comes before them, and even then, they are somewhat limited in terms of the scope of the decision they can make. However, because the Supreme Court cannot possibly entertain arguments for the several thousand cases that are petitioned to be heard each term, the justices' choices of which to hear and which to deny (thus rendering the lower court decision as final) is also a political action.

As we consider the various types of inequality that exist in America today, we will be attentive to times when court decisions have contributed to or challenged inequality. At this point, though, it is important to consider some Supreme Court decisions that directly relate to the notion of representation.

One Person, One Vote

Fundamental to the broadest notions of democratic theory is the idea that each citizen has an equal chance to influence government. As always, however, the devil is in the details. What does "equal" mean? Certainly it does not mean that each citizen has the same amount of money to donate each year to political campaigns. At a minimum, it means that each citizen gets the same amount of power at the voting booth. This can be achieved in a number of ways, but in the United States, we have settled on the one person, one vote model that was clearly affirmed by the Supreme Court in *Baker v. Carr*[16] and *Reynolds v. Simms*.[17]

In *Baker v. Carr* (1962), the Court considered whether it could address a political question such as the one brought forward by a Tennessee man named Charles Baker who complained that the state had not been dutiful in redrawing US House district borders following each census, even though there was significant movement within the state. At the time the case was filed, the district in which Baker lived (near Memphis) had nearly ten times the population of some of Tennessee's rural districts. Consequently Baker argued that he had less representation than someone who lived in a less populated district. The Court ruled that such questions were appropriate for courts to decide (a departure from earlier rulings), which opened the door for similar questions in the following years.

In *Reynolds v. Simms* (1964), the Court was asked to decide the constitutionality of an Alabama law that state legislative districts could not cross county borders. Consequently one state senate district had about forty-one times the population of another by the time the suit was filed. Although that number is very large, it was not unusual at the time for districts to vary greatly in population, as many rural districts featured sparse population and state laws regarding redistricting that were in place before urbanization led to vastly disproportionate representation for areas with higher populations. In *Reynolds*, the Court established the one person, one vote principle, which means that the power of each of us to affect government by having our representatives be responsive must be relatively equal.[18]

It might seem surprising that it took 175 years into the nation's existence under the current Constitution to officially establish a fundamental principle of democracy. Such is the nature of the way our brain processes information. For instance, it also seems ridiculous to many of us that it took the same amount of time to pass a federal law that prohibited states from excluding citizens from voting based on their race, or that it took 133 years to guarantee white women the right to vote. It is only because we take these rights as common sense today that we can be critical of past generations for not acting sooner, but, conversely, it is because the actions were taken that we now see those rights as nonnegotiable. It is difficult to predict what standards future generations will have that will cause them to judge us harshly (the right for LGBTQ couples to marry might be an example). We are still, for instance, not settled on the one person, one vote standard in practice. While few would argue that anyone should be in a district with a few thousand people while someone else in the same state should be in a district with a few million, the mechanism we use to count citizens—the census—is imperfect, and questions remain about who in fact is counted.

Everybody Counts

The Constitution requires a census every ten years, and because the US House of Representatives has members from states in proportion (roughly) to the size of their population, a process of reallocation of House seats and subsequent redrawing of district boundaries follows. Put another way, it would be impossible to appropriately apply the Court's standards from *Reynolds v. Simms* without a clear picture of how many people live in each state and where (within the state) they live.

After the 2000 census, Utah lost a House seat as a result of a decline in population over the previous decade. Believing that the loss was due to the Census Bureau's process of "imputation" in some states, which involves estimating population by way of statistical procedures when questions remain after all attempts to contact citizens have been exhausted,[19] officials in Utah sued[20] to have the imputed numbers removed from the allocation. The Court rejected Utah's arguments, effectively affirming the process of imputation.

Imputation matters in this context because citizens who have less power are more likely to be difficult to count in the census than those who have access to power. These hard-to-count groups include renters (as opposed to home owners), racial and ethnic minorities,[21] and homeless persons. If we can assume similarities in at least some characteristics based on geography (a proposition that I will question in a later section), then an undercounting of citizens in this category could result in less formal representation for them in government. If we consider the cyclical effects of reduced representation for Americans who are already struggling, we understand how these seemingly obscure questions come to life.

Symbolic Representation and Racial Minority Voting

Compared to many other nations, the United States is characterized by one of the largest gaps in voter turnout between rich and poor citizens.[22] The reasons for this are not straightforward, but at least some of it is likely attributable to race. In this section, we explore the importance of electing members of racial minority groups to public office and the related issue of voter turnout by and suppression of minorities.

After the Civil War, a number of African Americans achieved elected office, particularly in areas where the majority of citizens were non-white. After Reconstruction, however, the efforts to disenfranchise black Americans by way of literacy tests, white primaries, grandfather clauses, and poll taxes in the South made it difficult for blacks to run for office. As northern urban centers attracted black citizens during the Great Migration (1910–1930), African Americans began to concentrate in cities, which eventually led to electoral victories. In 1965 Congress passed and the president signed the Voting Rights Act, which abolished Jim Crow–era voter suppression and mandated federal oversight of elections in states with a history of such activity. With the passage of the Voting Rights Act, African American members of the United States Congress from Atlanta, Houston, Memphis, and New Orleans joined representatives from urban areas in the North, such as New York, Chicago, Detroit, Philadelphia, and St. Louis (as well as Los Angeles). The overwhelming majority of black elected officials today are still selected from so-called majority-minority districts.

To understand the importance and history of majority-minority districts to representing the interests of black and Latino voters, it is helpful to broaden our definitions of *majority* and *minority*. In the Madisonian sense, we can limit our understanding to the mathematical conceptualizations with which we are already familiar. A majority is 50 percent plus one. Anything less than 50 percent is a minority. But political scientists use these terms to refer to power as well as numbers. Perhaps the most vivid example is the system of apartheid in South Africa, which legally established whites as the dominant social, economic, and political group, even though they comprised only 10 percent of the population. In that situation, it does not make sense to talk about "the minority white" government in South Africa because whites comprise a power majority. Similarly, women are considered a "minority" in the United States because they have been disproportionately denied access to the levers of power (though they constitute a majority of the total population).[23]

Turning back to the first approach, majority-minority districts are those in which a numerical majority of voting-age citizens are nonwhite. Some of these districts do not have a clear numerical majority in terms of racial or ethnic groups (e.g., the plurality may be African American and the percentage of Hispanics combine to form more than 50 percent of the population), but the designation is meaningful because the majority of the citizens in the area are not a part of the racial group that disproportionately has access to power in the nation.

The establishment of majority-minority districts is linked both to the notion of symbolic representation discussed earlier in this chapter and to the historic reality that white voters generally do not vote for candidates of color.[24] Accordingly, the idea is that in order to make sure that people of color are represented in the national legislature, states that have a significant number of blacks, Hispanics, or Asians can draw district lines for the House of Representatives—by use of the concentration in housing patterns (discussed in Chapter 3)—such that a majority of the voters are nonwhite, with the expectation that they will elect a nonwhite person to represent them.

The Supreme Court has upheld majority-minority districts, though their utility is subject to criticism from several perspectives. For example, a number of states redrew congressional district lines with attention to this issue after the 1990 census (see Figure 1.1). Five white voters in North Carolina argued that the oddly shaped boundary of the Twelfth District (stretching some 160 miles, much of which was down an interstate highway) violated their rights because it took race into account at the expense of creating a cohesive geographical district.[25] The Supreme Court held that racially gerrymandered districts should be judged by the legal standard of "strict scrutiny" to determine whether a citizen's rights are violated on the basis of race. For a law to satisfy this standard, it must be deemed to have been made to further a compelling government interest and be narrowly tailored to achieve that interest. In other words, while it is permissible to draw majority-minority districts, a state must be attempting to avoid violation of the Voting Rights Act of 1965, and the district lines should be drawn in a way that takes other factors besides race into consideration so that white voters' interests are also protected. Justice Sandra Day O'Connor wrote the opinion of the Court in this case; she argued that the district violated the Fourteenth Amendment rights of the white voters who brought suit. O'Connor affirms the importance of states taking race into consideration as they draw district lines, but argues that the boundary in this particular case, while created with intentions to guarantee the rights of the minority (African Americans) in

FIGURE 1.1. Challenged Congressional Districts in the 1990s

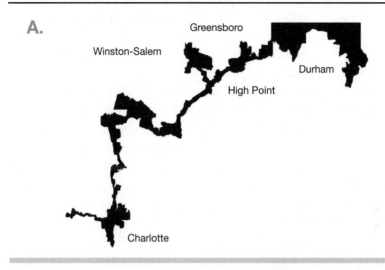

A.

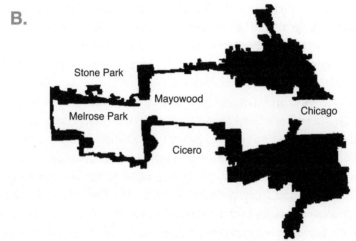

B.

A. "I-85" District: The 12th Congressional District in North Carolina, post–1990 census. This district was designed to create a majority-minority district for African Americans. These lines were overturned in *Shaw v. Reno* (1993).

B. "Ear Muff" District: 4th Congressional District in Illinois, post–1990 census. This district was designed to create a majority-Hispanic district without diluting African American voting in nearby districts. These lines were upheld upon challenge because they were deemed to be "narrowly tailored" to addressing a compelling state interest (of not violating the Civil Rights Act of 1965).

Source: Peter S. Wattson, "How to Draw Redistricting Plans that Will Stand Up in Court," State of Minnesota Senate, 2000. http://www.senate.leg.state.mn.us/departments/scr /REDIST/Draw/Draw992web.htm. Reprinted by permission from Election Data Services, Inc.

North Carolina, ultimately violated the rights of the majority (whites). Further, she argues in the opinion that African Americans might also be offended by the district as drawn because it makes assumptions about them based on their race that would be considered to be impermissible in other contexts:

> A reapportionment plan that includes in one district individuals who be-
> long to the same race, but who are otherwise widely separated by geograph-
> ical and political boundaries, and who may have little in common with one
> another but the color of their skin, bears an uncomfortable resemblance to
> political apartheid. It reinforces the perception that members of the same
> racial group—regardless of their age, education, economic status, or the
> community in which the live—think alike, share the same political inter-
> ests, and will prefer the same candidates at the polls. We have rejected such
> perceptions elsewhere as impermissible racial stereotypes.[26]

Yet exit polls show that African Americans, as well as Latinos from certain backgrounds, while not monolithic entities, do tend to vote similarly[27] and view their interests as linked (if not across racial and ethnic boundaries, at least within them).[28]

Voting by African Americans and Latinos, however, cannot be taken for granted. There have been significant efforts to disenfranchise African Americans throughout American history. Voting was prohibited to slaves, and many states—particularly those in the South—took extraordinary efforts (e.g., literacy tests, poll taxes, white primaries, grandfather clauses) to keep blacks from voting during the Jim Crow era.[29] Much of that changed after passage of the Voting Rights Act of 1965 (VRA),[30] but recent elections have seen renewed concerns about racial minority voters being inappropriately purged from voting rolls,[31] reportedly being stopped at police checkpoints on the way to the polls,[32] facing disproportionate ballot challenges,[33] and being asked to wait in unusually long lines in some urban precincts.[34] In 2013, the US Supreme Court heard a challenge by Shelby County, Alabama, to sections of the VRA that required nine states (and portions of six others) to obtain US Department of Justice clearance prior to making any changes in their election procedures. The Court agreed that the provisions of the law (which was reauthorized by Congress in 2006) requiring clearance were unnecessary at this time. Writing for a 5–4 majority, Chief Justice John Roberts argued that "our country has changed" and that these states are being unfairly punished for their mistreatment of racial minority voters in the past. Justice Ruth Bader Ginsburg disagreed, noting that the Justice Department blocked over seven hundred changes between 1982 and 2006, which suggested to her that there was still reason for concern about the targeting of minority voters.[35] The *Shelby* decision paved the way for more states to introduce laws that make voting more difficult (such as those that require voters to show valid identification).[36] The decision left open the possibility of Congress's writing legislation to require clearance, as long as the rationale was based on current evidence of discrimination. Some analysts have argued that Donald Trump's surprise win in the 2016 presidential election can be partially attributed to policies that several states adopted after the Court's decision in *Shelby*,[37] but such claims are difficult to substantiate, are overly simplistic (i.e., some states with voter ID laws were not previously covered by the VRA), and cannot explain losses in other traditionally Democratic states, such as Pennsylvania and Michigan.[38] Although Hillary Clinton far outpaced Donald Trump in the overall popular vote, the unique way that American presidents are elected resulted in a Trump victory. The Electoral College, however, is not the only mechanism that sets the United States apart from other democracies in terms of electoral systems.

The American Anomaly

In many ways, the dilemma of symbolic representation that persists is a result of the relative uniqueness of the way we elect officials in the United States, where geography tends to matter more than political attitudes.[39] Without a comparative perspective, it is easy to lose sight of explanations for and potential solutions to inequality in America. The way that we conceptualize and operationalize representation is an important component of the way we think about government officials' responsibilities and responsiveness to our collective needs. We are constrained by the system in which we were raised, and we generally believe that it is the only way to "do" democracy. A thorough discussion of different types of democratic governance is not possible here, but we will consider a few of our idiosyncrasies that are most relevant to understanding representation of majority and minority interests.

Americans generally think about voting as a choice between two individuals for one position. Because we have a two-party system in the

United States, that choice is usually between a Democrat and a Republican. We understand that primary elections or other selection mechanisms (such as the congressional party caucus) can be used to determine what candidate represents each of those parties in the general election, but for the most part, we view elections like tennis matches—someone will win and someone will lose. That sort of electoral system, known as single member district plurality (SMDP),[40] tends to lead to two-party competition (or a system where only two parties have a reasonable chance to control a branch of government). In a pluralistic society, such as the United States, each of the parties is thus left attempting to appeal to a broad range of interests so as to cobble together a coalition that will lead to electoral success. The result is that poor Americans do not have a party dedicated to representing their interests. Rather, Democrats have been successful in attracting union workers and racial minorities, whereas Republicans have attracted whites in rural areas. Of course, both parties must also be responsive to the wealthier members of their coalitions, and because the wealthy are more likely to be active (not to mention donate funds to electoral campaigns), it is difficult for the poor to have proportionate influence over either party, and thus the government.

Most democracies feature electoral systems that encourage multiple parties. Most prominent among these is proportional representation (PR), whereby voters choose parties, rather than individuals, to serve them in public office. As opposed to the winner-take-all (or first-past-the-post) nature of SMDP, each party that receives a minimum level of support is awarded seats in the legislature in proportion to the votes it receives. For instance, if there are one hundred seats available, and Party X receives 51 percent of the vote, Party Y receives 32 percent of the vote, and Party Z receives 17 percent of the vote, Party X would get 51 seats, Party Y would get 32 seats, and Party Z would get 17 seats. In an SMDP system, there would be one hundred districts drawn, with one member selected from each. If this electoral result occurred in each district, Party X would end up with all one hundred seats. While such an outcome is unlikely, what is equally unlikely is that Party Z would ever get a seat in an SMDP system, and if it did find some natural constituency in a limited regional area, the elected member would have no power in a legislature dominated by Parties X and Y. As a result, voters who support Party Z would be best served by voting for candidates from Party X or Y, which means that those parties would have to broaden their focus to appeal to those citizens. That scenario, of course, quite neatly describes the Democratic and Republican parties in the United States.

The result is that these two parties, who must attract broad coalitions to assemble a numerical majority, are generally unable or unwilling to address the needs of power minorities in the United States. As noted earlier, elected officials, particularly at the federal level, are disproportionately white and male, and they are better educated and wealthier than the average American.[41] While district lines can be redrawn to increase symbolic representation on the basis of race and ethnicity, there is no way to rectify the gender disparity in elected bodies within the confines of our current system. After all, housing in the United States is not segregated by gender but by socioeconomic status. As discussed further in Chapter 8, women, then, are unable to have their underrepresentation addressed through political or legal action beyond prohibition of overt discrimination. Because of these unique characteristics, we must bear in mind that our system of elections (rather than simply voter preference) contributes to the underrepresentation of minorities.

This dynamic came into focus during the 2016 presidential elections, as the Electoral College, which gives disproportionate voice to voters in rural states, selected Donald Trump as president, even though nearly 3 million more voters cast ballots for Hillary Clinton. (This was only the fifth time in history that the winner of the popular vote was not elected president, but it was the second time in five presidential elections.) While rural voters are advantaged by the system, the campaign revealed that many of them do not feel represented in general. As one voter from Kentucky noted, "A lot of us in rural areas . . . think people are talking down to us. What ends up happening is that we don't focus on the policy—we focus on the tones, the references, the culture."[42] The reality, then, is that many, if not most, Americans, might not particularly feel represented by the existing electoral structure.

Alternatives to Our Current System

Although the SMDP system is not mandated by the US Constitution, it is difficult to imagine Americans embracing proportional representation after two centuries of selecting leaders under this system. Consequently the two-party system is probably here to stay. And, as we will see later in the book, Americans tend to oppose the notion of quotas, so a system of racial or (as France instituted in 2000)[43] gender quotas is unlikely to attract support. There are, however, other alternatives to electoral choice that could work within the existing structure. These, too, are dramatic departures from what Americans have come to expect, but discussing them allows us to come closer to understanding the systemic barriers to racial and economic equality in the United States.

Legal scholar Lani Guinier[44] has argued that a cumulative voting system could be more advantageous to power minorities in the United States. Cumulative voting would violate the one-person, one-vote standard established by the US Supreme Court, but it is not undemocratic because each citizen retains the same voting power as every other citizen. It works like this: rather than casting a single ballot in an election, under a cumulative voting system, each voter has a number of votes equal to the number of candidates in the race and can cluster them as he or she sees fit. For instance, if the race for US Senate features seven candidates, each voter has seven votes for that contest. A voter who really liked the Republican candidate could cast all seven votes for him or her. If she likes the Republican candidate but sort of likes the Libertarian candidate, too, she can split her votes between them in a variety of ways (six for the Republican candidate and one for the Libertarian, four and three, etc.). During tabulation, the candidate with the most votes wins the seat. A voter who prefers a minor party candidate can vote for that candidate without "wasting" her vote because she can also give some of her votes to a major-party candidate. This type of system could encourage minor parties to run on platforms that focus on issues relevant to racial minorities and low-income Americans in ways that the big tent parties cannot.

Two other possibilities for changing electoral systems to encourage third-party involvement are Borda voting and instant runoff voting (IRV). Both of these systems ask voters to rank order their preference of candidates in a contest. A voter who liked the Republican candidate the most would place a number 1 next to that candidate's name. Unlike first-past-the-post voting, though, the voter would rank the other candidates in order of preference. The Borda system assigns weight to those preferences (e.g., four points for a first-place vote, three points for a second-place vote, etc.) and adds up all the points to determine a winner.[45] With IRV, after all first-place votes are tabulated, if no candidate receives a majority of votes cast, the candidate in last place is removed from the race, and the second-place votes for all those voters who chose him or her are redistributed to the other candidates in a process that continues until one candidate has a majority of support.[46]

These models encourage support for minor-party candidates because a vote for them is not "wasted." Even if they have little chance of winning, support for them is registered and the voter has a hand in choosing among the major-party candidates. With a highly polarized party climate like the one in twenty-first-century America, a gain of even a handful of seats by minor parties could force the Democrats and Republicans to notice the needs of small parties that represent minority interests. This could shift the balance of representation—perhaps significantly—away from the powerful. One can also imagine that a presidential election could be shifted with such a system. In 2016, there were two prominent third-party candidates on the ballot in most states. If voters who selected them in states that were decided by a small margin had the chance to indicate a second choice, the outcome might have been different. Americans are generally skeptical of this type of fundamental change, though. Even if such procedures were adopted, there is no guarantee that addressing these procedural matters will lead to more substantive equity or justice. Moreover, the current system of representation should not be viewed as inherently inadequate to address the needs of those with little power. Through substantive representation by elected leaders, potentially counter-majoritarian courts, and through the work of organized interests, ordinary Americans can affect government and politics in meaningful ways.

American Pluralism

America is pluralistic in the sense that it is characterized by many types of diversity (economic, gender, age, racial, geographic, ideological, etc.). The pluralist model of democracy emerged as a response to the elitist model, which was put forth in the 1950s by sociologist C. Wright Mills.[47] The elitist perspective did not argue that America should be controlled by elites, but rather observed that it is. Mills noted that a small group of important people (and families) have access to a disproportionate amount of power and thus are responsible for much of the formal and informal decision making in the United States. In such a system, it is difficult for individuals who are not born into the elite class to gain entrance. Consequently members of the elite are able to maintain their power generation after generation. Pluralism,[48] on the other hand, while not denying the existence of an elite class in the United States (it would be hard to argue that such a class does not exist), paints a more optimistic picture of American democracy by noting that individuals are in fact able to influence government through interest groups. These groups put pressure on the elites and consequently affect public policymaking in ways not available to individuals. From this perspective, the power minority—who are the numerical majority (or, as US senator Bernie Sanders would put it, the 99 percent)—is represented through the collective strength of voices, ballots, and pooled economic resources. In some cases, this approach has taken the form of social movements (such as the African American civil rights movement, the women's movement, the Chicano civil rights movement, the Native American civil rights movement, and the immigrant rights movement), whereas in other instances it has resulted in advocacy groups such as those we will encounter in the following chapters.

This brings us full circle to where we began this chapter. Recall that Madison warned of the potential "violence of faction" in *Federalist 10*, a concern that he certainly would have applied to the prevalence of organized interest groups in contemporary politics. The paradox, then, is how the pluralist model of democracy—which allows less powerful individuals to have their needs addressed through interest groups—can operate in a way that does not realize Madison's fears. Complicating the issue, powerful elements of American society such as wealthy individuals and corporations also (appropriately so) have the ability to form interest groups to pressure leaders to make decisions that will benefit them.[49] This marketplace of competition results in a similarly skewed power balance because wealthier individuals and groups gain disproportionate access and exert disproportionate influence in a political system where money (by way of organized lobbying and campaign contributions) matters. As we will see in the following chapter, this reality has resulted in a gap between those who have and those who do not have or who "have too little."[50] This gap has existed for generations but has grown very rapidly over the past couple of decades.

Conclusion

James Madison was among the elite in his day, and his concern to protect minority interests stemmed, at least in part, from a desire to protect the powerful few from the passions and preferences of the masses. But America has made great strides in opening the political system to more and more citizens in the past two hundred years, and the Framers' ideas and words have often grounded those struggles. Yet as Patricia Ireland, former president of the National Organization for Women, astutely notes, "progress is not equality."[51] It would be difficult for a reasonable person to argue that America is not a more equal place than it was even a generation ago; it would be just as difficult for a reasonable person to argue that America's promise of equality has been fulfilled. Capitalism assumes a certain amount of inequality with respect to wealth, but democracy promises each citizen some degree of control over his or her life. As we will see in the next chapter, it will be uncomfortable to hold onto the myth that Americans start off more or less on equal footing and that those who play by the rules and work hardest succeed.

Further, it is impossible to deny that poverty in America is primarily white, but it is disproportionately African American and Hispanic. We need to examine the root of that reality and ask why, nearly fifty years after the passage of landmark civil rights legislation and more than 150 years after the end of the Civil War, such a racial gap continues to exist. We also need to examine the ways that gender is related to both racial and economic inequality. Activists and public officials from across the ideological spectrum and from both parties have recognized systemic inadequacies that give tremendous advantages to some Americans while deeply disadvantaging others. This book offers insight into the nature of those problems and highlights just a few of the individuals who have worked hard to solve them.

Ultimately, we need to address the paradox of compromise as a guiding principle of American democracy. We generally celebrate the willingness of officials to work together to get things done, but incremental changes have not led to meaningful improvements in the lives of the poorest Americans. We must consider the importance of holding firm to such values as justice and equality, as well. As we move through this volume, we must repeatedly ask when it is appropriate to be unyielding in our desire to move toward increased social and economic justice and when it is important to work with those who seek to solidify or otherwise preserve the current structures that have led to and perpetuate injustice.

Discussion Questions

1. Consider Madison's dilemma. Can you think of specific contemporary policy issues where majority will has thwarted minority rights? What about the other way around? Are there times when the numerical minority seems to dominate the majority?

2. Donald Trump was elected president on a platform that emphasized the plight of the worker, even though he is, and has always been, very wealthy. What would the Framers (such as James Madison) say in regard to the wealth gap between the political leaders and the majority of citizens? Is it consistent with their ideal of democracy? If not, would you attribute the disconnect to a design error in the system, an implementation error, or something else?

3. How do you feel about the way David Yasskey's candidacy was received by members of the Congressional Black Caucus (see Box 1.2)? Can you understand Yasskey's position? Can you understand the CBC's position? What does this case teach us about the differences between symbolic and substantive representation?

4. Discuss how the judicial system has intervened with respect to issues of representation at various times throughout American history. Do these cases serve to enhance or detract from broad democratic principles, such as liberty, freedom, and justice? How so?

5. Do you generally prefer the delegate model of representation or the trustee model? Does the salience of the issue affect your preference?

6. Do you think that the single member district plurality model of elections is appropriate for American democracy? How does it compare to the proportional representation system? Discuss the benefits and drawbacks of each. How would Americans react to the adoption (or even the proposal) of a proportional model? What about an alternative voting system, such as IRV?

2

....

Income and Wealth

How can it be that it is not a news item when an elderly homeless person dies of exposure, but it is news when the stock market loses two points?

—Pope Francis, Evangelii Gaudium, November 26, 2013[1]

Today, after four years of economic growth, corporate profits and stock prices have rarely been higher, and those at the top have never done better. But average wages have barely budged. Inequality has deepened. Upward mobility has stalled. The cold, hard fact is that even in the midst of recovery, too many Americans are working more than ever just to get by; let alone to get ahead. And too many still aren't working at all. So our job is to reverse these trends.

—President Barack Obama, State of the Union Address, January 28, 2014[2]

I am proposing an across the board income tax reduction, especially for middle income Americans. This will lead to millions of new and really good paying jobs. The rich will pay their fair share, but no one will pay so much that it destroys jobs or undermines our ability as a nation to compete.

—Presidential candidate Donald Trump, August 8, 2016[3]

ST. JOHN'S UNIVERSITY EDUCATION PROFESSOR ALLAN ORNSTEIN argues that "no country has taken the idea of equality more seriously than the United States," though he notes that "we are witnessing the rise of a new aristocratic class, based on wealth and power, far worse than the European model our Founding Fathers sought to curtail."[4] Americans largely accept the notion that capitalism will produce unequal outcomes with respect to income and wealth, but we prefer a more equal distribution than currently exists. In 2011, a nationally representative sample of Americans was asked to (1) estimate the actual level of wealth inequality in the United States and (2) indicate preferences for ideal distribution of wealth. The researchers found that:

> Respondents vastly underestimated the actual level of wealth inequality in the United States, believing that the wealthiest quintile[5] held about 59% of the wealth when the actual number is closer to 84%. More interesting, respondents constructed ideal wealth distributions that were far more equitable than even their erroneously low estimates of actual distributions, reporting a desire for the top quintile to own just 32% of the wealth.[6]

The researchers also found that this preference existed across demographic groups (including participants' expressed presidential vote choice from 2004): "All groups—even the wealthiest respondents—desired a more equal distribution of wealth than what they estimated the current United States level to be, and all groups also desired some inequality—even the poorest respondents."[7] Finally, and perhaps most interesting, all groups agreed that the way to move toward this ideal is through redistributing wealth from the top to the bottom three quintiles.

The disconnect between what Americans of all ideological backgrounds desire and the reality of inequality is striking and calls into question the effectiveness of our representative system. So, why is this happening? One answer could be that our elected officials wish to make changes to bring the wealth gap more in line with what Americans want but are constrained by systemic forces that make such meaningful change possible. Another answer is that our elected officials, most of whom (at the federal level at least) are wealthier than the average American,[8] are trying to protect themselves and their elite friends and family members. More likely, though, as the researchers suggest, we generally are not aware that the gap is so large; we are optimistic about our chances of getting into higher quintiles; we are not clear about the causes of inequality; and we often do not make a connection between these beliefs and our public policy preferences.[9] In this chapter, we explore the statistical realities of income and wealth inequality, as well as the relationship between that inequality and race. We will focus on the various elements in American society that perpetuate economic inequality in an attempt to understand how the current gap has not only persisted but has been greatly expanded over the past generation or so.

Income

Economic inequality is customarily discussed in terms of two distinct but related concepts: income and wealth. Wealth is a person's (or household's) total worth (assets minus debt), whereas income is simply the amount of money a person (or household) earns in a year. We will explore wealth disparities later on, but in this section we consider the differences in annual household income and the ability to provide for oneself or one's family as a result.

Income and Employment

For most Americans, income is tied to employment; we only get paid when we work. Of course, there are exceptions. Disabled and retired individuals can collect Social Security from the federal government. Unemployed workers can receive benefits for a limited period after losing a job. Some wealthy individuals have invested money and earn from dividends and interest. For the most part, though, income is related to work.

Work is related to a number of factors that we will consider in more detail in the chapters that follow (specifically, education opportunities, immigration status, and incarceration rates). Most recently, though, attention has been focused on the sluggish economy and the degree to which it has affected Americans in the workforce. With respect to recessions, it has been said that when America catches a cold, African Americans get the flu. That sentiment was clearly reflected in the recession that began with the housing crisis in 2008. As Figure 2.1 reveals, there has been a persistent racial gap in unemployment for decades.

Unemployment rates for October 2016 indicated a nationwide level of 5.0 percent, but a closer look reveals that the rate for whites (4.4 percent) was lower than for Hispanics (5.8 percent) or African Americans (8.5 percent, or nearly double the rate for whites).[10] The gap has been even more pronounced among those with a college education. As a result of the Great Recession, which began in 2008, white unemployment among the college educated rose from 1.8 percent in 2007 to 3.9 percent in 2011, while black unemployment among the college educated spiked from 2.7

FIGURE 2.1. Unemployment Rate by Race, 2000–2016

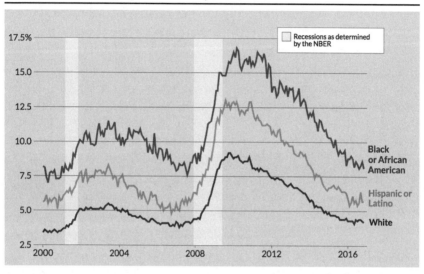

Source: Washington Center for Equitable Growth, "Equitable Growth's Jobs Day Graphs: November 2016 Report Edition," December 2, 2016, http://equitablegrowth.org/equitablog/equitable-growths-jobs-day-graphs-november-2016-report-edition/.

percent in 2007 to 7.0 percent in 2011.[11] By 2015, the overall numbers were much improved, but not much had changed in relation to the gap, with white, college-educated unemployment at 2.4 percent and African American, college-educated unemployment hovering at 4.1 percent—still higher than its white counterpart during the recession.[12]

Unemployment naturally has an effect on earnings. Data from 2011 demonstrate a notable income gap between white, black, and Hispanic families. In that year, the median household income for whites was $52,214, while the median income for African Americans was $32,229, and for Hispanics, $38,624.[13] Those numbers reflect a fairly stable gap over the past two decades.[14] More recently, after the recession had ended, the racial wage gap was still quite prominent. A 2016 study found that relative to white men, African American men made 22 percent less, and African American women made 34.2 percent less. Black women earned nearly 12 percent less than white women, a trend that was more pronounced for younger women.[15]

The income gap is most pronounced among Hispanics and African Americans, but its growth is notable among all segments of the population.

In 2015, the highest quintile (20 percent) of earners collected more than 50 percent of the total income in the United States. In contrast, the bottom three quintiles combined brought in just 25.6 percent of the total income that year (with the second-highest quintile earning 23.2 percent).[16] There has been a steady increase in this trend over the past forty years, such that the top 5 percent of earners in 1970 pulled in 16.6 percent. That number was stable a decade later but rose to 18.5 percent in 1990 and to 22.1 percent in 2000. In 2015, the top 5 percent of households earned 22.1 percent of the total income.[17]

This shift can be analyzed in a variety of ways. One notable trend is that incomes in all ranges rose steadily (and relatively evenly) between the end of World War II and 1979. However, the top 20 percent of earners saw a 49 percent increase (including a 73 percent increase among the top 5 percent and a 224 percent increase among the top 1 percent) since the early 1980s, while the bottom, second, middle, and fourth quintiles saw changes of 7 percent, 6 percent, 11 percent, and 23 percent, respectively.[18]

Gender is also related to income disparity. Much attention has been given to the wage gap in recent years, which stands today at about 20 percent. Put another way, women make an average of eighty cents for every dollar a man makes in the United States.[19] The gap is largest for Latinas (54 percent compared to white men) and smallest for Asian American women (85 percent compared to white men). The gap for African American women is 63 percent.[20] This wage gap holds at every level of educational attainment.[21] It should be noted that while the figure has fluctuated from year to year, based on differing indicators, some commentators have argued that the gap is most attributable to choices that women make compared to men.[22] As we will explore in Chapter 8, however, we must be careful in evaluating individual-level choices in a system where gender norms serve as a constraint.

On the opposite end of the spectrum, evidence of racial disparity is illustrated by an examination of the board members of America's top corporations. In 2012, white men comprised 86.7 percent of the board members at the largest Fortune 500 companies in the United States. African Americans held 7.4 percent of those seats, and Hispanics/Latinos held 3.3 percent. Those who identified as Asian/Pacific Islander accounted for just 2.3 percent of corporate board seats.[23] White women accounted for 15.9 percent of seats; nonwhite women held 3.9 percent.[24] It was not until 1999 that an African American became CEO of a Fortune 500 company,[25] and there have been only fifteen more since;[26] in January 2015, there were only five African American CEOs in such positions.[27] Women headed twenty-one Fortune 500 companies in 2016; the highest number was twenty-four in 2014.[28]

Further, there has been a tremendous shift in the ratio of Fortune 500 CEO pay to the income of an average worker. Although the ratios found on bumper stickers and pro-union literature vary (from as much as 500 to 1 to as low as 253 to 1),[29] the reality is complicated by the various types of compensation (besides monetary income) that CEOs receive. By one count, however, the ratio grew from 42 to 1 in 1980 to 107 to 1 in 1990 before spiking to 373 to 1 in the last two decades of the twentieth century.[30] In 2015, the median overall compensation of the top Fortune 500 CEOs was $12.4 million, which was slightly lower than the previous year.[31] The monetary portion of these figures relates to gross income (before taxes). Since the United States has a progressive income tax structure (higher annual incomes relate to higher tax brackets), some of this income inequality will ostensibly be resolved once taxes are collected. As we see in the next section, though, it is not that simple.

CEO pay is not the only indication that income inequality experienced a decrease in the past few years. Median household income rose 5.2 percent (to $56,500) between 2014 and 2015, and the gains were largest in the poorest households. These increases are likely more attributable to lower unemployment than an increase in wages.[32] While growth was slower in rural areas (3.4 percent) than metropolitan areas (6.0 percent) between 2014 and 2015, the increase in income across the geographical divide was perceived to be encouraging.[33] Whether it is an anomaly or the beginning of a trend will not be apparent for several years.

Taxes

There is no denying that the US income tax code is tremendously complicated. It is full of complex rules and regulations that are designed to add fairness to the system. But "fair" is in the eye of the beholder and open to interpretation by Americans with differing ideological leanings. Those who earn a lot often complain that the so-called progressive tax structure punishes (and, more important, deincentivizes) financial success, while those who earn less sometimes wish that a higher percentage of the nation's revenue would be paid by those who can most afford it. In sum, our tax code is a collection of deals and compromises between representatives who have different preferences—and who represent constituencies that have different preferences (see Box 2.1).

On the surface, the United States income tax system is progressive in that it appears to tax those who earn more at a higher rate than those who earn less. In 2015, the rate began with a base of 10 percent, with a married couple earning more than $18,450 paying an increasingly higher rate on the money they make over the first 10 percent—from 15 percent to 39.6 percent (for those earning more than $464,851).[34] The effective tax rates (which includes all forms of income tax, not just taxes on wages) for the highest earners have been reduced over the past forty years, from 66.4 percent after World War II to 47.7 percent in 1982 to 36.4 percent in the 1990s. The George W. Bush tax cuts further reduced the top bracket to 32.4 percent.[35] In 2015, it was 33.4 percent.[36] However, before the tax rate is applied, the taxable income amount can be reduced by a host of deductions that are disproportionately available to higher earners. A recent study found that more than half of all tax benefits went to the wealthiest 5 percent of taxpayers and that "the top 1 percent of taxpayers, those making more than $1 million, received an average $95,000 in assistance. . . . By contrast, the poorest taxpayers, including families making $50,000, received less than $500 in benefits."[37] The most widespread of these policies is the mortgage interest deduction, which allows for a reduction in taxable income related to money paid toward interest on a home mortgage. The more expensive the home, the larger the deduction. There are also deductions for contributions to retirement plans, and a flat 15 percent tax on income made from the sale of capital assets held for more than a year.[38] Mitt Romney, the 2012 Republican presidential candidate, revealed that he paid 14 percent in 2010 and 2011 (the only years for which he released returns during the campaign), even though he earned $13.7 million and $21.7 million in those years, respectively, because most of the income was from investments.[39] Multi-billionaire Warren Buffett has famously quipped that his secretary pays a higher percentage of her annual income than he does as a result of these complicated regulations.[40] Donald Trump famously refused to provide his tax returns during the 2016 campaign, but a leak obtained by the *New York Times* suggested that despite his estimated $3.7 billion estimated wealth,[41] he may have paid no federal income taxes for nearly twenty years.[42] Clearly, the income tax structure can disproportionately benefit those with the most income.

Box 2.1. *Representing:* Steve Forbes and the Flat Tax

The publisher of *Forbes* magazine, Steve Forbes, championed a flat tax in his bids for president of the United States in 1996 and 2000, as well as in a 2005 book called *Flat Tax Revolution: Using a Postcard to Abolish the IRS.*[a] While some progressives worry that a program touted almost exclusively by wealthy conservatives will not ultimately benefit the neediest Americans, the underlying premise addresses one of the more egregious inequalities about the current tax structure: those who are able to hire tax professionals benefit most because of the complicated nature of the process.

For individuals, the proposed tax form has just twelve lines and can literally fit on a piece of paper the size of a postcard. After reporting wages and salary earned, a taxpayer deducts for adults ($13,200 each) and children ($4,000 each) in the household, calculates 17 percent of the remaining amount, and then earns an additional $1,000 deduction for each child under age sixteen. The Earned Income Tax Credit (EITC) could also be claimed by those who qualify.[b]

While conservatives call the plan "simple, fair, and good for growth,"[c] progressives call it "a game of three-card monte that deliberately confuses the issues of simplicity, fairness, and the total tax burden on society."[d] Nonetheless, it is an idea that has some intrinsic appeal to anyone who has filed a federal tax return. Because most of the wealthiest individuals pay others to compute their taxes, Forbes's proposal would likely generate

At the same time, other taxes that disproportionately affect those who are not wealthy have increased. These are called regressive taxes. For example, Social Security is funded by a flat payroll tax (12.4 percent in 2016), with half paid by the employee and the other half by the employer. Individuals pay only on the first $118,500 earned.[43] Those who earn more make no further contributions. That means that higher earners pay a smaller percentage of their overall income to help fund the program than do lower earners. Sales taxes are applied by state and local governments to products and services. Everyone needs to buy food and necessities, so everyone, rich and poor, is subject to these taxes. But a 3 percent tax on milk or an 18 percent excise tax on gasoline (in addition to local gas taxes) will have a more significant impact on a working family's budget than on a millionaire's. In this manner, increases in regressive taxes to make up for revenue lost from providing income tax breaks to the significant mass appeal if elected officials ever took it seriously. Whether the result would be an increase in economic equality is unclear, but some scholars[e] have argued that it ought to be adopted to eliminate the complicated (often nearly invisible) benefits that the current system provides to those who need it least.

After his party's candidate won the presidency for the first time since 2004, Forbes repeated his call for a simplified tax system. Although he did not call for President-elect Trump to adopt a flat tax, he offered a plan with only two tax brackets, in addition to reduction in capital gains taxes and taxes on corporations.[f]

---

a. Steve Forbes, *Flat Tax Revolution: Using a Postcard to Abolish the IRS* (Washington, DC: Regnery, 2005).

b. Ibid., 73. Other versions of the plan do not include the additional deductions for children under 16 or the EITC. See Daniel Mitchell, "A Brief Guide to the Flat Tax," Heritage Foundation, July 7, 2005. http://www.heritage.org/research/reports/2005/07/a-brief-guide-to-the-flat-tax.

c. Mitchell, "A Brief Guide to the Flat Tax."

d. Michael Kinsley, "Steve Forbes's Flat Tire," *Washington Post*, August 7, 2005, http://www.washingtonpost.com/wp-dyn/content/article/2005/08/05/AR2005080501490.html.

e. Dorothy Brown, "Let's Kill the Progressive Tax Rate System," CNN.com, April 17, 2012, http://www.cnn.com/2012/04/17/opinion/brown-progressive-tax-rates/index.html.

f. Steve Forbes, "Why Trump's Tax Cuts Should Be Big and Bold," *Forbes*, December 14, 2016, http://www.forbes.com/sites/steveforbes/2016/12/14/why-trumps-tax-cuts-should-be-big-and-bold/#1f0df9186298.

---

wealthy can cause a significant burden for those who are already economically vulnerable.

On the other hand, a number of provisions in the US tax code provide tax breaks that benefit low earners disproportionately (such as the deductions for children, tuition, and government-backed low-interest student loans) or solely (such as the low-income housing tax credit and credit for rent paid). One such program, the Earned Income Tax Credit (EITC), was expanded between 1984 and 1996 to provide an incentive for single mothers to work.[44] The EITC benefits working families (particularly those with children) by providing a reduction in taxable earnings for families earning less than $53,505 (in 2016, married with three children or more).[45] The mortgage interest deduction program also benefits Americans in a variety of income ranges. So, while it is not the case that the high earners are the sole beneficiaries of US tax policy, they benefit disproportionately, even though they represent a distinct numerical minority of citizens.

Minimum Wage and the Poverty Line

In 1938, Congress set a federal minimum wage (at twenty-five cents per hour),[46] but it was not indexed to increase with inflation. As a result, there have been significant lags in the buying power of the dollar for minimum wage workers. The current federal minimum wage, set in 2009, is $7.25 per hour, though the highest level (in real dollars) was in 1968 ($10.04 in 2010 dollars).[47] Twenty-nine states and the District of Columbia have minimum wages higher than the federal level.[48] Individuals in occupations where tips are expected are not protected by minimum wage laws.

A full-time worker at the federal minimum wage will fall below the poverty line for a family of four. In 1968, a full-time minimum wage worker earned about 90 percent of the poverty level, but from the mid-1980s until Congress raised the minimum wage in 2006, full-time minimum wage workers with a family of four only earned between 50 and 60 percent of the federal poverty level.[49]

The poverty line (technically "poverty threshold") is not without its critics (those who think it is too low and those who think it is too high). The poverty threshold was developed in the 1960s and is based on the cost of food, under the assumption that a family of three or more spends about one-third of its income on food.[50] In 2015, the poverty threshold for an individual was $11,880; the threshold for a family of four was $24,300.[51] In 2010, the poverty rate in the United States was the highest since 1993, with 15.1 percent of individuals living in poverty. Twenty-seven percent of African Americans and 26.6 percent of Hispanics lived below the poverty threshold in 2010; less than 10 percent of non-Hispanic whites and 12.1 percent of Asians lived in poverty that year.[52] By 2014, the rate declined a bit: 14.8 percent of all persons in the United States lived in poverty.[53] Once again, gender matters, and its effect is intersectional:

> Poverty rates are highest for families headed by single women, particularly if they are black or Hispanic. In 2014, 30.6 percent of households headed by single women were poor, while 15.7 percent of households headed by single men and 6.2 percent of married-couple households lived in poverty.[54]

Poverty rates are even higher for women of color who are the head of a household: In 2015, 39.9 percent of female-headed African American households, 41.9 percent of female-headed Hispanic households, and 48.4 percent of female-headed Native American households with children were living in poverty, as compared to 30.6 percent of female-headed white households.[55] Because women earn less than men, and because women of color are more likely to be the head of a household, a portion of the racial gap in income is related to gender.

Children are also disproportionately affected by poverty. Nearly one in five American children is poor, and as for women, there is a racial component: The child poverty rate for white children is 12.1 percent, compared to 32.9 percent for African American children, 28.9 percent for Hispanic children, 30.7 percent for Native American children, and 12.3 percent for Asian children.[56]

As is always the case with statistics and classifications, there is disagreement about how to appropriately operationalize poverty. Those who argue that the existing formula sets the level too low point to the fact that income from federal programs (often referred to as welfare; see below) is not counted in this calculation.[57] Those who argue that the level is too high note that while the rationale for calculating based on food as one third of a family budget might have been appropriate a half-century ago, housing prices in particular (not to mention transportation and utility costs) have increased at a rate disproportionate to food.[58]

Similarly, there are competing ideas about whether raising the minimum wage would help relieve income inequality. By one calculation, if the minimum wage had risen proportionately with CEO compensation, it would be more than $23 per hour.[59] The wisdom of raising the minimum wage can be considered in terms of our shared American values (*should* the minimum wage rise at the same level as CEO compensation?), as well as in terms of more practical considerations. A *New York Times* editorial in March 2011 argued for a raise, noting that even with the 2009 increase, in real dollars, the minimum wage is still lower than it was thirty years ago.[60] In his 2014 State of the Union Address, President Obama called on Congress to raise the federal minimum wage to $10.10 per hour.[61] Both Bernie Sanders and Donald Trump supported a minimum wage increase in their respective 2016 presidential election campaigns.[62]

Business groups who oppose raising the minimum wage argue that doing so would harm job creation, force layoffs, or lead to hours being cut back for those earning the minimum wage.[63] They note, for instance, that many minimum wage workers are not trying to support families—they have a second earner, have supplemental income (such as Social Security retirement for seniors working part-time), or are students. In combination with other government programs, advocates of this position feel as if there is enough of a safety net in place to protect low-wage workers and that the government should not meddle with the invisible hand of the economy.

Welfare

Many advanced democracies have expansive welfare states that are designed to provide a safety net so that no citizen falls into economic despair. Such societies are generally characterized by high tax rates and active central governments that are involved in many segments of the economy.[64] The United States has sponsored a number of programs over the years that are designed to provide such protections, but the scope and duration of those programs was dramatically reduced in the 1990s.

Welfare is a catchall term for government-funded and -operated programs that provide different forms of financial assistance to those who need it. While various levels of assistance have been in place since colonial times, New Deal programs established during the Great Depression were more expansive than their predecessors. Many of these programs, such as unemployment compensation, Aid to Families with Dependent Children, and the program that we now know as Social Security are still in place.[65] Although not income per se, health care programs, such as Medicare (for senior citizens) and Medicaid (for needy persons who are not seniors) provide additional assistance to offset costs associated with taking care of oneself and one's family.

There has been great debate in the United States about how much assistance should be provided to the needy and under what circumstances. These debates involve conflict of several core values to which Americans subscribe.[66] While Americans have a commitment to equality in a broad sense, they also have a commitment to individualism that has roots deep into US history. Further, the language used to discuss welfare in the 1980s was highly racialized, causing persistent inaccuracies in perceptions about whom these programs benefit and how much money is spent in this area.

Ronald Reagan's reference to a "welfare queen" in Chicago with "80 names, 30 addresses, 12 Social Security cards and is collecting veterans' benefits on four nonexisting deceased husbands" to the tune of $150,000 per year[67] created an enduring image of poverty in America that is characterized by undeserving African Americans who are cheating the system to get rich on the backs of hardworking (white) taxpayers. The story he told on the campaign trail in 1976 about Linda Taylor was likely an exaggeration,[68] but the retelling of the story suggested that she was typical. As a result, the welfare queen script came to dominate the imagination of white Americans who were asked to consider reforms to the welfare system in the following decade.[69] As political scientist Martin Gilens notes:

> The connection between "poor" and "black" exists simply because African Americans account for a disproportionate number of poor people in the United States. Only one in ten white Americans falls below the official government poverty line, but three out of ten blacks are poor. Still, blacks are a small segment of the American population, and even though they are disproportionately poor, they comprise only a minority (currently about 27 percent) of all poor people.[70]

Gilens's study reveals that white respondents who viewed blacks as hardworking were much less willing to decrease welfare spending than those who viewed blacks as lazy.[71] In this way, it is very difficult to disentangle Americans' views of the poor generally with their perceptions of poor persons of color. Deservedness lies at the heart of welfare policy debates. In a political culture that values individualism and has a history that is deeply rooted in racial animosity toward African Americans in particular (and more recently Latinos), support for benefits to veterans, retired persons, and the physically disabled is more plentiful than support for the working poor, the homeless, or the mentally ill. Further, we must consider that Reagan chose to focus on a welfare queen, not a welfare king. The public disdain for the poor that is reflected in Gilens's study and that led to reforms in the 1990s is rooted in patriarchal views of personhood that marginalize women's voices and delegitimize their lived experiences.[72] In other words, Reagan's simplistic and atypical story resonated with Americans because of preexisting sexist and racist narratives that we hold in our subconscious.

Public attitudes about welfare drove significant reforms in the mid-1990s. Congress now provides grants to states to distribute to needy citizens. This procedural change, along with federal guidelines, has resulted in a dramatic decrease in the number of Americans who receive cash assistance to offset their poverty. In 2014, only 23 percent of poor families received cash assistance, compared to 82 percent in 1980. It was 60 percent in 1996.[73] Twenty years after the reforms, there is mixed evidence about the results: "The new program did work for millions of families, but not all. Many of the most disadvantaged people have been unable to get or keep jobs, and they're worse off than they were before, in part because there's now a five-year lifetime limit on welfare benefits—and in some states, it's lower."[74]

The reality, of course, is much more complicated. Government "handouts" do not only go to the needy. So-called corporate welfare refers to tax incentives and subsidies for businesses.[75] Most Americans may not be aware of these policies, and even if they are, such programs as these are generally not lumped into the category of welfare. Although subsidies and tax breaks to corporations (even if they are profitable) are not income in the individual sense of the word, they help to make businesses successful, which sometimes translates into job creation (and thus income for workers) and often results in increases in wealth for top executives and major stockholders.

Wealth

Whereas income is the amount of money a person or household earns in a year, wealth is the value of that person or household overall. Wealth is calculated by subtracting debt from assets, and in many ways it is a more accurate window into economic and racial inequality in America. Although it is important to understand income gaps as part of the cycle of disadvantage (and advantage) in the United States, wealth signifies the command over financial resources that a family has accumulated over its lifetime along with resources that have been inherited across generations. Such resources, when combined with income, can create the opportunity to secure the "good life" in whatever form is needed—education, business, training, justice, health, comfort, and so on.[76]

Some Americans (both rich and poor) earn no income on an annual basis. In that respect, they are equal in terms of income even though their opportunities may be quite different. Further, wealth and income are not highly correlated, and there is great variation in wealth within income categories.[77] In this section, we will briefly consider some markers of wealth inequality before turning our attention to the systemic factors that reflect and perpetuate the growing gap between the wealthy and the poor in the United States.

Wealth Gap

While the income gap is large (and growing), the wealth gap is even more dramatic.[78] Median household wealth in the United States grew from $79,100 in 1989 to $126,400 in 2007 before falling dramatically to $77,300 in 2010.[79] In 2015, the median household wealth has rebounded to $81,450.[80] Rather than accumulating wealth throughout a lifetime, a sizable percentage of Americans struggle through their senior years, living primarily on Social Security. Nearly half of Americans die with less than $10,000 in assets.[81] Research over the past decade has demonstrated that the gap between the rich and poor in America has been increasing over the past thirty years and that it is more exaggerated when race is factored in.[82]

Specifically, the top 10 percent of US households now control 76 percent of the nation's total wealth (up from 49 percent in 2005), leaving the bottom half of the population controlling a mere 1 percent of that wealth.[83] That increase, however, somewhat masks the reality that is faced by persons of color. Between 1989 and 2013, whites' median family wealth rose about 3 percent (to $134,008). Conversely, African American and Hispanic family wealth rose dramatically (44.6 percent and 50.6 percent, respectively), yet the actual amount is still significantly lower ($11,184 for black families and $13,900 for Hispanic families).[84] If we use average (mean) wealth, rather than median wealth, the results are even more dramatic: whites' average household wealth was $656,000 in 2013, up from $355,000 in 1983. For African Americans, average wealth increased over that same period from $67,000 to $85,000; for Hispanics, the increase was $98,000 from $58,000.[85] As the authors of one report noted,

> [I]f the past 30 years were to repeat, the next three decades would see the average wealth of White households increase by over $18,000 per year, while Latino and Black Households would see their respective wealth increase by about $2,250 and $750 per year. . . . If average Black family wealth continues to grow at the same pace it has over the past three decades, it would take Black families 228 years to amass the same amount of wealth White families have today.[86]

At this point, it should come as no surprise that gender is also relevant with respect to wealth, though it is much more difficult to measure since wealth is most often reported at the household, rather than individual, level. The data that are available center on nonmarried households and tend to show that women are less likely than men to own almost every type of asset. The median value of assets held by women is almost always lower than that of their male counterparts. A smaller percentage of women own stocks, bonds, and other financial assets compared to men. Women are also less likely to hold retirement accounts and a woman's pension is typically smaller than a man's.[87]

When married couples divorce or when a spouse dies, women often face a disproportionate financial burden. If they were not in the labor force during marriage, they are disadvantaged when competing for positions with more experienced candidates. Children most often live with their mother after a separation or divorce, and men are not always willing or able to pay child support.[88] Women are also more likely than men to lose health insurance after a divorce,[89] which, as we will see later, can result in significant, even debilitating, financial strain. A woman whose husband dies tends to own only fifty-nine cents for every dollar of wealth that men have when a wife dies.[90] As we saw with income, because women of color are more likely to be heads of households, there is an interactive effect between race and gender, as well.

The very wealthiest Americans lost a lot during the Great Recession: "The 10 richest Americans lost a combined $39.2 billion" between September 2008 and September 2009 (which represents a 14 percent reduction).[91] One way to look at this, then, is to consider that the wealthiest were hit hardest by the housing crisis and resulting economic troubles. We must ask, though, how the day-to-day life of those Americans were affected compared to the life of the poorest Americans. Put another way, if given the choice, would we rather be one of those individuals who lost the most money, or an American living in poverty who either lost a low-wage job or had a harder time finding one as a result of the recession?[92]

Gifts and Inheritance

Some individuals get a head start on the road to financial security by having parents or other relatives with money. Whether gifts are made early in one's adult life or assets are left after a relative dies, being able to count on money that one has not personally earned can be a tremendous help. While many people who are wealthy have parents who were not as wealthy, the majority of poorer Americans come from poor families and thus do not have the opportunity to get a head start in this way.[93]

The racial gap with respect to inheritance is significant. While slavery and legal racial segregation seem to be in the distant past, when we consider the passing of wealth through generations, it becomes clear that African Americans who are alive today who trace their heritage to slaves have been systemically disadvantaged because accumulation of wealth was illegal or nearly impossible given the conditions in which their ancestors lived. Researchers Gittelman and Wolff conclude that "African Americans would have gained significant ground relative to whites [between 1984 and 1994] if they had inherited similar amounts."[94] Similarly, Menchik and Jianakoplos estimate that white households are at least twice as likely to receive an inheritance and that "racial differences in inheritances can explain between 10 percent and 20 percent of the average racial difference in household wealth (in 1989)."[95] A windfall inheritance—even if it is modest—can help to offset existing debt, be invested in a major purchase (such as a home), or be put aside for an emergency or to plan for retirement. Because whites are, on average, able to count on inheritance or financial help from family members more than persons of color, their starting line is closer to the finish line (economic security). This should not obscure the reality, however, that millions of whites have also not been able to rely on significant family support or inheritance and, as well, have lived for generations in poverty, at least partly due to the rapid decrease in manufacturing jobs.[96]

Savings and Investments

Children are often encouraged to save their money for a rainy day. As adults, we have historically been expected to have some sort of reserve in the event of a job loss, an illness, or some other unforeseen event that affects our earning (see Box 2.2). But savings and investment can only occur after basic needs (housing, food, utilities, school supplies, etc.) are satisfied. Savings of disposable income (money available after basic needs are met) dropped to just over 1 percent in 2001, which is much lower than the average rate of nearly 8 percent between 1959 and 2001.[97] In 2009 (during the Great Recession), savings increased to between 3 and 6 percent, but those rates were much lower for poorer Americans, as one might expect.[98] In 2015, a survey found that 62 percent of Americans have less than $1,000 in savings.[99]

Box 2.2. *What Can I Do?:* Community Education

Understanding personal finance is difficult for everyone, irrespective of educational background. Even those of us with advanced degrees have trouble making sense of tax forms, understanding the difference between an IRA and a 401(k), knowing what mutual fund to consider, and choosing a savings account or certificate of deposit. If you have a good grasp of these matters, you can be helpful to people in your local community. See whether your college (or another local college) has a community program related to finance, or check with the library to see whether it has programs designed to educate the public (often these pop up around tax time in March and April).

There are also a number of not-for-profit groups that offer this sort of assistance. Foundation Communities (www.foundcom.org) in the Austin, Texas, area, for instance, sponsors a program, Community Tax Centers, that provides free income tax preparation help to low-income families in the area. Participants work with volunteers who have a detailed understanding of tax law and who, in turn, educate additional volunteers to give hands-on assistance. The Community Financial Education Foundation (CFEF) is a nationwide group whose mission is "to educate the American public and reach underserved communities by teaching meaningful financial life skills, encouraging positive financial behaviors, and providing access to outcome-based, educational resources over the long-term" (www.communityfef.org). It works with volunteers and community partners to provide these services in a number of communities, as well as through online educational tools.

Whites' real estate assets are generally worth more than nonwhites' (which is a function of housing values in each neighborhood, as will be discussed further in Chapter 3).[100] This is significant because for most Americans, a home is their most significant asset. Only one in four African Americans have any non–real estate assets (such as stocks, bonds, or mutual funds); only one in six Hispanics hold any of these types of assets. Less than half of black Americans and less than a third of Hispanic Americans reported having an individual retirement account in 2011. Further, 18 percent of African Americans and nearly one-third of Hispanics reported having no checking or savings account. Half of whites reported having some form of non–real estate assets, two-thirds have a retirement account, such as an IRA or 401(k), and 95 percent had a checking or savings account.[101] As will become clear in Chapter 3, home ownership is a significant asset for many white Americans, but far fewer African Americans and Latinos own a home (and those who do have less equity than whites).[102]

Credit and Debt

The ability to get credit—borrow money—both reflects wealth and determines one's ability to accumulate it. Automobile commercials frequently promise low (or no) finance charges for "well-qualified" buyers—those whose high credit score and income are deemed sufficient by the lender. Of course, someone who fits that categorization will certainly *appreciate* a better deal on the car, but he or she probably does not *need* the better deal nearly as much as someone who is not "well qualified" by those criteria. The person with less income or worse credit thus pays more for the car, which only contributes to his or her unsteady economic circumstances. Banks often charge fees on checking accounts that fail to maintain a minimum balance throughout the billing cycle, give stiff fines for overdrafts, and place restrictions on savings account withdrawals if there is not a minimum balance. While all of these practices can be justified from the perspective of the banks in terms of their ability to conduct business, there is a potential for very adverse effects on those with limited funds in their accounts.

Missing a payment or making a late payment can trigger a higher interest rate, which only exacerbates the problem for borrowers with financial uncertainty. (As detailed in Chapter 3, adjustable-rate mortgages can leave families in financial trouble even if bills are paid on time.) Missing payments or paying late, with the accumulation of late fees and interest, can harm credit scores or lead to bankruptcy.

Calculations of creditworthiness are complicated (sometimes including up to one hundred variables),[103] but are essentially based on factors such as income, available existing credit, and history of repayment. Other factors such as zip code, marital status, and length of time at the present address may also be considered.[104] It is not difficult to understand how poorer Americans—those who live in less desirable zip codes, rent their home, earn relatively low income, and so on—are disadvantaged by a system that is used by middle-class folks to increase their wealth. Credit scores do not affect only consumer financing or credit card applications. They are often used in determining whether a person is granted a lease for an apartment, rates for automobile and homeowner's insurance, and sometimes for evaluating candidates for employment.

Ability to secure conventional loans or access to credit, like other measures of economic inequality, is not unrelated to race. Because African Americans and Latinos are poorer on average than whites, there is a disproportionate tendency for persons of color to be victimized by predatory lending with respect to all aspects of consumerism.[105] Those who cannot secure traditional forms of credit often turn to riskier (and more costly) alternatives to stay afloat.[106]

Predatory Practices and Gambling

While gambling (betting on sporting events, at a casino, or through state-sanctioned lotteries) is available to and enjoyed by Americans from all social and ethnic groups, there is a tendency for those who are the most needy to turn to these potentially quick sources of revenue. Problem gambling can be so debilitating because the more desperate people are, the more likely they are to gamble.

Type of gambling is related to income. For instance, while only 6 percent of individuals with a household income under $30,000 per year gamble on sports, 17 percent of those with a household income between $30,000 and $75,000 do.[107] In general, gambling is much more common among higher-income than lower-income Americans.[108] However, individuals who play the lottery and have a household income of under $10,000 per year bet nearly three times as much on lotteries as do those with a household income over $50,000 per year.[109]

More systematic than gaming, however, is the existence and persistence of predatory loan businesses that are disproportionately located in communities that are most likely to use them (i.e., poorer communities). Payday loan shops offer quick access to cash in exchange for a commitment to have the amount (and an interest fee) deducted from the customer's next paycheck. There is no credit check or lengthy application. One must generally produce a valid form of identification and proof of employment (with wages and pay date). Payday loans are mostly for small amounts (less than $300), but the fees range from $15 to $30 for each $100 borrowed,[110] an interest rate that exceeds that of most credit cards. Researcher Michael A. Stegman describes the market for such services:

The core demand for payday loans originates from households with a poor credit history, but who also have checking accounts, steady employment, and an annual income under $50,000. . . . A 2001 survey of low-income families in Charlotte [North Carolina] . . . estimated that African Americans were about twice as likely to have borrowed from a payday lender in a two-year period as whites . . . , and that, after controlling for a wide range of socioeconomic characteristics, blacks were five times more likely than whites to take out multiple payday loans.[111]

In 2016, the United States Consumer Financial Protection Bureau imposed new regulations on payday loan establishments,[112] but it is expected that the industry will respond to these guidelines with creative options that are no less predatory.[113]

Americans who lack access to traditional forms of credit may also turn to rent-to-own (RTO) establishments to furnish their homes and buy appliances or such items as televisions. RTO programs allow customers to pay a small amount on a regular basis (rent) and then have a chance to buy (own) the item at the end of the contract. The majority of RTO customers earn less than $25,000 per year,[114] and those customers understand that they are going to end up paying more for the item than they would if they were able to pay cash outright.[115] *Consumer Reports* explains that customers are generally unaware, however, that they are paying what amounts to a 250 percent annual interest rate on some RTO transactions.[116] Further, a recent study showed that inflation was rising at higher rates on goods that are disproportionately consumed by poorer Americans, placing those Americans with less wealth at an even greater disadvantage as a result of market forces.[117]

Not everyone sees such systemic disadvantage as victimizing the poor, however. Historian Thomas Woods Jr. asks why poor Americans are not more responsible with money.[118] He suggests that Americans who cannot afford such luxuries as television sets should not purchase them or should save money so that they can purchase them later. He argues that consumers who pay RTO prices have "character flaws" that cause them to spend irresponsibly. Woods raises a valid point in terms of the wisdom of such purchases, but he is inattentive to the tremendous psychological pressure placed on all consumers—not just those who are economically disadvantaged—to appear to be in the middle class by, well, *consuming*. Each of us should practice frugality, spend wisely, and not live beyond our financial means.

Those who have significant amounts of disposable income, however, can be financially irresponsible without life-altering consequences; those who do not, cannot. If we all had the same income, it would be difficult to argue with such commentators as Woods, who make reasonable points without considering the inherently unreasonable nature of the circumstances.

Such a position fits neatly within the myth of American meritocracy explained in the previous chapter: those who are able to access traditional methods of credit (and secure reasonable interest rates to borrow) are considered to be in such a position because of their wisdom, hard work, and perhaps some good luck. In exchange, they deserve to have beneficial terms for borrowing and spending, whereas poorer Americans do not, ostensibly because they have contributed to their own poverty. This individualistic view of inequality is convenient for those who have privilege because it removes any concerns about either the legitimacy of their own financial comfort or the responsibility to take action against a system that is flawed. As this chapter demonstrates, however, the convenient response is too simplistic to capture the reality of contemporary economic and racial inequality in the United States.

Representing the Poor

Thomas Woods's position is closest to that of most Americans: empathy for the poor does not run particularly high. In the abstract, most Americans believe that poverty is an important problem that is facing government,[119] but studies have also found that Americans believe there are multiple determinants of poverty but that individualistic or "internal" causes (e.g., lack of effort, being lazy, low in intelligence, being on drugs) tend to be more important than societal or "external" ones (e.g., being a victim of discrimination, low wages, being forced to attend bad schools).[120]

Further, polls have shown that an overwhelming majority of those who are doing well financially claim responsibility for their success, whereas less than half of those who believe they are doing poorly economically take responsibility for that condition.[121] Consider, then, the position of elected officials, who are responsible for responding to public opinion on policy issues as they seek to represent their constituents. If most Americans do not think that the system needs to be adjusted, then there will be little pressure on policymakers to make adjustments. Consequently, the belief that poorer Americans are largely responsible for their own financial condition has led to an unwillingness to address systemic barriers to greater equality. After all, if we do not believe it is broken, we will not try to fix it.

Race's relationship to wealth and poverty is a central theme of this book. Because of the way hegemonic power systems operate, the word *race* generally invokes images of persons of color in the mind of white Americans. When most people speak of "poverty and race," they assume that the conversation is about racial minorities. But poverty is widespread in the United States, and while it disproportionately affects communities of color, millions of poor whites, primarily living in rural areas, are disadvantaged by systemic forces. Because our system of representation in the United States is primarily based on geography, and because housing patterns are influenced by economic circumstances, there are some dramatic differences in the constituencies of some representatives as opposed to others. While many elected officials represent diverse economic areas (US senators, for example, represent entire states, most of which have both rich and poor families, and big-city mayors often have very economically diverse constituencies), many others represent areas that are overwhelmingly wealthy or overwhelmingly poor. In the strictest sense, these representatives are responsible for giving voice to the poorest Americans in national and state legislatures, even (and especially) if other elected officials fail to do so. In attempting to understand the relationship between representation and inequality, we will consider the demographics of some of the poorest areas in the United States and the officials who are charged with representing them.

As reflected in Figure 2.2, the highest percentage of poverty occurs in nonmetropolitan areas of southern states. According to the most recent census, in terms of median income, the three poorest counties (as well as 4 of the top 10, and 22 of the top 100) are in Kentucky.[122] In terms of percentage of residents living below the poverty line, the poorest county in the United States is Ziebach County in South Dakota (more than 54 percent of households are below the poverty line).[123] The number of residents within a county vary greatly, so perhaps a more appropriate way to examine the representation of the economically disadvantaged in America is to consider congressional districts (each of which contain approximately 710,000 people).[124] Congressional districts contain more people than most counties but fewer than large cities, which results in members

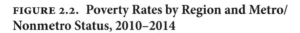

FIGURE 2.2. Poverty Rates by Region and Metro/ Nonmetro Status, 2010–2014

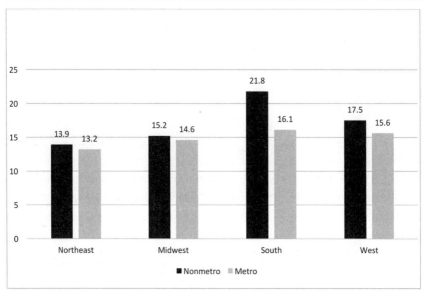

Source: US Department of Agriculture, "Geography of Poverty," October 17, 2016, https://www.ers
.usda.gov/topics/rural-economy-population/rural-poverty-well-being/geography-of-poverty.aspx.

of the US House of Representatives representing relatively, but not entirely, homogeneous geographical areas.

The poorest congressional district in the contiguous United States
is New York's Fifteenth, with an annual median household income of
$26,047. Thirty-eight percent of its residents (and 49 percent of children)
live below the poverty line.[125] José Serrano, who is a Democrat, represents
this district.[126] Kentucky's Fifth District, represented by Harold "Hal"
Rogers, who is a Republican, is also among the most impoverished congressional districts in the nation with an annual median household income of $31,339 (see Box 2.3). Twenty-nine percent of its residents live
below the poverty line.[127] Serrano's district is distinctly urban (covering
the South Bronx); Rogers's is rural. Serrano's district is 63 percent Hispanic and 36 percent African American; Rogers's district is 98 percent
white. Of the ten poorest congressional districts, only Rogers's is majority
white. Four are majority Hispanic (Arizona 4, California 30, New York 15,
and Texas 28), three are majority black (Michigan 13, Michigan 14, and
Mississippi 2), one is plurality Hispanic (Texas 30), and one is plurality

Box 2.3. *Representing:* José Serrano and Hal Rogers

US representatives José Serrano (D-NY) and Hal Rogers (R-KY) have been elected to Congress from the two most impoverished districts in the United States. Serrano, who is Latino, represents the South Bronx, whereas Rogers, who is white, represents a rural area in southeastern Kentucky.

On his website (http://serrano.house.gov/our-district), Congressman Serrano offers a lengthy, detailed explanation about how his district fell into economic despair. According to Serrano, the current conditions are attributable to several factors: changes in rental policy beginning in the 1960s, regional economic downturns, the installation of the Cross Bronx Expressway, cutting through the borough, and the resulting exodus of those residents who were able to move. Serrano responds to the interests of his Latino constituents by sponsoring legislation relevant to their needs, such as a bill that would allow judges to take children with citizenship into consideration when considering deportation against undocumented parents.[a]

Since 1981, Congressman Rogers has advocated for his constituents by attempting to attract jobs to his district and encouraging the community to work together. Through a number of initiatives, he encourages residents of southeastern Kentucky to resist drugs, support small businesses, and attract tourism to what he calls "one of the most beautiful regions of the country" on his website (http://halrogers.house.gov/Biography/). As chairman of the powerful Appropriations Committee from 2011 to 2016, Congressman Rogers has helped oversee the use of taxpayer funds, which is consistent with his conservative philosophy.

Although they represent vastly different areas with respect to race, political orientation, and geography, Serrano and Rogers both serve as a voice for poorer Americans and use their influence to advocate for the issues that disproportionately affect those with minimal political influence.

---

a. Albor Ruiz, "Immigration Reform Needed to Stop Heartbreaking Separations," *New York Daily News*, July 6, 2011. http://articles.nydailynews.com/2011–07–06/local /29759431_1_citizen-children-immigration-status-immigration-laws.

black (Pennsylvania 1).[128] Eight of the districts are represented by Democrats. Two of the representatives of America's poorest congressional districts are Hispanic, four are African American, and four are white. Eight of the representatives are men (Representatives Eddie Bernice Johnson of

Texas's Thirtieth District and Brenda Lawrence of Michigan's Fourteenth District are the exceptions to this current trend).

Leaving aside questions about voting behavior of constituents,[129] it is important to consider what this means at a policy level. All ten of these House members have constituents who are very poor but differ from one another in many ways. How might these representatives work together to consider policies that could help their citizens? Should they? If inequality is a result of individual shortcomings and behavioral elements, it is difficult to argue that there should be any governmental solutions to alleviate it. If, however, systemic factors contribute to and perpetuate economic and racial inequality, then it would seem that these officials, as well as others who represent large numbers of poor families, would have their sights set on advocating for meaningful change that will result in more opportunities for Americans who are suffering the most.

Conclusion

It is tempting to think of income as fluid (relating to securing a job, losing a job, getting a raise or a promotion, etc.) while wealth is more or less stable, growing over time (where possible). This characterization is inappropriate, though, as losses in income or an unexpected rise in expenses (due to an illness, a death in the family, etc.) can lead to a sudden and dramatic drop in wealth. According to sociologist Dalton Conley, "a significant proportion of individuals in the U.S. experience at least one drop in wealth."[130] Whites and African Americans have approximately the same number of drops (on average), but African Americans are more likely to have a greater drop.[131]

Researchers Shapiro, Meschede, and Sullivan argue that while America's racist past is certainly a driving factor behind the existence of the racial wealth gap, the fourfold increase in such a short time reflects policies, such as tax cuts on investment income and inheritances, which benefit the wealthiest, and redistribute wealth and opportunities. Tax deductions for home mortgages, retirement accounts, and college savings all disproportionately benefit higher income families. At the same time, evidence from multiple sources demonstrates the powerful role of persistent discrimination in housing, credit, and labor markets.[132]

They note that persons of color pay more to access credit and are particularly susceptible to predatory lending in the mortgage industry. In

FIGURE 2.3. Cycle of Advantage and Disadvantage

short, while there may be overt, individualized bigotry involved in shaping income and wealth inequality, such incidents cannot come close to explaining these larger trends. First, while income and wealth inequality are pronounced between whites and persons of color, there is a tremendous gap between the highest earning whites and all other whites, as well. Second, the policies that perpetuate and exacerbate these trends are ostensibly colorblind. That is, they are not infused with explicit advantages for whites or disadvantages for persons of color.

Taking a color-blind approach to policy within a racist systemic context cannot lead to increased equality. As Figure 2.3 indicates, there is a cycle of advantage and disadvantage that centers on three major elements of American life: jobs, education, and housing. To earn access to the middle class in the twenty-first century, a college degree is increasingly necessary. Gaining admission into and succeeding in college is more difficult if one does not have a rigorous education in high school (which begins in elementary school). Because most areas fund the local public school districts disproportionately through property tax revenues, the neighborhood in which one lives is strongly related to the quality of education that is available. Of course, most people live in the neighborhood they can afford, so having money in the first place is important. This can be thought of as a cycle of disadvantage, but it is also a cycle of advantage. That is, if one is disadvantaged, it is quite difficult to break the cycle and gain access to economic security (let alone prosperity). Conversely, those who are privileged to be in an advantageous position have numerous opportunities to avoid falling into economic despair.

The cycle is not a guarantee of success or failure. There are many Americans who started in poverty and became financially comfortable and even wealthy, and there are wealthy individuals who fall on hard times and are unable to recover. The idea, however, is that the starting line is not the same for everyone, and that far from simply being behind (as the foot race metaphor suggests), there are systemic obstacles that are difficult to overcome. Many ideas and programs have been designed to interrupt this cycle at various points. As will become clear in the following chapters, the reasons for its persistence are complicated and affected by other related elements (such as disparities in health and in the criminal justice system). Solutions are multifaceted and present opportunities and challenges for ordinary Americans to become involved and make a difference.

Discussion Questions

1. St. John's University professor Allan Ornstein claims that the United States is witnessing the rise of an aristocratic class. Do you agree or disagree with this observation? What evidence can you offer to support your position? In what ways might the rise of an aristocratic class hinder or improve American democracy?

2. Does the existence (and persistence) of wealth and income gaps in the United States lend support for substantive representation or symbolic representation? Why?

3. In the welfare section of this chapter, we encounter some negative stereotypes about poverty and wealth. To what extent have you heard these claims? By whom? In what ways can average Americans work to dispel these myths and stereotypes? What can be done at the elite level? Does the government have a role to play in helping citizens to think beyond stereotypes like these?

4. Discuss Thomas Woods's argument regarding the source of poverty. Is his opinion likely to resonate with Americans? Is it consistent with American values? If so, which? Does it contradict any core American values? If so, which? Discuss how these core values affect the discussion of poverty in the United States.

5. Consider the heterogeneity of America's impoverished regions. Do you perceive this to be a barrier to combating poverty? Why or why not? If you believe that it is an issue, what could possibly be done to help overcome it?

6. Discuss each element of the cycle of advantage and disadvantage (Figure 2.3). Provide examples of salient policy issues that are relevant to the various elements.

3

. . . .

Housing

PERHAPS WE SHOULD BEGIN OUR EXPLORATION OF HOUSING IN-equality with some normative questions that can serve as a baseline. Af-ter all, we are interested in not only the *difference* in housing that exists in America, but the degree to which there is access to *sufficient* housing. Are Americans entitled to any housing at all? If so, what sort? Basic shel-ter (i.e., protection from the weather)? Security from harm? Is access to electricity a right? Plumbing? Internet? If so, is it enough to make sure that Americans are not denied these services? Should they be provided to those who cannot afford them? Does everyone have a right to live in a mansion? Does anyone? What about two mansions? Or ten? Should some Americans have two or three homes when others do not have even one? If not, would it be fair to prohibit wealthy individuals from buying addi-tional homes? What if they rent them to those who cannot afford to buy? Should there be a limit on how much rent they can charge or how much they can raise it from lease to lease? Where do we draw the lines in the proverbial sand? What is reasonable to expect from a wealthy nation such as the United States, and how much should be left to the free market? It is hard to argue against the notion that access to shelter is a basic human right, but how is "shelter" defined, and to what lengths are we willing to go to protect all citizens' housing rights? Answers to these questions form the basis for guidelines to which policymakers must be attentive in a rep-resentative democracy. Simply considering them is the first step to pro-viding a blueprint for how we want our leaders to act.

The Roots of Disadvantage

For most Americans, their home is their largest asset, though many Amer-icans are unable to achieve home ownership at all, and many own a home in an area (rural or urban alike) that is substandard by a number of criteria. It has been estimated that "upwards of 100 million people in the United States live in housing that is physically inadequate, in unsafe neighborhoods, over-crowded or way beyond what they can reasonably afford."[1] In addition, discriminatory redlining (see below) policies during much of the twentieth century resulted in greatly segregated housing patterns that feature wealthy suburbs and poorer inner-city neighborhoods and rural areas.

As indicated in Figure 2.3 (page 69), one of the elements of systemic inequality is housing.[2] The route to economic security runs through our neighborhoods for three reasons: (1) our system of representation is based on geography; (2) access to quality education is related to place of residence; and (3) access to jobs—especially for those who do not have reliable transportation—relies on affordable housing near employment centers. After emancipation, and especially since the Great Migration, African Americans became concentrated in America's largest urban centers[3] while continuing to live in rural areas of former slave states. Latinos, who are now the second largest ethnic group in the United States (17 percent of the population),[4] live in every state but most prominently in rural areas in the South, suburban and urban areas in the Midwest and Northeast, and, most heavily, in the Southwest (particularly Southern California, New Mexico, Arizona, and Texas) and southern Florida.[5]

These broad geographical guidelines are helpful in terms of understanding issues of representation, as state legislators often take racial and ethnic housing patterns into account when drawing legislative district lines (see Chapter 1). With respect to systemic advantages and disadvantages, however, smaller units of analysis are relevant. School districts are organized mostly around neighborhoods in densely populated areas, and access to schools, healthful food, and jobs is often more limited in low-income areas (both urban and rural). And homelessness has adverse consequences that extend beyond lack of shelter. In this chapter, we will explore historic and current patterns of housing inequality in order to understand the relationship between housing and opportunities for equality in education, employment, and health.

Opportunities for Home Ownership

Owning a home is a core component of the American Dream, but on any given day, more than half a million Americans are sleeping outside or in

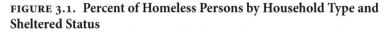

FIGURE 3.1. Percent of Homeless Persons by Household Type and Sheltered Status

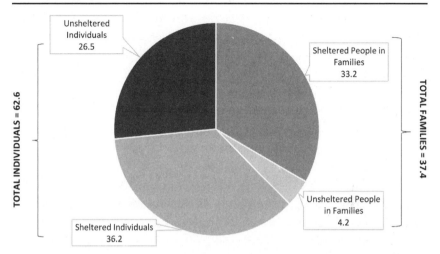

Source: Meghan Henry, Alvaro Cortes, Azim Shivji, and Katherine Buck, "The 2014 Annual Homeless Assessment Report to Congress," US Department of Housing and Urban Development, October 2014, https://www.hudexchange.info/resources/documents/2014-AHAR-Part1.pdf.

an emergency shelter, or participating in a transitional housing program.[6] Many others are staying with friends or relatives on a temporary basis. Figure 3.1 shows the percentage of homeless individuals by the type of shelter they had (or did not have). More than one third of the homeless population includes families with children, including an estimated 1.2 million public school students and 2.5 million children overall.[7] This figure—one in every thirty American children—represents a historic high,[8] even as overall numbers have shown a gradual reduction.[9] Although the vast majority of homeless persons are not chronically homeless,[10] being without shelter for even a couple of days presents challenges that can quickly accumulate and prove to be debilitating.

People are homeless for a number of reasons, including (but not limited to) job loss, domestic abuse, medical or other emergency in the family, mental disorders, and addiction. About one fifth of homeless adults are mentally ill[11] or are addicted to drugs or alcohol, though advocates point out that addiction is often a result of homelessness rather than a cause.[12] Most homeless persons have worked within the past month.[13] These facts, however, deeply cut against most Americans' image of the homeless as being on the street as a result of being insane, addicted, and/or lazy. Such stereotypes undermine empathy for homeless Americans, which in turn makes it difficult for policymakers to place the issue atop the list of those to be addressed. After all, if individuals are homeless because of bad choices they made (assuming they had a reasonable start in life), few Americans would support using governmental resources to help them. If there are systemic reasons for homelessness that put individuals at a distinct disadvantage from a very early age or because of situations beyond their control (e.g., returning home from military service or an illness), then it is more likely that we would turn to our elected officials for help.

In addition to various state initiatives, the federal government has been involved in helping Americans to find affordable housing since the Great Depression. In 1934, Congress created the Federal Housing Administration (FHA) to encourage banks to offer home loans to individuals and families. That program has resulted in some 34 million home loan mortgages. The Housing Act of 1937 established the United States Housing Authority (USHA) to subsidize the building of low-rent public housing. In 1938 and 1970, Fannie Mae and Freddie Mac were created, respectively, to increase the amount of home ownership money available in the lending market.[14] In 1965, the Department of Housing and Urban Development (HUD) was created as a cabinet-level agency (see Box 3.1).[15] These efforts were largely successful for decades, but when the housing bubble burst in 2008, ushering in the Great Recession, millions of Americans found themselves either in foreclosure or in a home that was worth less than the amount owed on it.[16] This means that many home owners—particularly those who have not been in their home for very long—owe more than their home is worth, which makes refinancing more difficult or impossible, contributing to the debt cycle for these families and individuals. By the summer of 2012, home ownership had reached its lowest level since 1965,[17] and it has continued to decline since 2006, reaching another historic low in the summer of 2016.[18]

The 2008 housing crisis was created by risky lending practices and complex financial arrangements among lenders and traders that greatly overvalued the properties they were backing.[19] While that created a housing boom for a period of time, which resulted in a record number of Americans owning a home in the early part of the twenty-first century (largely as a result of low interest rates), many of the loans had adjustable interest rates. When the initial offering rate expired, home owners faced monthly payments that they could not afford. Complicating this was an

Box 3.1. *Representing:* Mel Martinez

Melquíades "Mel" Martinez, a Republican senator and trial lawyer from Florida, was born in Cuba in 1946 and immigrated to the United States when he was a teenager. He is the first Cuban American to serve in a president's cabinet and the first to serve in the US Senate.

As secretary of Housing and Urban Development (HUD), Martinez focused on increasing home ownership, promoting affordable housing, strengthening communities, and improving management, accountability, and ethics at the agency. Martinez proposed the American Dream Downpayment Initiative, which authorized up to $200 million per year to help low-income, first-time home buyers with money for down payments and closing costs. He also awarded a $900,000 grant to the International Code Council to help with housing construction designed to be accessible to people with disabilities.

Under Martinez, HUD urged Congress to pass a law that would strengthen colonias, which are rural settlements along the US-Mexico border. The Colonias Gateway Initiative focused on developing affordable housing and infrastructure in regions of the American Southwest that are home to migrant farmworkers and their families. (The bill never became law.) Martinez significantly increased funding for protection of children from health and safety hazards in the home—conditions that disproportionately affect poorer Americans. Consistent with his politically conservative roots, Martinez also instigated open-door policies that made local housing agencies more receptive to faith-based organizations that wished to provide social services to residents.

Progressive-leaning not-for-profit groups that advocate for housing rights were not pleased with everything Martinez did (or did not do) as HUD secretary. However, considering that his political philosophy (as well as that of his boss, then president George W. Bush) tends to oppose any federal involvement in housing, it is reasonable to conclude that he spent his three years in charge of the department representing the interests of low-income Americans in a way that was consistent with his values and ideology.[a]

---

a. James B. Goodno, "House of Cards: What Exactly Did Mel Martinez Accomplish at HUD—and Will It Be Enough to Get Him Elected to the U.S. Senate?" *Shelterforce*, May-June 2004, http://www.nhi.org/online/issues/135/martinez.html; "Mel Martinez," *Orlando Sentinel*, http://www.orlandosentinel.com/topic/politics/government/mel--martinez-PEPLT007461.topic; US Department of Housing and Urban Development, American Dream Down payment Initiative, 2011, http://www.hud.gov/offices/cpd/affordablehousing/programs/home/addi/.

increasing demand for packages of securities backed by these mortgages. Several large investment firms fell apart, and a domino effect was instigated.[20] Even though mortgage rates remained low through the Great Recession, the housing market stagnated because investors were hesitant to lend, especially to borrowers with less than stellar credit ratings, and existing home owners had trouble selling their home to buy another.

In some areas, renting is a safe and affordable option, but it is not optimal for a number of reasons. First, although renters do not need to have the same credit rating or income as home buyers, they may find it difficult to produce the up-front money necessary to rent a desirable unit. Often a lump sum equal to two months' rent and an additional month's rent in security deposit is required before occupancy. This forces many to rent more costly (and often less desirable) motel rooms by the week or by the month. Similar to the rent-to-own and payday loan practices described in Chapter 2, these arrangements have short-term utility, but they are costly over the long term. For the money spent, more stable accommodations in a traditional rental unit might have been purchased, but saving enough for the deposit can be impossible. Second, not all landlords maintain their property well (including cities responsible for maintaining public housing). Living quarters can deteriorate without regular maintenance. Renters are not responsible for repairs and cannot afford to make them or are prevented by the lease from doing so. Whereas home owners receive a deduction on their federal income taxes for the interest they pay on their mortgage, renters are not similarly rewarded. Finally, although renting may be initially affordable, rent prices can increase from year to year, and moving is often expensive as well. As a result, Americans with few resources to begin with can be stuck in a costly cycle of disadvantage that home owners can avoid. More than that, renting produces no equity to draw on for the future. Add to that the adverse effects on property values when a high percentage of units are rentals and the increased sense of community that many believe to exist when individuals have long-term investments in homes, and one can see how becoming a "nation of renters" has effects beyond the ability to access the American Dream.

The USHA continues to work with local housing authorities to provide low-rent options for America's poorest citizens. Through the Section 8 program, landlords can secure low-interest loans to rehabilitate a property in exchange for their promise to rent a percentage of the units to low-income residents. Individuals and families who qualify for Section

8 assistance can rent apartments in designated properties (or, through the Housing Choice Voucher Program, any available unit) at a rate below market value. The local housing authority, by way of grants from USHA, pays the difference in value directly to the landlord.[21]

In 1977, Congress passed the Community Reinvestment Act (CRA), which requires lenders to consider the rate of lending in low-income rural and urban communities when it seeks federal government approval for opening new branches, acquiring other banks, or mergers. There were scattered rumblings that the 2008 housing crash was a result of banks being forced to lend to poorer Americans in these communities, but a bipartisan congressional commission's investigation into the crash found that the CRA "was not a significant factor in subprime lending or the crisis."[22] While direct accusations that people of color were responsible for the crisis were limited to the blogosphere, it was not surprising to many to detect undertones of racism as lawmakers, economists, and pundits searched for answers.[23]

Racial Inequality and Housing

Even though African Americans comprise only 13 percent of the US population, they represent a majority or near majority of the nation's homeless.[24] As minority home ownership rose during the housing boom, it still remained lower than rates for whites, and the Great Recession increased the gap to 45 percent for African Americans compared with 74 percent for whites; the foreclosure rate for black Americans who bought a home between 2005 and 2008 was double that of whites.[25] When black and Hispanic Americans do own a home, the median value is far less than that of white Americans.[26] The reasons for disproportionately low home ownership among African Americans and Hispanics are several:

> Because blacks, Mexicans, and other Hispanics face distinct demographic, economic, and educational disadvantages in the housing market they may be less able to afford a home. Because these minority groups are younger on average and, in the case of blacks, less likely to be married, the life-cycle situation may also contribute to a lower demand for owned housing.[27]

People of color comprise a disproportionate share of the rental market as well.[28] We are in the midst of a decade-long boom in demand for rental

Box 3.2. *Representing:* ACORN

Before it disbanded in December 2010, the Association of Community Organizers for Reform Now (ACORN) was the "largest grassroots community organization of low- and moderate-income people."[a] With some 1,200 local organizations in 75 cities (in 40 states), the interest group, created in 1970, advocated for housing opportunities and civil rights broadly in urban areas.

In 2010, a series of videos that were secretly filmed and edited by two conservative activists were posted on the Internet and covered by major news organizations. In the videos, ACORN workers were seen providing fraudulent tax advice to the activists, who presented themselves as a pimp and a prostitute. Conservative groups argued that the tapes were evidence of widespread misbehavior by the group, which had been in trouble previously for questionable practices relating to voter registration, as well as financial problems.[b] The videos put strong pressure on the group, as well as on Barack Obama, whom the group supported in his 2008 presidential bid.[c]

ACORN assisted America's poorest families—officials claim that the group helped more than 150,000 low-income families prepare tax returns and receive some $190 million in refunds between 2004 and 2009—but few organizations could withstand such accusations. Ultimately, most of the videotaped allegations were demonstrated to be the result of creative editing and partial information,[d] but the damage was done. Suggestions that a group that largely represented poor black and Latino families was engaged in illegal activity were easy for many whites to accept, as it fit preexisting

units, largely fueled by the sharp and persistent decrease in home ownership.[29] But the increases in demand have resulted in an uptick in average rental prices, which has not been matched by an increase in the salary of renters.[30]

Irrespective of the reasons, inequality in housing opportunities has implications beyond wealth calculations. In the epilogue to the tenth anniversary edition of *Black Wealth/White Wealth*, Melvin Oliver and Thomas Shapiro argue that residential segregation is the lynchpin of race relations in America. . . . [Residential] segregation structures the "segregation tax" producing far less housing wealth in African American communities and the way in which substandard, inferior schools are located stereotypes about persons of color being prone to criminality, looking out for one another, and being dishonest. A decentralized organization can be greatly harmed when its chapters or individual members behave inappropriately. The "bad apple" narrative often attributed to inappropriate behavior in corporate America is rarely applied to the poor or to minorities.[e] The important question is not whether ACORN's fate was deserved but rather what group will fill the role that ACORN served for two generations advocating for urban communities. To date, none has, though its legacy has been helpful to those who seek to make voting more challenging: an August 2016 poll found that 40 percent of Donald Trump's supporters in North Carolina believed that ACORN would steal the election for Hillary Clinton.[f]

a. ACORN, "Who Is ACORN?" 2010. http://www.acorn.org.

b. John Fund, "More ACORN Voter Fraud Comes to Light," *Wall Street Journal,* May 9, 2009, http://online.wsj.com/article/SB124182750646102435.html; Ian Urbina, ACORN on the Brink of Bankruptcy, Officials Say," *New York Times*, March 19, 2010, http://www.nytimes.com/2010/03/20/us/politics/20/acorn.html.

c. http://www.cbsnews.com/stories/2009/09/21/politics/main5326235.shtml; Stanley Kurtz, "Planting Seeds of Disaster: ACORN, Barack Obama, and the Democratic Party," National Review Online, 2008, http://www.nationalreview.com/articles/225898/planting-seeds-disaster-stanley-kurtz#./us/politics20acorn.html.

d. Scott Shifrel, "B'klyn ACORN Cleared over Giving Illegal Advice on How to Hide Money from Prostitution," *New York Daily News*, March 1, 2010, http://www.nydailynws.com/news/crime/b-klyn-acorn-cleared-giving-illegal-advice-hide-money-prostitution-article-1.176119.

e. George Lakoff, *The Political Mind: Why You Can't Understand 21st-Century Politics with an 18th-Century Brain* (New York: Viking, 2008).

f. Public Policy Polling, "Clinton Leads in NC for First Time Since March," August 9, 2016, http://www.publicpolicypolling.com/pdf/2015/PPP_Release_NC_80916.pdf.

predominantly in neighborhoods where minorities and low-income families are concentrated.[31]

Racial inequality, like income and wealth inequality, is widespread and complex. With respect to economics, the housing crisis that began in 2007 and 2008 has led to record numbers of foreclosures, so by that measure, we can identify a parallel with the increasing income and wealth inequality addressed in the previous chapter. On the other hand, neighborhoods are integrating with respect to race in a number of areas, though that story too is a bit complicated.[32]

Racial segregation in housing has existed since the end of the Civil War, but the stories of segregation in the North and South are quite different. There were high levels of integration in the South before the turn of the twentieth century because prior to emancipation, free blacks were intentionally scattered so that they would not be able to organize or form strong communities.[33] Between the end of Reconstruction and the 1960s[34]—an era commonly referred to as Jim Crow—the racial separation of neighborhoods in the South was officially written into local and state law.[35] Jim Crow affected every element of public life—buses, railroads, restaurants, bathrooms—including housing.

In contrast, most prejudice and discrimination in the North at the end of the nineteenth century affected employment, not housing: "the typical black resident of a nineteenth-century northern city lived in a neighborhood that was upward of 90 percent white."[36] In the early twentieth century, black migration to rapidly industrializing urban centers led to housing segregation in the North. European immigrants were also ushered into their own areas, but intermarriage and entrance into the middle class resulted in more notable integration patterns for those Americans.[37] In contrast, white reaction to the Great Migration was more rigid:

> Northern whites viewed this rising tide of black migration with increasing hostility and considerable alarm. Middle-class whites were repelled by what they saw as uncouth manners, unclean habits, slothful appearance, and illicit behavior of poorly educated, poverty-stricken migrants who had only recently been sharecroppers, and a resurgence of white racist ideology during the 1920s provided a theoretical, "scientific" justification for these feelings (Zuberi 2003). Working-class whites, for their part, feared economic competition from the newcomers; as first- or second-generation immigrants who were themselves scorned by native whites, they reaffirmed their own whiteness by oppressing a people that was even lower in the racial hierarchy (Ignatiev 1996).[38]

These attitudinal and behavioral components became manifested in structural elements that began as legal guidelines and informal practices and persist to the present. In 1933, a federal agency created maps that indicated creditworthiness based, in part, on the race of residents. The FHA adopted the maps, resulting in a policy that became known as "redlining,"[39] which reinforced segregated neighborhoods.[40] African Americans were also kept out of white neighborhoods by violence (including bombings) and threats[41] and by the formation of "neighborhood improvement organizations" that influenced local policymakers, boycotted real estate agents who did not respect their preferences, and bribed black residents to leave.[42] The most prominent aspect of the neighborhood association was the restrictive covenant, a legally enforceable contract among white home owners who promised not to sell or lease to African Americans and members of other racial and ethnic minority groups such as Asians and Jews.[43]

Where legal documents were not in place or were ineffective, whites responded by fleeing urban centers. Even the presence of a single middle-class black family could set off panic selling by whites, often resulting in a white neighborhood turning black. White property owners dug in deliberately in their new neighborhood firmly establishing lines that created what are often referred to as ghettos.[44] After World War II, segregation in housing remained, but white flight, aided by public transportation systems and highways that provided access to employment, continued away from inner cities, forming the beginnings of the suburbs.[45] Such trends exemplify the difference between de jure (by law) and de facto (by fact) segregation. While the former was rendered illegal by federal legislation and Supreme Court decisions in the middle of the twentieth century, the latter has persisted as a result of Americans' attitudes and behaviors, as well as the economic realities of disproportionate poverty in communities of color.

Today, our cities are highly segregated on the basis of race, but there are trends toward integration, particularly in urban centers, as whites seek to live in the inner cities to take advantage of cultural opportunities and affordable housing.[46] This, however, creates a new set of dilemmas that must be resolved.

For example, the notorious Cabrini-Green public housing center in Chicago was dismantled in 2010, replaced with mixed-income town homes, and zoned for retail development. The housing project (as public housing clusters are often called) was more than fifty years old when it was demolished, housing up to fifteen thousand residents.[47] The high-rises were not properly maintained by the Chicago Housing Authority, became dilapidated, and were grounds for gang activity and other crime. While the units provided shelter for Chicagoans who might otherwise have been homeless, the conditions were horrifying. Individuals can disagree about whether graffiti is art or is used by violent gangs to mark territory (or both), but inoperable elevators inarguably make life difficult for senior citizens living on a high floor. Persistent problems with rats and cockroaches further compromised living standards and residents' health.[48] Still, people resisted eviction when the orders came to close the complex, noting that the community was tight-knit in some ways and was the only home many residents had ever known. Further, residents learned important organizing and advocacy skills as part of a community organization.[49] While some of the residents would be invited back to live in publicly subsidized apartments (next door to units whose owners paid market value), many others were forced to move to different areas of the city or the state.[50] The shift in focus—from clustering poor families together to dispersing them among middle-income families—presents new issues for public officials to consider. The hope is that the higher property values will maintain, largely because of the desirability of urban housing. If that happens, opportunities for better education and jobs could follow. If history repeats itself, however, whites and middle-class persons of color, who have more choices, could avoid the mixed-income complexes, forcing nearby businesses to close, and public officials will be once again faced with the dilemma of what to do with the beautiful 70-acre site that once housed Cabrini-Green.

If middle-class families decide to stay, however, low-income residents will be displaced as rents and property values are inflated. Columnist Eugene Robinson has referred to those in the latter situation as "the Abandoned."[51] To make matters even more complicated, employment opportunities have increasingly moved to the suburbs, further disadvantaging low-income residents who remain in the inner cities,[52] unable to chase the jobs that they (or their ancestors) moved to the city to be near. Higher-income individuals are increasingly making reverse commutes from their urban homes to their suburban jobs on the very highways and public transportation systems designed to facilitate the opposite commute over the past half-century.

Poverty and Housing in Rural America

It is sometimes tempting to think about substandard housing as a function of inner-city life. While public housing projects and ghettos often form the public face of housing inequality in the United States, millions of Americans living in rural areas are burdened with conditions that rival Third World countries (see Box 3.3).[53] For example, in McDowell County, West Virginia:

Box 3.3. *Representing*: Justin Maxson

With generations-deep Kentucky roots, Justin Maxson might be perceived as a natural voice for rural Americans living in poverty. His lifelong commitment to bringing attention and finding solutions to economic challenges in rural areas is anything but typical. For over a decade, Maxson served as director of the Mountain Association for Community Economic Development (MACED), an organization that works to reduce poverty in Kentucky and Central Appalachia through programs related to energy and conservation.[a] Although common wisdom would lead us to believe that citizens in these areas would be averse to energy suggestions that could be seen as competitors to coal, Maxson's projects have focused on "creating a new sense of what is possible [by creating] tangible examples on the ground of sustainable development at work."[b] These efforts, however, run counter to the direct representation of Kentucky's powerful voices at the national level—Senate majority leader Mitch McConnell, Congressman Hal Rogers, and US senator Rand Paul—all Republicans who tend to oppose environmental regulation and efforts to shift the energy conversation to include renewable sources.[c]

In 2015, Maxson left his position at MACED to serve as executive director at the Mary Reynolds Babcock Foundation in North Carolina.[d] In this position, he has been a vocal advocate for private and public funding for programs that will disproportionately benefit rural Americans. A recent study[e] found that rural communities received only 6 to 7 percent of private foundation grants between 2005 and 2010, even though nearly one fifth of the US population lives in rural areas.[f] He notes that because of the vast expanse and lack of population density in rural communities, it is common for big-city foundations to believe that their funds cannot have a significant effect on economic growth. However, Maxson points out that there is evidence that, by working with local leaders and slowing down enough to learn, then meaningful progress can be made.[g]

a. MACED website, http://www.maced.org/overview.htm.

b. Quoted in Andrew Leonard, "Justin Maxson: An Appalachian Trailblazer for Sustainability," Grist, December 8, 2011, http://grist.org/energy-efficiency/2011-12-07-justin-maxson-an-appalachian-trailblazer-for-sustainability/.

c. Leonard, "Justin Maxson."

d. Susanna Hegner, "New Executive Director Named at Babcock," Mary Reynolds Babcock Foundation, January 14, 2015, http://mrbf.org/blog/new-executive-director-named-babcock.

e. Tim Marema, "Rural Gets Less Foundation Money," *Daily Yonder*, June 29, 2015, http://www.dailyyonder.com/rural-gets-less-foundation-money/2015/06/29/7893/, cited in Betsey Russell, "Bringing People Together: Rural Is 'Different,' Not 'Less,'" *Daily Yonder*, May 25, 2016, http://www.dailyyonder.com/bringing-people-together-rural-is-different-not-less/2016/05/25/13230/.

f. Russell, "Bringing People Together."

g. Ibid.

- The poverty rate is 33 percent; nearly half of all children live in poverty.

- Unemployment is over 30 percent.

- Fewer than 50 percent of adults age 25 or older have a high school diploma.

- 67 percent of households have no wastewater treatment.[54]

The US Census Bureau and the US Department of Agriculture report that the nonmetropolitan poverty rate since 1967 has been consistently higher than poverty rates in cities and suburbs[55] (and recall Figure 2.2 on page 66). Further, "the most significant problem facing rural households is housing affordability." The poverty rate in rural areas in 2013 was 1.5 percent higher than the national average, and the rural income gap has been persistent: median household income is highest in metropolitan areas outside of major cities and lowest in nonmetropolitan areas.[56] In addition, according to the US Department of Agriculture,[57] the welfare reform policies discussed in Chapter 2 have posed disproportionate challenges for individuals and families in rural communities.

In rural America there are more whites in poverty than persons of color. But as is the case nationwide, poverty in those areas is disproportionately black and Hispanic. According to the Housing Assistance Council,[58] African Americans living in rural areas have the highest poverty rate (32.8 percent), followed by Hispanics (29.1 percent), whites (13.3 percent), and Asians (8.1 percent). The child poverty rate in nonmetropolitan areas is also greater (25.2 percent) than in metropolitan areas (21.1 percent).[59]

Even though the challenges faced by impoverished rural Americans are similar in many ways to those faced by poor Americans in metropolitan areas, they are less visible because major media outlets are farther from them and tend to cover them less frequently. Because of the structure of government at the federal level, there are fewer members of the representatives with rural constituents; US senators—all of whom have rural families in their states—are responsible for representing a much broader spectrum of citizen concerns than their counterparts in the House. As a result, poverty often feels urban in the United States, although in reality it is more widespread and reflective of American diversity than stereotypes allow.

Box 3.4. *What Can I Do?:* Graduate Degrees in Public Policy and Urban Planning

Postgraduate degrees are proliferating in the twenty-first century. As the perceived value of a bachelor's degree diminishes and colleges and universities struggle with budgets in poor economic contexts, graduate programs are increasing.[a] Hundreds of colleges and universities offer graduate programs or certificates in areas related to housing and socioeconomic/political issues. Finding the one that is right for you could open the door to a rewarding career advocating for increased equality of opportunity in urban and rural settings.

The programs vary in terms of focus, requirements, outcomes, and even names (do a search of the terms "urban planning," "urban affairs," "urban politics," "rural development," or "rural studies"). Some programs can lead to a doctoral degree in sociology, political science, or a related field, but also offer a gateway into public- or private-sector jobs centered on improving the lives of people in rural or urban areas. Further, there are a number of master's level degrees available. For example, Morgan State University (Maryland) offers a master of city and regional planning (MCRP) degree; the University of California, Davis offers a master of science (MS) degree in community development; the University of Akron (Ohio) offers a master of arts (MA) degree in geography, planning and geographical information science; and Oregon State University offers a master of public policy (MPP) degree with a rural policy concentration. Most doctoral programs are in traditional fields with concentrations in urban or rural studies, but others are more specific, such as the PhD in agricultural history and rural studies at Iowa State University and the PhD in urban studies at Temple University.

a. Laura Pappano, "The Master's as the New Bachelor's," *New York Times*, July 22, 2011, http://www.nytimes.com/2011/07/24/education/edlife/edl-24masters -t.html.

Conclusion

Our examination of inequality in America centers on disparities in wealth and, to a lesser extent, income, but central to those components is availability of housing and the benefits that availability provides (as well as the disadvantages that accompany a lack of access). Although home ownership is considered to be an important component of the American Dream, many policymakers and commentators do not believe that every American should be able to own a home because everyone cannot afford it. In fact, there have been a number of claims that the government's desire to help low-income families own a home was a primary cause of the Great Recession.[60] Such criticisms return us to the normative questions that opened this chapter. What should be expected with respect to housing in America? What is deserved by all? What is reserved for some? And, most important for political scientists, what measures (if any) should be taken to help low-income Americans gain security, invest in their futures, and take part in middle-class American life?

Even if we agree that all adults do not deserve to achieve middle-class comfort (presumably because of poor choices they made at some time in their lives), it is difficult to reconcile core American values of opportunity with the notion of punishing children who live in substandard conditions and, as we explore in the next chapter, start out at a further disadvantage because of the way the United States structures and funds its elementary and secondary educational institutions. With a college degree being more important than ever in a postindustrial society, housing patterns and inequality—and the resultant effect on educational opportunities—will continue to serve as the linchpin to our ability to achieve social justice for all.

Discussion Questions

1. Consider the list of normative questions from the beginning of this chapter. To what extent do you agree or disagree with each idea presented?

2. Use examples from this chapter to explain how housing inequality intersects with other elements of inequality discussed in previous chapters. Then project forward to estimate how housing inequality interacts with education, employment, criminal justice,

immigration, and health to perpetuate the cycle of advantage and disadvantage (see Figure 2.3).

3. Discuss the case of the Cabrini-Green housing complex as compared to public housing in your city or town. What are the similarities and differences with respect to living conditions and public perception? What specific public policy complexities does public housing highlight? How should we, as a community, approach public housing today and in the future? Does government have any role at all in helping Americans to find and afford housing? If so, what are the minimal standards that should be expected for residents with respect to both quality of accommodations and their role as tenants or owners?

4. Compare and contrast urban and rural poverty while trying to avoid stereotypical thinking. Do the differences and similarities simplify or complicate public policy questions that center on housing inequality?

5. The boxes in this chapter present different approaches to addressing housing inequality: top-down (HUD) and grassroots (ACORN and the Babcock Foundation). Discuss the pros and cons of each approach and offer your opinion of which can be most effective.

4

. . . .

Education

EDUCATION HAS BEEN CALLED THE GREAT EQUALIZER, AND THERE is little doubt that it can be (and often is). Particularly in a postindustrial age, most Americans who achieve economic and social success after being born into poverty do so as a result of their educational achievements. Reasonable people can disagree about whether equality in educational *outcomes* is a fundamental human right, but there is near consensus—at least in theory—that access to educational *opportunity* is. Even so, American schools remain segregated on the basis of income and race, and educational opportunities are quite unequal.

In this chapter, we explore the roots and persistence of education inequality in the United States. To that end, we start with a set of normative questions. To what quality of education are Americans entitled? Does everyone deserve to earn an advanced degree? A four-year college degree? Advanced vocational training beyond high school? If all Americans are not guaranteed such outcomes, are they at least promised access to programs that lead to those degrees? Or does the circumstance of each child's parent appropriately determine the quality of education he or she receives? If many of our schools really are failing, who is to blame? Teachers (some, most, or all)? Parents? Government agencies that fund schools and set standards? The mass public (for not putting appropriate pressure on policymakers to improve educational opportunities)?

Recall Figure 2.3 (page 69). Educational opportunities are determined in a significant way by housing patterns, and educational opportunities, in turn, help to determine one's ability to succeed in higher education and secure a well-paying job. Accordingly, we will focus most of our attention on elementary and secondary education, but will conclude the chapter with an examination of disparities in college performance, as well. Along the way, we will see evidence of systemic disadvantage perpetuated by and within the American institution (education) that is designed to interrupt it.

The Roots of Inequality in Education

As we discovered in the previous chapter with housing inequality, disadvantages in educational opportunities are similarly concentrated in rural and inner-city areas, whereas suburban schools, by and large, show the strongest performance by a number of indicators. Also consistent with our exploration to this point is the fact that limited educational opportunities disproportionately affect African Americans and Hispanics. Before we move to a discussion of funding inequality, we consider the purely racial nature of school segregation that traces to the arrival of the first slave ships in the seventeenth century.

The idea of public responsibility for education has roots that run deep in the United States. Thomas Jefferson strongly believed in the importance of education and advocated for it during his lifetime. Compulsory education for all children (not just children of wealthy parents) was in place in Massachusetts in the middle of the nineteenth century, and by 1918 mandatory attendance through elementary school was in place in every state.[1]

Slave owners largely prohibited education of any type. After all, if slaves learned to read, write, and think critically,[2] it would be difficult to consider them property (and thus, inhuman). And educated slaves would have a much greater chance of organizing to demand rights or freedom.[3] At the time of the Emancipation Proclamation, black literacy rates were estimated at 5 percent.[4] The transition from slavery to freedom was quite slow, so it is not surprising that beliefs about the proper role of education for African Americans was similarly slow to evolve to the point where no reasonable person in a position of power believes (or at least expresses) that a child's race or ethnicity should determine his or her educational opportunities.

Such acceptance of educational opportunities was ushered in at the turn of the twentieth century by such African American leaders as Booker T. Washington and W. E. B. Du Bois (see Box 4.1). By 1910, literacy among African Americans was 70 percent,[5] but there was disagreement about schooling beyond the elementary level. Washington focused on vocational training for black men, but Du Bois argued for a more broad-based education that included such liberal arts staples as science, mathematics, and literature.[6] This disagreement on specifics did not prevent a push toward full citizenship facilitated by education and training.

The US Supreme Court's 1896 decision in *Plessy v. Ferguson*[7] established a legal precedent for having "separate but equal" public facilities—
including schools—for white and black citizens. For more than fifty years,
elementary and secondary schools were segregated throughout the southern states, and institutions of higher education (both private and public) openly denied admission to African American students. Even in the
North, opportunities for free black citizens to attend college were rare, so
during Reconstruction, a number of black colleges (what are now referred
to as historically black colleges and universities) opened their doors.[8]

In 1950, the Supreme Court heard the case of an African American applicant to the University of Texas Law School who was denied admission
because he was black.[9] Heman Sweatt asked a state district court to compel
university officials to admit him because his qualifications were sufficient.
In view of the fact that the Texas state constitution prohibited integration
of educational facilities, the court continued the case for six months so
that the state could build a new law school for African Americans. When
Sweatt refused to attend the new school, he appealed, and the US Supreme
Court heard the case. The Court ruled that Sweatt must be admitted to
the University of Texas Law School, and in the opinion, Justice Frederick
Vinson set the stage for the more famous case (*Brown v. Board of Education*)[10] that came four years later. Rather than simply note that the newly
created school violated the separate-but-equal doctrine based on tangible
inequalities (which clearly existed and were enough to lead to Sweatt's
victory in the case), Justice Vinson explained that more harm comes from
racial segregation than disadvantage based on unequal facilities:

> In terms of number of the faculty, variety of courses and opportunity for
> specialization, size of the student body, scope of the library, availability of
> law review and similar activities, the University of Texas Law School is su-
> perior. *What is more important, the University of Texas Law School pos-
> sesses to a far greater degree those qualities which are incapable of objective
> measurement* but which make for greatness in a law school. Such qualities,
> to name but a few, include reputation of the faculty, experience of the ad-
> ministration, position and influence of the alumni, standing in the commu-
> nity, traditions and prestige. It is difficult to believe that one who had a free
> choice between these law schools would consider the question close. . . .
> The law school to which Texas is willing to admit petitioner excludes from
> its student body members of the racial groups which number 85 percent

Box 4.1. *Representing:* Booker T. Washington and W. E. B. Du Bois

At the turn of the twentieth century, when women were still largely ex-cluded from public and intellectual life, Booker T. Washington and W. E. B. Du Bois disagreed publicly about the proper route to political and economic justice for black Americans. Washington, who was born a slave on a plantation in Virginia, attended school after emancipation and went on to found Tuskegee Normal and Industrial Institute in Alabama. Although he believed wholeheartedly in the deserved freedom of African Americans, his approach was at times conciliatory and tentative, particularly in comparison to his contemporary, Du Bois.

In his most famous address, Washington discussed the state of race relations and the possibilities of mutual progress among black and white Americans at the Cotton States Exposition in 1895. He explained that southern whites should not look to newly arriving European immigrants for labor but to African Americans to help pull the South out of its postwar economic troubles. He similarly told his fellow African Americans that they could find prosperity in the South, just as many of them were considering moving north to escape harsh treatment and to find opportunity. The most notable passage in the address has come to be known as the Atlanta Compromise: "In all things that are purely social we can be as separate as the fingers, yet one as the hand in all things essential to mutual progress."[a] He continued the speech by noting that the "wisest" blacks of his time under-stood that equality would not come from force or demands but rather from earned respect, and that vocational training for African Americans was pre-ferred over liberal arts education.

Du Bois, while indicating his respect for Washington's work on behalf of African Americans, was unsettled by these suggestions. Du Bois was born free in Massachusetts, but faced his share of racist intimidation and harassment. After being educated at Fiske College in Nashville and later at Harvard, he studied in Germany, where he gained a global perspective on

of the population of the State and include most of the lawyers, witnesses, jurors, judges and other officials with whom petitioner will inevitably be dealing when he becomes a member of the Texas Bar. With such a sub-stantial and significant segment of society excluded, we cannot conclude that the education offered petitioner is substantially equal to that which he would receive if admitted to the University of Texas Law School.[11]

racial oppression and inequality. He completed a doctorate at Harvard. For Du Bois, suggestions that African Americans had to earn rights that were assumed to be granted "by our creator" to whites in America's founding documents reaffirmed the racist notion that blacks were not morally equal to whites. In response to Washington's philosophy, Du Bois wrote, "Mr. Washington represents in Negro thought the old attitude of adjustment and submission."[b] Responding to Washington's accepting attitude toward Jim Crow policies, such as literacy tests and poll taxes, Du Bois wrote:

"The way for a people to gain their reasonable rights is not by voluntarily throwing them away and insisting that they do not want them; . . . the way for people to gain respect is not by continually belittling and ridiculing themselves; . . . on the contrary, Negroes must insist continually . . . that voting is necessary to modern manhood, that color discrimination is barbarism, and that black boys need education as well as white boys."[c]

Du Bois argued that the most gifted African Americans—whom he called the "Talented Tenth"—could, with proper education, lead black Americans through the transition from slavery to full participation.

While some contemporary scholars and activists regard Washington as overly submissive (and read through twenty-first-century eyes, he certainly was), most note that his pragmatism was driven by the reality of race relations of his day, and that he was being strategic in his attempts to gain full citizenship for African Americans. Du Bois continues to be a tremendous influence to scholars and activists who value education of the whole person and an approach to racial justice that considers fundamental psychological and structural barriers to equality.[d]

a. Washington, *Up from Slavery*, 221–222.
b. Du Bois, *The Souls of Black Folk*, 50.
c. Ibid., 54–55.
d. Ibid.; Louis R. Harlan, "Booker T. Washington, 1856–1915," Documenting the American South, 2004, http://docsouth.unc.edu/fpn/washington/bio.html; Gerald C. Hynes, "A Biographical Sketch of W. E. B. Du Bois," W. E. B. Du Bois Learning Center, http://www.duboislc.org/html/DuBoisBio.html; Washington, Up from Slavery.

It is this additional attention to the intangible inequalities that result from racially segregated education that Chief Justice Earl Warren (see Box 4.2) relied on in the Court's unanimous decision in *Brown*, as he concluded that "in the field of public education, the doctrine of 'separate but equal' has no place. Separate educational facilities are *inherently* unequal."[12] This statement—indicating that there is no remedy that maintains

Box 4.2. *Representing:* Chief Justice Earl Warren

People often are surprised to hear that presidents used to appoint US senators, governors, and even a former president (William Howard Taft) to the US Supreme Court. Today, most appointments come from lower courts, which helps perpetuate the myth that members of the Court are above politics. When President Eisenhower nominated Earl Warren, the governor of California, to become chief justice of the Court in 1953, however, it was no secret that politics was at work, as Warren had supported Eisenhower in his presidential bid in 1952.

While neither Eisenhower nor Warren was considered particularly conservative, it would have been difficult to predict that Warren would preside over a Court that, just a year after his appointment, would make one of the most controversial decisions in history. Warren convinced all eight of his colleagues to support the decision in *Brown v. the Board of Education*, and the chief justice himself wrote the opinion.

There was widespread dissatisfaction and noncompliance throughout the South. One of the most notable instances was when Governor Orval Faubus ordered the Arkansas National Guard to block nine black students from entering Little Rock Central High School in 1957. Days of protest ensued and angry white parents gathered outside the school, shouting racist

segregation—was revolutionary and set the legal tone for the civil rights movement that was to begin, rooted in the moral principles outlined by African American thinkers dating back to before emancipation.

Much as de jure segregation in housing ended as a result of legislation and subsequent attitude shifts in the latter part of the twentieth century, legally mandated racial segregation in public schools ended in the decades following the *Brown* decision. And just as de facto segregation has continued in housing, it continues in K–12 education;[13] as reflected in Figure 4.1, white students, on average, attend schools that are 9 percent black, whereas black students attend schools that are 48 percent black. America's elementary and secondary schools are more racially segregated today than they were in the 1960s.[14] If facilities at majority-white schools were equal to those at majority-minority schools, the rationale in *Sweatt* and *Brown* would still hold that children of color are being denied their Fourteenth Amendment right to equal protection as a result of the segregation. As will become clear in the following sections, however, intangible inequality epithets at the black students. In response Eisenhower issued an executive order that sent members of the army's 101st Airborne Division to make sure that the students entered the school safely. The protests continued for weeks, and the students faced harassment inside the school as well.

Earl Warren was persistently criticized. Calls for his impeachment appeared on billboards and bumper stickers throughout the South. Eisenhower would call Warren "the biggest damned-fool mistake" he ever made, but most people now regard his actions as not only brave but morally justified. Despite continuing racial inequality, few Americans believe that forcing African American children into separate schools was an appropriate policy. The Supreme Court, operating with full awareness of, but mostly immune from, public pressure made a decision that would have been politically impossible for elected officials to make. Earl Warren's actions represented the part of Madison's dilemma that is so often overlooked: minority rights must be respected, even if they conflict with majority will.[a]

---

a. "Civil Rights: The Little Rock School Integration Crisis," Dwight D. Eisenhower Presidential Library, http://www.eisenhower.archives.gov/research/online_documents /civil_rights_little_rock.html; Ed Cray, *Chief Justice: A Biography of Earl Warren* (New York: Simon & Schuster, 1997); John Fox, *Earl Warren*, PBS, 2007, http://www.pbs.org/wnet /supremecourt/democracy/robes_warren.html.

is only part of the disadvantage that African American and Hispanic students face in school.

Inequality in Funding

In his comprehensive treatment of educational inequality in the United States, researcher Richard Rothstein notes that the overly simplistic commonsense approach to addressing so-called failing schools (i.e., placing the blame and burden on teachers alone) is inadequate because it ignores how social class characteristics in a stratified society like ours may actually influence learning in school. Low income and skin color themselves don't influence academic achievement, but the collection of characteristics that define social class differences inevitably influences that achievement.[15]

As Rothstein and others have noted, the amount of money flowing into schools is not the only concern. While it poses a significant challenge for

FIGURE 4.1. **Percentage of Students, by Race, in Each Black Density Category, 2011**

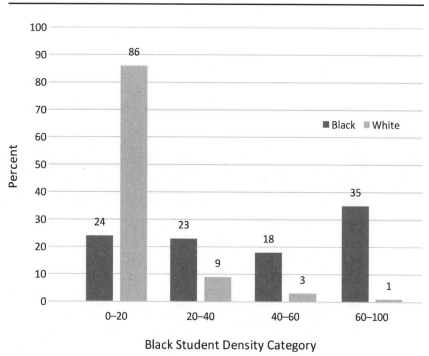

Source: US Department of Education, "School Composition and the Black-White Achievement Gap," NCES 2015-018, June 2015, https://nces.ed.gov/nationsreportcard/subject/studies/pdf/school _composition_and_the_bw_achievement_gap_2015.pdf.

educators, it is also a reflection of deeper socioeconomic hardship, which, as will become clear, also affects student learning.

The problem of vastly disproportionate funding in education stems from relying on local property taxes as the primary source of revenue for most public schools. The proportions in each state vary, but the federal government provides only 10 percent of the funding for K–12 public schools in the United States. The rest is composed of a combination of statewide distributions and funding from local taxes. As a result, there are tremendous per-pupil spending disparities between states,[16] as well as within states.[17]

The issue of education funding is fundamental to broad American principles in a number of ways. First, there is the obvious interest in having an informed and intelligent citizenry as a necessary condition for a participatory democracy. If citizens are unaware of how government works, unsure of their role in it, and confused about the issues of the day, those who have such knowledge (and skills to process it) are at a distinct advantage in terms of controlling public policy. Second, there is an element of federalism that complicates the first principle. If we believe that all Americans deserve to have access to quality education, who should pay for it? If some states think it is important to spend tax revenue on education and others prioritize infrastructure or services, should the federal government intervene? Finally, beyond the state-national division, there is the popular philosophy that the government closest to the people governs most effectively. Even if taxpayers within a state have a commitment to education, they must reconcile that preference with the idea that people can choose to live where they want—which is often at least partially determined by the quality of the school district—and that local areas will have vastly different levels of resources that must be distributed among the various budget items (police, social services, road maintenance and snow removal, etc.) that are important to a community.

The result, of course, is that even if the percentage of revenue is equal in different neighborhoods, the amount of funding available can differ substantially because of the amount of money in the community. Further, as state revenues have been affected by the Great Recession and property taxes have fallen, there are increased challenges for funding public schools at all income levels.

Inequality in Outcomes

Much of the public discourse about education policy over the past decade has focused on outcomes and accountability, two concepts that are difficult to oppose in principle. The outcomes portion is clear: there are achievement gaps that can be measured in a variety of ways. Beginning with the *A Nation at Risk* report[18] in 1983, policymakers and the public have been concerned about how the nation is slipping with respect to student learning. There is a gap in achievement between the United States and other nations, as well as increasing evidence of educational attainment disparities between white students and students of color.[19] Data from 2013 were examined as part of an *Education Next* series commemorating the fiftieth anniversary of James S. Coleman's landmark study "Equality of Educational Opportunity." The findings are sobering:

In both math and reading, the national test-score gap in 1965 was 1.1 standard deviations, implying that the average black 12th grader placed at the 13th percentile of the score distribution for white students. In other words, 87 percent of white 12th graders scored ahead of the average black 12th grader. What does it look like 50 years later? In math, the size of the gap has fallen nationally by 0.2 standard deviations, but that still leaves the average black 12th-grade student at only the 19th percentile of the white distribution. In reading, the achievement gap has improved slightly more than in math (0.3 standard deviations), but after a half century, the average black student scores at just the 22nd percentile of the white distribution.[20]

In short, as with the racial wealth disparity that we discussed in Chapter 2, the gap is narrowing, but at a very slow rate. Disparities persist:

- According to the 2013 National Assessment of Educational Progress report, white students in twelfth grade held a 29-point[21] advantage over black students in reading and a 30-point advantage in math scores. White students held a 21-point advantage over Hispanic students in both reading and math.[22]

- According to the 2009 National Assessment of Educational Progress report, white students held a 21-point advantage over Hispanic students in mathematics in fourth grade; the gap widens to 26 points in eighth grade. White students held a 25-point advantage over Hispanic students in reading in fourth grade and in eighth grade [23]

- According to the 2007 National Assessment of Educational Progress report, white students hold a 26-point advantage over African American students in mathematics in fourth grade; the gap widens to 31 points in eighth grade. White students hold a 27-point advantage over African American students in reading in fourth grade; the gap is twenty—6 points in eighth grade.[24]

- One in four African American middle and high school students without a learning disability were suspended from school (compared to one in fourteen white students) during the 2009–2010 school year.[25]

FIGURE 4.2. Average SAT Scores for the 12th Grade SAT Test-Taking Population, by Subject, Race/Ethnicity, and Sex, 2011

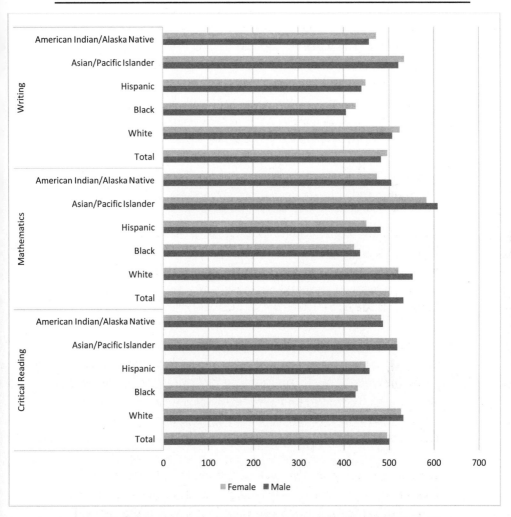

Source: Institute of Education Sciences, "Average SAT Scores for the 12th-grade SAT Test-taking Population, by Subject, Race/Ethnicity, and Sex, 2011," https://nces.ed.gov/pubs2012/2012046 /figures/figure_24-2.asp.

Figures 4.2, 4.3, and 4.4 depict racial gaps with respect to SAT scores, dropout rates, and expected degree attainment, respectively.

The accountability portion of the argument is very controversial, as citizens and public officials look to identify the source of unsatisfactory outcomes so that remedies can be devised and implemented. The

FIGURE 4.3. **Dropout Rates of 16- to 24-Year-Olds, by Race/Ethnicity, 1990–2014**

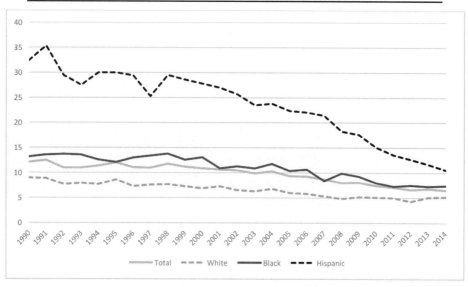

Source: Institute of Educational Sciences, "Status Dropout Rates," May 2016, http://nces.ed.gov/programs/coe/indicator_coj.asp.

manifestation of this dilemma has been high-stakes testing[26]—standardized testing where the results are not only made public but tied to funding decisions in a variety of ways. This approach has intuitive appeal but has received persistent criticism from educators and educational researchers. The most notable of the policies to emerge from this philosophy is the federal No Child Left Behind (NCLB) law ushered in by President George W. Bush in 2001.[27] NCLB was designed to provide stronger accountability, more local freedom, and choices for parents by way of proven methods.[28] But no reduction in achievement gaps were documented,[29] and Congress replaced it with a new law—Every Student Succeeds Act (ESSA)—in 2015. Unlike NCLB, the new law does not contain top-heavy incentives from the federal government based on standardized test scores. Rather, local districts and schools are empowered to craft interventions to improve student learning, and there are particular provisions in place to support schools with traditionally underserved students.[30]

For many scholars, the move away from standardized testing as a benchmark tied to funding is welcome. There was a sense that teachers were encouraged to "teach to the test" so as to secure (or not lose) funding

FIGURE 4.4. **Public High School Graduation Rates, by Race/Ethnicity, 2013–2014**

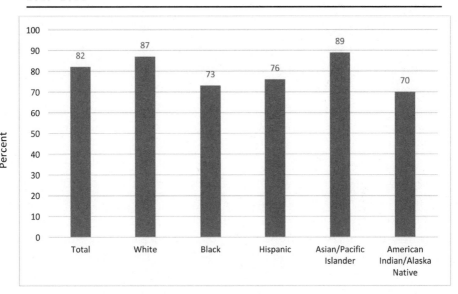

Race/Ethnicity

Source: Institute of Education Sciences, "Public High School Graduation Rates," May 2016, http://nces.ed.gov/programs/coe/indicator_coi.asp.

under NCLB. To further complicate matters, it is not clear that the standardized assessments of student learning are accurate and unbiased. While seemingly objective test scores would appear to be a fair marker to determine how much students are learning (and how well teachers are teaching), there are several disadvantages to this approach.[31] Both race[32] and economic circumstances[33] have been found to affect test scores, but not directly. Children from economically disadvantaged families often go to school hungry, which can affect their performance.[34] Students who have a stressful home life—whether because they live in a dangerous neighborhood or because adults in their life face high levels of stress and may be abusive—have more difficulty with academic performance.[35] To the extent that America is characterized by racially segregated housing and a racial wealth and income gap (as well as nutrition and health disparities, which we explore in Chapter 7), we must acknowledge the interrelationship between these factors and academic performance. Further, as we consider the way that representation matters with respect to such policies, it is interesting to note that many of the strongest voices for charter schools, vouchers, and high-stakes testing in public schools were actually educated in elite private schools.[36] Even if they did attend public school, few grew up or currently live in areas with inadequate school funding.

If we reject standardized testing because it is problematic, however, we must replace it with another form of assessment because we must have some way to compare students against one another. In particular, institutions of higher education need to find ways to choose applicants for admission. Grade point average (GPA) is not necessarily an appropriate indicator. Consider a scenario in which one student, among the brightest in her high school, earns mostly A's, many of them in advanced placement courses. This results in her earning 5 grade points (rather than the standard 4) for each A, so she can graduate with a GPA greater than 4.0, even if she earns a B or two. Another student at a different school, who is similarly gifted, may not be able to take advanced placement courses because her high school does not offer them. Therefore, even if she earns all A's and scores as well as the first student on her board exams (ACT or SAT), her application may not look as attractive to colleges, even though both students took full advantage of their natural abilities and opportunities.

In fact, data from a number of studies reveal significant socioeconomic and racial disparities in students' access to and success in higher education settings. Finishing high school (which is a precursor to being admitted to college, absent completion of a GED) is largely dependent on socioeconomics and family history. The school dropout rate for sixteen- to twenty-four-year-olds is 6.5 percent nationally; for whites, it is 5.2 percent; for African Americans, it is 7.4 percent; and for Hispanic students, it is 10.6 percent.[37] General Social Survey data reveal that children whose father did not graduate from high school are eight times more likely to not graduate either (a 22.2 percent chance of dropping out, compared to 2.9 percent for children whose father graduated).[38]

Enrollment in college has also been characterized by racial disparity, though recent evidence suggests that the gap is narrowing, at least among high school graduates.[39] While overall college enrollment rates in 2012 (66.2 percent of high school graduates) were the lowest they had been since 2006, the one-year drop among African Americans that year was particularly notable—58.2 percent in 2012 as compared to 67.5 percent in 2011.[40]

By 2014, however, the gap had closed completely; in fact the percentage of black high school graduates attending college (70.9 percent—the highest proportion since the United States Bureau of Labor Statistics began keeping track in 1959) edged white graduates (67.3 percent); Hispanics followed closely, with 65.2 percent of high school graduates attending college.[41] A recent study found that white students were five times as likely as African American students and three times as likely as Latino students to attend a highly selective college, even controlling for income. This pattern was extended between 1982 and 2004 (the last year for which data were available). Low-income students of any race were much less likely to attend these types of colleges.[42]

Besides the fact that poorly funded high schools may not prepare students for college as well as some better funded public schools in wealthy neighborhoods (let alone expensive private schools), poor students of color may face additional hurdles that white students who attended underfunded schools might not. For example, one study revealed that African American students who experienced stereotype threat, which is "a disruptive apprehension about the possibility that one might inadvertently confirm a negative stereotype about one's group," performed far worse on a language test than African American students who did not experience it.[43] In other words, simply being African American or Latino in America—all other things being equal (and they rarely are)—can serve as a disadvantage:

> The stark inequities manifest in inner-city and some rural schools help to explain the low achievement rates of large numbers of poor children, a disproportionate number of whom are African American and Latino. Left unexplained is the lagging performance of middle class and poor African American and Latino children who have access to better schools.[44]

This is an example of the systemic meeting the psychological. Even though middle-class minority children may escape the systemic disadvantage of underfunded schools, they may face other barriers to achievement. For instance, racial imbalances with respect to discipline have been well documented. A recent study found that African American public school students were more than three times as likely to be assigned out-of-school suspension as white students. Latino students were suspended at a rate slightly higher than their white classmates.[45] In an effort to explain that

Box 4.3. *Representing:* Jonathan Kozol

Jonathan Kozol has conducted gripping research on inequality in America's schools. Having worked as a public school teacher, Kozol provides heart-wrenching depictions of America's most underfunded inner-city schools. In *Savage Inequalities*,[a] we meet children, teachers, and administrators at poorly funded, dilapidated schools in six cities. In addition we learn about standing raw sewage in neighborhoods, rat-infested apartment complexes, and an ice-cream man who sells condoms. In *Amazing Grace*,[b] we read more stories of crumbling schools and residences, as well as about the violence that awaits so many inner-city kids after the final bell.

Kozol's *The Shame of the Nation* (2005),[c] is his most pointed criticism of K–12 educational inequality. The book's provocative subtitle, *The Restoration of Apartheid Schooling in America*, primes the reader to think more deeply about our national priorities by using a word that is not commonly associated with the United States. Kozol explains that most inner-city black and Latino students attend schools with few or no whites. These students are "tracked" into curriculums that anticipate their failure and prepare them to overcome mistakes in their lives (such as committing a felony) in a way that predominantly white suburban schools would never consider. Corporations fund school-to-work programs that do not even suggest college, but rather put students squarely on a path to low-skill employment and, optimistically, management. Federally mandated testing with financial

disparity, a 2016 Yale University study found that implicit associations on the part of teachers contributes to disparate treatment of racial minorities in preschool, as well.[46]

Researchers Pedro Noguera and Antwi Akom report that a desire for peer acceptance, combined with "racial images rooted in stereotypes . . . diminish the importance of intellectual pursuits" among young minority students.[47] This internalized racism works as a self-fulfilling prophecy. It is a powerful but often misunderstood aspect of systemic oppression.

Finally, as might be expected given all these trends, there is a race gap with respect to college graduation rates, even as the enrollment gap has narrowed: 60 percent of white college students earn a bachelor's degree within six years, compared to 40 percent of African Americans and 49 percent of Latinos.[48] A recent study of 232 institutions that have improved overall graduation rates between 2005 and 2015 showed that the rate for penalties tied to failure and the resulting test-based lessons exacerbate the trend. This, Kozol argues, leads to a race-based economy where whites are trained for advanced degrees and higher paying jobs (with access to power) while racial minorities by and large are not.

In contrast to a public discourse that often blames teachers and administrators for school failure, Kozol portrays teachers who love their job, love their students, and set high expectations, but are hampered by low investments (in the schools and the communities broadly) that result in few examples of success that can be used to motivate students to high academic achievement.

Through his writing, Kozol strives to make the families and school officials visible to those of us who do not have personal experience with such conditions. By educating America about the state of education in America, Jonathan Kozol is representing those whose voices too often go unheard.[d]

---

a. Jonathan Kozol, *Savage Inequalities: Children in America's Schools* (New York: Harper Perennial, 1991).

b. Jonathan Kozol, *Amazing Grace: The Lives of Children and the Conscience of a Nation* (New York: Harper Perennial, 1996).

c. Jonathan Kozol, *The Shame of the Nation: The Restoration of Apartheid Schooling in America* (New York: Three Rivers Press, 2005).

d. American Entertainment International Speakers Bureau, Jonathan Kozol, 2009, http://www.aeispeakers.com/speakerbio.php?SpeakerID=579; Kozol, *Savage Inequalities*; Kozol, *Amazing Grace*; Kozol, *Shame of the Nation*.

---

black students improved 4.4 percent over that time period, compared with a 5.6 percent improvement for white students.[49] Of course, race alone does not explain the disparity. University of Michigan economists Martha Bailey and Susan Dynarski report that low-income students born in the early 1980s had a higher college completion rate than those born in the early 1960s (9 percent and 5 percent, respectively). However, among high-income students, the rate of those who completed college jumped from 36 percent for those born in the early 1960s to more than half (54 percent) for those born in the early 1980s. Essentially, over two decades, the college income gap widened to 45 percentage points from 31 percentage points, a phenomenon that was observed even after the researchers accounted for differences in students' cognitive skills.[50]

Stated in reverse, students who drop out of college before earning a degree are characterized by disproportionate poverty: about one third

Box 4.4. *What Can I Do?:* Teach for America

In her senior thesis at Princeton University in 1989, Wendy Kopp suggested training outstanding college graduates to spend at least two years teaching in America's poorest schools. Today, Teach for America[a] has an annual budget of over $200 million and a staff of 1,400. Each year, nearly 20,000 applicants compete for 2,500 positions.

Some of the best teachers have not only earned degrees in education but have spent years developing classroom skills, which calls into question the potential effectiveness of teachers who majored in other areas, received limited training (just five weeks), and will likely stay in the classroom for only a couple of years. The point of Teach for America is for participants to make a difference in the lives of children for a few years in the classroom and then go on to other professions and leadership positions, effecting broader change when the opportunity to do so arises. In other words, people who have spent two years in struggling schools will be less likely to make decisions that perpetuate inequality in education.

Donna Foote, who followed four Teach for America participants in her book *Relentless Pursuit*,[b] believes that while these teachers face obstacles (including resentment from experienced teachers), the lesson of the program is clear: do not "dismiss these children or relegate them to the ghetto. If you teach them, they will learn. They have something to offer, and we have an obligation to give it to them. This is a national disgrace—we should be ashamed that 20 minutes from my comfortable home, there are children that have no future."[c]

of poor students finish college, compared to two thirds of students from wealthier families.[51] Recently graduation rates at many historically black colleges and universities have risen,[52] though data do not reveal socioeconomic factors in that trend.

Conclusion

As is true with most important political issues, finding consensus on how to rectify the situation is difficult. First, some believe that inequality in education is appropriate, as it reflects inequality in other segments of American life, which is part and parcel of capitalism. In other words, if

Still, Teach for America has received criticism over the years, for example, that it is little more than a résumé booster for privileged white students[d] and that the teachers do not do a good job in the classroom. While such criticisms were valid in the earliest days of the program, today nearly a third of Teach for America teachers are persons of color, and many come from state schools rather than Ivy League private colleges.

As large as the organization has become, it is only a small part of a larger national effort by teachers and administrators to provide the best education possible to all students, irrespective of their working conditions. Teach for America demonstrates how not-for-profit entities can fill gaps in social and political institutions and that attitudinal shifts, particularly among those who will be in positions of power, can lead to more thoughtful and sophisticated consideration of the reasons for inequality.[e]

a. http://TeachforAmerica.org.

b. Donna Foote, *Relentless Pursuit: A Year in the Trenches with Teach for America* (New York: Knopf, 2008).

c. Quoted in Lucia Graves, "What Is Teach for America Really Like?" *U.S. News & World Report*, March 5, 2008, http://www.usnews.com/education/articles/2008/03/05/what-is-teach-for-america-really-like.

d. Mark Naison, "Why Teach for America Is Not Welcome in My Classroom," *LA Progressive*, July 18, 2011, http://www.laprogressive.com/education-reform/teach-america/.

e. Graves, "What Is Teach for America Really Like?"; Andrew J. Rotherham, "Teach for America: 5 Myths That Persist 20 Years On," *Time*, February 10, 2011, http://www.time.com/time/nation/article/0,8599,2047211,00.html.

the adults in a family are economically successful and move to a neighborhood where the schools are strong, that is part of the American way. Without these sorts of consequences, the theory goes, individuals would not be motivated to work hard, take risks, and be productive. Most Americans, though, believe in equality of opportunity for all, even if one's parents have not been financially successful (for whatever reason).

A recent survey reveals that there is an appetite among the general public—at least in the abstract—to rectify the educational opportunity and achievement gaps. Nearly two thirds of American adults agreed that it is "essential or a high priority" to close the gap between wealthy and poor students (though only about half that many agreed that it is a priority to close the racial gap). In fact, empathy for black and Hispanic students was low among these respondents; nearly half said that the gap could not be explained by discrimination or injustice.[53] Still, whether the desire is driven by economic or racial considerations, there seems to be some level of public support for more educational equality.

This desire for equality of opportunity, however, leads to a second difficulty in finding consensus: We cannot agree about who or what deserves the blame for failing schools. For some, it is mostly about funding; if we can just make per pupil funding more equal, each student will have a chance to succeed. Others, however, feel that "throwing money at the problem" is not an effective solution.[54] For these folks, teachers (usually teachers' unions) are often blamed for protecting bad teachers who are not using the resources they do have effectively. Third, if there is agreement that there needs to be more equality in terms of funding, how should that be achieved? Should the federal Department of Education provide supplemental resources? Should it come from the state (which is essentially a redistribution of tax money from wealthier neighborhoods to poorer ones)? Should we discontinue the practice of using property taxes to fund schools?

Among the more dramatic solutions proposed are voucher programs that would provide a certain amount of money to families to offset the cost of private school education. Those who support vouchers argue that they are effective because they force schools to compete for students or risk closing, which should increase the quality of education at schools or eliminate schools that cannot attract students. Opponents argue that putting vouchers in the hands of parents drains resources from schools that might be struggling precisely because they are underfunded.[55] Additionally, the voucher amount is rarely enough to cover the entire cost of school tuition, so only families who have enough resources to cover the difference can escape a failing school.

In January 2011, Kelley Williams-Bolar spent nine days in jail after being convicted of lying about her address so that her daughters could attend better schools near Akron, Ohio.[56] The case caught national attention because it vividly illustrated the desperation so many parents feel as they try to provide the best educational opportunities for their children. Charter schools have become increasingly popular, allowing parents to group together to form quasi-public schools on their own with the blessing (and funding) of the state. However, many states limit the number of charter schools that can form, which leads to overenrollment that is often rectified by a lottery system. As dramatized in the documentary film *Waiting for Superman*,[57] there is a cruel irony to hoping for a random number to be called to be able to secure a good education in a country with so much wealth and an avowed dedication to providing (and mandating) education for all of its children. In fact, in 2016, the National Association for the Advancement of Colored People (NAACP) and a collective of groups organized by Black Lives Matter called for a moratorium on charter schools, arguing that they have "exacerbated segregation, especially in the way they select and discipline students."[58]

The case for school choice (whether through private school vouchers or charter schools) does not cut neatly across ideological lines. Conservatives champion the competitive nature of the process, forcing schools to produce measurable outcomes or close their doors if they (and their teachers) cannot attract students. Progressives who advocate for the poor note that the wealthy in America already have school choice—it is only the poor who do not.[59] Any program that does not relegate students to underfunded, deteriorating, and physically unsafe (both in terms of health concerns and the risk of violent crime) schools is a welcome shift in policy for poorer Americans who want better for their children. Progressives who oppose such programs highlight larger systemic issues in school funding, unfairness in testing, and dedication of teachers even in the poorest schools. They believe that every school should be well funded and provide quality education. Put another way, no child should be left behind. Because those left behind are not just left behind at the schoolhouse door; they are left behind at the college admissions desk and in the employment line as well. Some may resort to illegal activities to earn money and the respect of peers, further complicating prospects for employment, which could otherwise be an escape route from the cycle of disadvantage depicted in Figure 2.3 (see page 69). Kelley Williams-Bolar was studying to be a teacher when she was convicted of altering her address so that her daughters could go to a better school. She will now have to search for another career, which, as we will see in the next chapter, is no easy task for a convicted felon.

Discussion Questions

1. Discuss the concept of education as a great equalizer. How do educational opportunities and educational outcomes play into this concept? Do our public officials have a responsibility to help secure either (or both)?

2. Does the federal government have a role in determining how states prioritize their funding? What about in extreme circumstances (such as when states spend significantly less than the nationwide average)? How does educational funding demonstrate an intersection between liberal and conservative ideological values?

3. What are some ways that capitalist principles rub against access to education? For example, while we value and seek to reward both hard work and success, in what ways are children vicariously rewarded and punished by the status of their parents? Discuss ways that we might address this friction if we wish to have more equal access to quality education for American children.

4. Consider the inequalities surrounding K–12 education and higher education separately. How are the challenges in addressing these inequalities different from one another? How are they similar? Does government have a role to play in attempting to rectify inequalities in either or both contexts?

5. Reflect on the ways that Booker T. Washington and W. E. B. Du Bois fought for the rights of African Americans. Does one approach seem more appropriate to you? Which seems more productive in today's political context? Consider how your own social standing and learned values inform your opinion about these different perspectives. Do modern leaders appear to be closer to Washington's approach or Du Bois's? Give specific examples.

5

....

Crime and Criminal Justice

NOW THAT WE HAVE EXPLORED THE INTERRELATIONSHIP BETWEEN the wealth gap and housing, as well as the relationship between housing and education, we will examine how the criminal justice system is related to poverty and racism. Certain types of crime are associated with poverty, and as we have established, poverty in the United States disproportionately affects citizens of color. Felony convictions make securing employment much more difficult. We need to ask very pointed and complex questions about the way the criminal justice system operates in the United States. Of course, we collectively believe that persons guilty of committing crimes should be punished while those who are not are never falsely accused or convicted. If that ultimate goal is impossible (and it is), how should the system be structured to minimize the number of false convictions and maximize the number of offenders who are punished? Irrespective of the answer, we most likely agree that race and ethnicity should have no bearing. To the extent that there are disproportionate arrests, convictions, or deviations in sentencing between whites and persons of color, we must consider the reasons for such disparities and the relationship to employment opportunities.

Social contract theorists have considered for centuries how to explain the way that societies are organized. Our Framers borrowed most heavily from John Locke, who viewed the arrangement as an implicit contract between the people and government. This arrangement is necessary because absent formal rules (a "state of nature"), individuals retain the rights they have by virtue of being human ("natural rights"), but do not have protection from those who might seek to infringe upon them. Channeling Locke, the Framers wrote in the Declaration of Independence that "all men are created equal [and] they are endowed by their Creator with certain inalienable Rights, that among them are Life, Liberty and the pursuit of Happiness." While that sounds reasonable enough, if my pursuit of happiness involves killing someone who is bothering me, that infringes on that person's fundamental right (life), which is problematic. The Framers recognized this and followed the aforementioned phrase with another reference to Locke: "That to secure these rights, Governments are instituted among Men, deriving their just powers from the consent of the governed. . . . " Collectively, we enter into an arrangement with government—not members of government, but the very notion of government. Like all contracts, there is a quid pro quo, which means that each side both gives and receives something of value. In this case, citizens receive protection of their natural rights from government, and government receives a voluntary relinquishing of some liberty (i.e., agreeing to follow the rules). If citizens break their end of the contract, it—to the extent that it applies to that individual—is void (at least for a period of time), and the government can impose punishment. If government breaks its end of the agreement, the citizens can overthrow the government. This delicate balance manifests in many varied ways, and as we will see, unequally.

James Madison famously wrote in *Federalist 51*, "If men were angels, no government would be necessary."[1] Since we are not, societies must have rules, and members of society should be incentivized to abide by those rules. The normative questions we face as we embark on this chapter, then, center on how we should punish those who do not follow the rules. How should we decide if someone has broken the law? Who should decide? Do context or extenuating circumstances matter? Who decides that? What is an appropriate punishment? Death? Disfigurement? Public humiliation? Seizing of personal assets? If removing one's liberties (i.e., imprisonment) is an essential element of punishment, we need to decide what that looks like. For how long? In what conditions? With what provisions for release? Should prisoners have available programs that might help them avoid committing crimes when they are released (see Box 5.1)? Or do we believe that individuals are fundamentally either good or bad, and no amount of work can keep a bad person out of trouble? Answers to these questions are no simpler than those posed in previous chapters, and they are important to consider as we seek to better understand inequality in the criminal justice system.

Box 5.1. *What Can I Do?:* Veterans Healing Veterans from the Inside Out

Volunteering for organizations dedicated to addressing elements of inequality can be rewarding. Some, such as Goodwill (www.good will.org) or the Salvation Army (http://www.salvationarmyusa.org), are widely known and work to address economic inequality broadly, but others have unique missions that address specific aspects of the cycle of disadvantage.

Veterans Healing Veterans from the Inside Out (http://www.veterans healingveterans.com/) emerged in 2012 at San Quentin State Prison in California. Ron Self, a former marine who was serving time for attempted murder at the prison,[a] was working on understanding the complexities of the effects of the trauma he faced as a combat veteran. Moved by the high rate of veteran suicides,[b] he was motivated to develop a way for incarcerated veterans to work together.[c] In meetings rooted in narration therapy, participants respond to writing prompts and share personal stories to instigate insight into their struggles. Combined with yoga and meditation, the aim is to help incarcerated veterans "foster . . . self-awareness and behavioral change that allow veterans . . . to make successful transitions back into society."[d]

---

a. Sha Wallace Stepter, "A Combat Veteran and a Veteran of the Streets Deal with PTSD," KALW Public Radio, November 11, 2013, http://kalw.org/post/combat-veteran-and-veteran-streets-deal-ptsd#stream/0.

b. Although they comprise only 9 percent of the US population, veterans accounted for 18 percent of all suicides in 2014. Leo Shane III and Patricia Kime, "New VA Study Finds 20 Veterans Commit Suicide Each Day," *Military Times*, July 7, 2016, http://www.militarytimes.com/story/veterans/2016/07/07/va-suicide-20-daily-research/86788332/.

c. http://www.veteranshealingveterans.com.

d. Ibid.

Due Process v. Crime Control Models

We are confronted with a stark reality that presents a fundamental dilemma: How do we know whether someone has broken a law? A seemingly obvious way would be for the person to confess to the crime. In June 2015, a young white man joined a prayer group at a predominantly African American church in Charleston, South Carolina. Partway through the meeting he rose, declared his hatred of African Americans, and opened fire, killing nine people.[2] The man confessed to the crime after he was arrested, and his attorneys did not argue for his innocence during the trial.[3]

However, not everyone who commits a crime confesses, of course, and not everyone who confesses has committed a crime. A notable case of wrongful conviction based on a false confession is that of the so-called Central Park Five, a group of black and Hispanic teenagers who were convicted of raping and brutally beating a young white woman as she was jogging in New York City in 1989. The boys (aged fifteen to eighteen at the time) confessed and served between six and thirteen years in prison before DNA evidence (unavailable at the time of their trial) exonerated all of them in 2002.[4] The case garnered renewed interest during the 2016 presidential election because Donald Trump had taken out a full-page ad in the *New York Times* after the attack, arguing that the death penalty be reinstated in New York. He has never apologized for the mistake and, indeed, when asked about it during the campaign, said that he still believed that the boys were guilty because they confessed.[5] Yet false confessions have been involved in about a quarter of convictions that have been reversed by DNA evidence.[6] Most of us cannot imagine ever confessing to a crime that we did not commit, so why would anyone do so?

The way we empower law enforcement officials to do their work is at the heart of the fundamental dilemma captured by the due process and crime control models of criminal justice. If we assume that (1) society has an obligation to punish those who break the law; and (2) there will not always be a clear way to know when someone has broken the law, then we need to agree on a set of guidelines that strives to punish everyone who commits a crime yet avoids punishing anyone who has not. While this goal is impossible in a practical sense, we can consider a continuum with these perfect scenarios at the poles. Our task as a society, then, is to decide where on that continuum we should position ourselves. If we move too far to one side, too many criminals will remain on the street, unpunished; if we move too far the other way, we might capture most of those who commit crimes, but we also risk punishing too many innocent people. The former approach is known as the *due process* model.[7] Here, the most important thing is for government to follow its own rules, even if that means some guilty people are never punished. In this model, law enforcement officials have very strict guidelines for what they may and may not do, and deviation from those guidelines results in important sanctions.

The other approach is the *crime control* model, whereby priority is given to punishing those who commit crimes,[8] even if that means that innocent people are sometimes wrongly convicted. Here, law enforcement personnel have wider latitude in terms of their own procedures in an attempt to not disadvantage them as they work to apprehend those who have committed crimes.

At this point, a wise reader will be thinking, "That's a false dichotomy; we can both limit government power and apprehend criminals." In theory, that is accurate, but in practice, it is much more difficult. The Founders were very interested in having a safe society, but they also desired to make sure that government (which includes law enforcement) would not abuse its power over citizens. Rights of the criminally accused (or suspected) are codified in many portions of the Bill of Rights: protection against illegal search and seizure (Fourth Amendment); the right to not have to incriminate oneself (Fifth Amendment); the right to counsel, speedy trial by jury of one's peers, ability to confront witnesses (Sixth Amendment); and protection against excessive bail and cruel and unusual punishment (Eighth Amendment). The axiom that individuals are innocent until proven guilty is relevant for the judicial branch (the courts), but would be impossible to implement for the executive branch (in this case, the police or other law enforcement agents). The notion that officers would not be permitted to arrest anyone until they were proven to be guilty is preposterous. On the contrary, law enforcement officials must decide whom they believe is guilty and then, within the rules we have established, work to capture them and attempt to bring them to justice.

The most powerful restraint on police officers is the *exclusionary rule*, which holds that officers are required to observe the rights of those suspected of crimes while collecting evidence to be used against the suspected at trial. If any evidence is collected in a way that does not protect the rights of the suspected, that evidence cannot be used at trial. While it all seems rather neat here in these pages, in practical application, it is quite a murky area.

One notable case highlights the dilemma between the crime control and due process models. After a ten-year-old girl went missing from a YMCA (where she was watching her brother participate in a wrestling match) in Des Moines Iowa on Christmas Eve 1968, a man who was living at the YMCA was arrested in connection with her murder. The arrest was made in Davenport, Iowa, some 160 miles from Des Moines, and the

Box 5.2. *Representing:* Bryan Stevenson

As founder and executive director of the Equal Justice Initiative (EJI; http://eji.org), attorney Bryan Stevenson has dedicated his life and talents to providing legal representation to the most economically vulnerable. The EJI has been responsible for reversing convictions for over one hundred wrongfully convicted prisoners on death row.[a]

Stevenson's grandfather was murdered in a Philadelphia housing project when Stevenson was a teenager growing up in Delaware. When he graduated from Harvard Law School, he began representing poor clients in Georgia, and later in Alabama.[b] Since then, his work has attracted international attention; South Africa's Archbishop Desmond Tutu called him "America's Nelson Mandela," referring to the icon who worked to bring an end to the brutal system of apartheid in that nation.[c] Stevenson is hopeful that his work will lead to a broader examination of systemic inequality, not merely a focus on individual miscarriages of justice. Recently, he has been involved in local efforts in southern cities to erect markers recognizing the role of slavery, so as to provide a fuller picture of the history of those cities and towns.[d]

Stevenson has been recognized many times for his work, including with the MacArthur "Genius" Award in 1995 and the Olaf Palme Prize for international human rights in 2004.[e] In 2016, he was featured on an episode of the acclaimed podcast *Criminal*,[f] and his TED Talk has been viewed millions of times.[g]

---

a. http://eji.org.

b. Ted Conover, "'Just Mercy,' by Bryan Stevenson," *New York Times*, October 17, 2014, https://www.nytimes.com/2014/10/19/books/review/just-mercy-by-bryan-stevenson.html.

c. Tim Adams, "Bryan Stevenson: 'America's Mandela,'" *Guardian*, February 1, 2015, https://www.theguardian.com/us-news/2015/feb/01/bryan-stevenson-americas-mandela

d. Adams, "Bryan Stevenson: 'America's Mandela.'"

e. "Bryan A. Stevenson Biography," New York University School of Law, n.d., https://its.law.nyu.edu/facultyprofiles/index.cfm?fuseaction=profile.biography&personid=20315

f. Episode 45, "Just Mercy," http://thisiscriminal.com/episode-45-just-mercy-6–17–2016/.

g. Bryan Stevenson, "We Need to Talk about an Injustice," March 2012, https://www.ted.com/talks/bryan_stevenson_we_need_to_talk_about_an_injustice.

suspect, Robert Williams, contacted attorneys in both Davenport and Des Moines. When the police who arranged Williams's return to Des Moines refused to let an attorney accompany them on the car ride, the lawyer asked them not to talk to him about the case during the trip. Knowing that Williams was deeply religious, one of the detectives began a conversation about religion during the trip, and ultimately told Williams that he wanted him to "think about" the snowy conditions and that the little girl's family would be able to provide a Christian burial for her if only they could locate her body. Williams subsequently led the detectives to where the body was buried in the woods, and that fact was used in his conviction.

Brewer v. Williams[9] is a challenging case because while it appears that Williams's rights were, in fact, infringed upon (he was questioned outside the presence of counsel), we know that he is guilty because he was able to take police to the body. Further, though Williams was informed of his rights to counsel and to remain silent, he chose to take the officers to the body (that is, to effectively confess). The Supreme Court ruled, in a 5–4 decision, that the speech by the officer constituted a form of subtle interrogation and, therefore, should have been excluded from trial. (On retrial without the confession included, Williams was convicted anyway.)

These blurred lines present challenges for law enforcement officials, citizens, and defense attorneys alike. While some rules are well established, others remain in flux. Moreover, officers are routinely put in a position to make split-second decisions while pursuing suspects or investigating crimes, and those decisions form the basis of what will be the outcome of a case. To the extent that procedures are administered equally across subgroups of Americans, there is much to be debated; however, far too often data reveal that suspects who are poor and those who are black or Hispanic are treated disproportionately more harshly than their wealthy or white counterparts, and that leads us to another area of concern.

Police Brutality and Black Lives Matter

The most significant popular attention with respect to race and criminal justice in recent years has been focused on police brutality. Anecdotes of officers harassing and brutalizing African American men have abounded for decades—immortalized in popular music recordings such as NWA's "Fuck tha Police," Body Count's "Cop Killer," Rage Against the Machine's

"Killing in the Name," and System of a Down's "Deer Dance." But it was the extrajudicial killing of eighteen-year-old Michael Brown, who was African American, by a police officer in Ferguson, Missouri, on August 9, 2014 that propelled Black Lives Matter to prominence, a movement cofounded by Alicia Garza, Opal Tometi, and Patrisse Cullors in the wake of the shooting death of seventeen-year-old Trayvon Martin by George Zimmerman (and Zimmerman's subsequent acquittal), into the national spotlight. Black Lives Matter seeks to call attention to inequality in the criminal justice system, as well as dismantle structures that have perpetuated the unequal treatment of African Americans in all areas of society.

On August 9, 2014, Michael Brown, a black man living in Ferguson, was suspected of shoplifting from a convenience store in the north St. Louis community and was walking on the street when Officer Darren Wilson, who was notified of the theft, encountered Brown and his friend and confronted them, believing they matched the description of the suspects. A struggle ensued with Wilson inside his police car, and Brown outside, at the window. Wilson's weapon fired during the struggle. When Brown and his friend fled, Wilson gave chase, and when Brown turned around, Wilson fired a dozen shots, hitting him with six and killing him. Brown was not armed.[10] His body remained on the street for four hours after his death.[11]

In the days that followed, a number of protests—most peaceful, but some violent—erupted in Ferguson, in nearby St. Louis, and then all over the country. A month before Brown was killed, another black man, Eric Garner, was strangled to death by police officers on the street in New York City. The protests and national uproar that followed their deaths caused the hashtag #BlackLivesMatter, first used by Garza after Zimmerman's acquittal, to trend on several social media platforms. A powerful indictment of systemic racism, the phrase has come to symbolize not only the struggle against police brutality but broader struggles for racial justice.[12]

Unpacking the phrase, we can note that it appears to state an obvious fact. This feature provides much of its poetic power. It ought to be intuitive that every life "matters," so the need to state that black lives do, in fact, matter, is jarring. In fact, an empathetic onlooker would affirm that all lives (should and do) matter, and indeed, that was the refrain from those who embrace a post-racial approach to American political and social life.[13] Social justice advocates quickly pointed out the inherent racism and privilege in such a response, however, noting that "all lives matter" is a theoretical and hopeful statement, but it does not square with the reality of many black Americans' lives. Worse, some argued that Black Lives Matter—as a movement, as well as a phrase—was racist itself, as it suggests that the only lives that matter are those of African Americans. This sentiment was heightened as a number of police officers were killed by African American men, prompting the additional slogan Blue Lives Matter.[14] That, of course, brings the topic full circle in a cruel, ironic way, since the original phrase originated in the wake of police killings of unarmed black men. Activists and scholars have argued that the disproportionate number of exonerations of (or refusals to even indict) police officers in these conflicts is further evidence that black lives do not matter.[15]

There have been real effects of this increased attention. A recent survey of nearly eight thousand officers found that 86 percent believed that their jobs are harder as a result of these killings (and the subsequent media attention); 93 percent think that officers worry more about their personal safety than they had previously.[16] More striking, however, is the discrepancy in the ways that white and black police officers view race relations. That same survey found that 92 percent of white officers agreed that African Americans have equal rights in the United States; only 29 percent of black officers concurred; and "[w]hile 60 percent of white and Hispanic officers said that police relations with blacks were either excellent or good, only 32 percent of black officers agreed."[17] The degree to which officers' attitudes about race and African Americans in particular leads to increased killings is yet to be fully examined. "Shooter bias" studies are designed to examine implicit biases and the relationship between these beliefs and behavior. Simulating the life-or-death context of a real-world situation in the laboratory, of course, is challenging, and a recent overview of shooter bias studies found that the results are too inconclusive or contradictory to rely upon.[18]

Since Black Lives Matter emerged as a movement, there has been increased media focus on persons of color—usually men—being shot and/or killed at the hands of police officers.[19] At the moment, this is the most visible relationship between race and the criminal justice system, but it is not the only connection. Systemic disadvantage and implicit bias within the system is at once reflective of and a perpetuation of both racism and economic disadvantage.

Criminal Justice and the Perpetuation of Inequality

America imprisons more citizens per capita than any other nation,[20] and convicted felons are not proportionally distributed across racial and ethnic groups. Approximately 2.1 million Americans were incarcerated, and another 4.6 million were on parole or on probation in December 2015.[21] This total figure represents a 1.7 percent decrease from 2014.[22] Approximately 7.7 percent of African American men between the ages of twenty-five and fifty-four are in prison or jail, compared to 1.6 percent of white men in that same age bracket.[23] More than two thirds of the federal prison population is black (37.6 percent) or Latino (33.8 percent), which is striking compared to their population percentages (12 percent and 9 percent, respectively).[24] Approximately 93 percent of incarcerated persons are men, but there are racial disparities among the female prison population, as well; women in state and federal prison are disproportionately African American (30 percent) and Latina (16 percent).[25]

Disparities in convictions are most dramatic with respect to drug violations. Before Chicago decriminalized small amounts of marijuana in the summer of 2012, 78 percent of marijuana possession arrests in the city were African Americans. Eight-nine percent of convictions and 92 percent of those jailed for small amounts of marijuana possession were black.[26] And according to one *Washington Post* article:

> In 2003, black men were nearly 12 times more likely to be sent to prison for a drug offense than white men. Yet national household surveys show that whites and African Americans use and sell drugs at roughly the same rates. African Americans, who are 12 percent of the population and about 14 percent of drug users, make up 34 percent of those arrested for drug offenses and 45 percent of those serving time for such offenses in state prisons.[27]

In addition to the difficulty they experience in seeking employment after release, convicted felons in many states lose their voting rights.[28] While reasonable people can disagree as to whether such a policy is appropriate, it is important for this discussion because the disproportionate rate of African American incarceration subsequently affects the numbers of potential voters in the electorate, which can have significant electoral consequences that in turn can affect substantive and symbolic representation for black Americans.[29]

Apart from convictions,[30] arrests are also disproportionate in black and Hispanic communities. In 2015, for example, 26.6 percent of all arrests were of African American suspects, which is more than double the proportion of African Americans in the population.[31] This disproportionate rate of arrests and convictions—even stops and detainments[32] that do not result in arrest—for racial minorities is facilitated by stereotypes that link African Americans and Hispanics with criminality.[33] The statistics in turn perpetuate those stereotypes.[34] Further, media portrayals of violent crime exaggerate these numbers, which results in a distorted view of the relationship of minorities to crime among the mass public.[35]

White Americans tend to overestimate black criminality,[36] and race of the victim is relevant. For all the fear of interracial crime, most black victims are killed by black assailants (89.3 percent of black victims were killed by African Americans in 2015), and the same is true for whites (81.3 percent of white victims were killed by whites in 2015).[37] In the midst of the national outcry over police killings of black men, several observers noted that more African Americans are killed by other African Americans than are killed by whites, let alone by white police officers.[38] This claim, while accurate, is problematic for at least two reasons. First, violent crime is proximate; because America is racially segregated, it is more likely for a victim of a violent crime to be the same race as his or her attacker. Second, the argument serves to shift focus away from unarmed black men being killed at the hands of armed government officials and places emphasis back on persistent problems in neighborhoods that are characterized by high levels of poverty. Similar to the claim that "all lives matter," urging a renewed focus on "black-on-black" crime rings hollow when it comes from individuals, groups, or news agencies who were not focused on relieving such suffering until they were asked to consider police abuse.

This complicated relationship between facts and perception must be considered in context. The numbers cannot be detached from the broader racial and socioeconomic factors that both affect and are affected by the presentation by the media and absorption by the public. Such fears and resentments undergird public opinion, which has an effect on public policy such as police tactics and procedures. For example, even before our focus turned to killings by police officers, racial profiling and stop-and-frisk policies had been under increased scrutiny for at least a decade. Defense of these policies are often justified by such cyclical logic.[39]

These trends have a striking effect on the ability of convicted felons to secure employment after release. Former inmates are "one-half to one-third as likely to receive initial consideration from employers as equivalent applicants without criminal records."[40] Here, as in every other area we have examined, race matters. Whites with no criminal record receive job interview callbacks about 34 percent of the time compared to blacks, who receive callbacks about 14 percent of the time. Whites with criminal records receive callbacks about 17 percent of the time (still higher than blacks with no criminal record), but African Americans with a criminal record receive callbacks only 5 percent of the time.[41]

There are a number of government-sponsored programs designed to help convicted felons to (re)enter the workforce. The Work Opportunity Tax Credit is a federal program that provides tax incentives to businesses for hiring individuals from groups who have historically faced challenges in gaining employment.[42] The federal bonding program "guarantees honesty for 'at-risk' hard-to-place job seekers" in the form of a six-month bond with no cost to the applicant or employer.[43] The federal Workforce Reinvestment Act funds education programs and the development of regional workforce investment boards, which are designed to be collaborations of businesses, labor unions, and policymakers focused on economic development.[44] While these programs are not specific to convicted felons, the holistic approach they take can be a positive influence on the job prospects for individuals with criminal records. Finally, there are a number of state-specific programs—both governmental and not-for-profit—that are designed to help bridge the gap between job seekers and employers (see Box 5.3).

Conclusion

As of this printing, two states permit marijuana to be used legally (Colorado and Washington), and 28 states and the District of Columbia permit marijuana to be used for medicinal purposes.[45] There is disagreement about the effect of the war on drugs on the spike in incarcerations,[46] so estimating how decriminalization and legalization of marijuana will affect arrests and convictions is difficult. This trend, however, raises important questions about our core thoughts concerning what is permissible and, conversely, what behaviors are appropriate to punish. It is important to remember that laws are written and enforced by people, and in a democracy, people can change laws and the policies for enforcing them.

Box 5.3. *What Can I Do?:* Together We Bake

Founded in 2010 by two women with training in mental health and a desire for social justice, Together We Bake (www.togetherwebake .org) seeks to "provide a comprehensive workforce training and professional development program to help women gain self-confidence, transferable workforce skills, and invaluable hands-on experience" to help them transition to the workforce and become self-sufficient.[a]

Previously incarcerated women are invited to participate in the training programs and work at the bakery, which is located in Alexandria, Virginia. Together We Bake is not only a training ground but a successful business operation that makes products sold in local restaurants, cafés, and grocery stores.[b] Graduates of the program sometimes return to lead groups and provide training to others, establishing a scaffold-type model that serves to encourage and inspire. Eighty-nine percent of women who have been through the program pass the exam for the ServSafe Food Protection Manager's Certification Course from the National Restaurant Association's Educational Foundation.[c] Holding this credential affords opportunities for supervisory positions in the industry.

---

a. www.togetherwebake.org.

b. Allison Aubrey, "This Bakery Offers a Second Chance for Women After Prison," National Public Radio, April 15, 2016, http://www.npr.org/sections /thesalt/2016/04/15/469942932/this-bakery-offers-a-second-chance-for-women -after-prison.

c. Ibid., www.togetherwebake.org.

It is tempting to think about racial disparities in the criminal justice system as being purely a function of blacks and Hispanics committing more crimes and, appropriately, being disproportionately punished. Such a view legitimizes our system as fair and race-neutral. As we continue to explore the intersection of race and economic opportunity with other aspects of social life, however, it becomes increasingly difficult to explain away the multitude of statistical evidence as being rooted in individual choice or behavior or in cultural norms. As we turn our attention to employment and immigration status, we should keep in mind the effect that being involved in the criminal justice system has on one's ability to interrupt the cycle of disadvantage.

Discussion Questions

1. What do you make of the phrase "Black Lives Matter"? Given the context in which it emerged, are you supportive of its use in attempting to bring attention to and ultimately reduce systemic inequality? Has it outlived its utility? Have responses such as "all lives matter" and "blue lives matter" served to erode or strengthen its effectiveness?

2. Are you more likely to favor a crime-control model of criminal justice, or a due process model? Given that a perfect combination is desirable but impossible, on which side should we err? What sorts of policies should be put in place to reflect your decision?

3. What do you think about the fact that some states revoke voting rights for citizens if they have been convicted of a felony? What core American values come into play with these policies? To what extent do individuals convicted of felonies deserve to have a voice in the way they are represented when they are incarcerated? What about after they have served their time?

4. How and to what extent do the media influence inequality related to crime? Do the media have the ability to help reduce inequality in the criminal justice system? Do they have the responsibility to do so? Why or why not?

5. The United States is one of the only industrialized democracies to use the death penalty (it is legal in thirty-two states). What are your thoughts as to its appropriateness? If you are supportive, do you believe that it is likely to serve as a deterrent (to prevent crime) or an appropriate punishment for the most heinous crimes? If you are opposed to the death penalty, on what grounds do you find it problematic? Is the emergence of DNA evidence relevant to this discussion?

6

Immigration and
Employment

Now that we have explored the interrelationship between the wealth gap and housing, the relationship between housing and education, and the importance of the criminal justice system, we will examine inequality in employment opportunities and the ways that immigration status intersects with those challenges. Whereas some very wealthy individuals can rely on investments to provide a revenue stream, the vast majority of Americans rely on work—either their own or that of a family member—to be able to afford everything from basic needs to luxury items. The ability to find and keep a job is at the core of democracy's promise.

The normative questions relevant to this chapter are even more complicated than in the previous chapters. While it is difficult to deny that each American has a right to a quality education, a safe place to live, or protection against improper punishment, guarantees of employment are thorny. First, in a capitalist economic system, it is expected that there will be some level of unemployment, underemployment, and discrepancy in compensation based on experience, training, performance, and so on. While an honest consideration of the employment dynamic in any system would lead to an appreciation of each and every component, we might agree that jobs requiring certain skills or that can be performed by a relatively small group of people should earn more than jobs that most people could be trained to do. That is, even though surgery could not be performed without the surgical assistants, the electricians who wired the room for lighting, the plumbers who installed the pipes, the contractors who built the hospital, and the custodians who clean and sterilize the operating room, surgeons will be paid more because they have abilities that comparatively few others possess.

Thus, we need to focus on more fundamental questions: Does each American deserve a job? If so, should a basic standard of living be expected with the compensation from that job? Should all Americans simply have a fair chance to have the job they would like to have? Beyond the basic standard of living, how should wages be determined? As we wrestle with these questions, we keep in mind Figure 2.3 (page 69) and the previous chapters so that we are mindful that all Americans do not begin with the same opportunities.

Discrimination in Hiring

In Chapter 4, we considered the role of education in Americans' quest for financial security. Education is one—and increasingly the most important—form of training that situates candidates for employment in comparison to one another. In theory, the person most qualified for a job opening will get the opening. Neither race nor ethnicity, nor any other characteristic unrelated to the position, will be taken into account.

Reality, of course, does not match this abstract goal. In January 2009, at the beginning of the Great Recession, the unemployment rate for white Americans (7.8 percent) was lower than for Latino Americans (11 percent) or African Americans (13.4 percent).[1] By July 2010, unemployment grew overall, with black unemployment at 15.8 percent—nearly double that of whites (8.1 percent).[2] (This disparity is related in part to cuts to federal, state, and local budgets since the start of the Great Recession. Black Americans are 30 percent more likely to work in government jobs than are members of other racial/ethnic groups.[3]) As noted in Chapter 2, unemployment rates for whites in October 2016 was 4.4 percent, compared to 5.8 percent for Hispanics and 8.5 percent for African Americans.[4] This discrepancy is not a function of the Great Recession, however; the gap between white and black Americans has been shown to be persistent and impervious to the narrowing gap in educational attainment.[5] Further, black men, who have the most difficult time with respect to employment discrimination, tend to experience higher rates of long-term unemployment as compared to their white counterparts.[6]

White women and persons of color face discrimination in employment and promotion. Although there are documented examples of blatant discrimination in employment,[7] the US Constitution has been interpreted as prohibiting the government from discriminating against citizens without due process and requiring equal protection of citizens, and overt discrimination in the private sector has been addressed by a series of laws and court rulings. The most notable is Title VII of the Civil Rights Act of 1964, which makes it unlawful for employers to discriminate based on race, color, religion, sex, and national origin. A number of court cases and pieces of legislation (such as the Lilly Ledbetter Fair Pay Act of 2009) have reinforced these principles and provided remedies for victims of such discrimination. As sociologist Devah Pager notes, while overt forms of discrimination are shocking, they have become relatively rare; however, "contemporary forms of discrimination may be simply more subtle and covert, leading to less frequent detection and awareness by the general public."[8] The most widespread incidents relate to these hidden biases. Absent "gotcha" cases where there is evidence of explicit prejudice at work in hiring or promotion, it is therefore important to reflect on the ways that subconscious processes can affect employment decisions.

As noted in the Introduction to this book, implicit prejudice can be equally damaging (if not more so, since it is often somewhat invisible).[9] To demonstrate this dynamic with respect to hiring, let us consider a series of innovative studies[10] that involve sending fictitious résumés and cover letters to potential employers, using traditionally "white-sounding names" on some and "African American–sounding names" on others, keeping the qualifications the same. The authors of one of these studies report a 50 percent gap in callbacks such that "a white name yields as many more callbacks as an additional eight years of experience" on a résumé.[11] A separate study found that the race of hiring managers affected the racial composition of new hires,[12] but that does not necessarily mean that the discrimination was intentional, explicit, or conscious. Although it is tempting to believe that such results are attributable to overtly bigoted individuals responsible for the hiring at these companies, we must consider the effects that hidden or unconscious racism has on such decisions.

Additionally, there are systemic elements of the racial wage gap as it relates to employment. African Americans (both men and women), for instance, are largely segregated in job markets in a way that leads to inequality, particularly in geographical areas where there are heavy concentrations of African Americans.[13] One study found that "blacks are systematically segregated into jobs with disproportionate black representation" and that "jobs with more black workers . . . tend to pay less than other jobs, even with stringent controls."[14] While there is certainly an attitudinal component to these patterns,[15] such that whites living in areas with high concentrations of African Americans have been found to perceive a greater racial threat, these dynamics work at the macro level as well. For instance, when a job is perceived to be "black" (or "women's work"), the perceived value of the work decreases.[16] If the difference in pay is related to that market-based perceived value, as opposed to being directly related to the race or ethnicity of the person in the position, it is much harder to demonstrate that there is *discrimination* (even though there is clearly *segregation*), as it does not fit our colloquial understanding of racism.

Finally, there is the problem identified in Chapter 3—jobs moving to the suburbs while persons of color primarily live in urban areas (particularly in the North).[17] Such a reverse commute would require access to reliable transportation; that is, individuals living in areas that lack extensive public transportation systems would need a car even to submit an application or get to an interview, as well as to get to work on a regular basis.[18]

One proposed solution to these interrelated problems is the creation of enterprise zones. Championed by former professional football player and congressman Jack Kemp (see Box 6.1), enterprise zones are designed to provide tax incentives to businesses to open (and thus create jobs) in urban and rural centers. When an area is identified as economically depressed, it can be designated as an enterprise zone, which means that businesses operating there qualify for lower taxes and possibly less government regulation.[19]

There is mixed evidence regarding the effectiveness of enterprise zones to create employment opportunities; even when opportunities do exist, white males tend to have an advantage in learning about them.[20] Further, even controlling for other relevant factors, African Americans are employed less frequently in areas that have high proportions of racial segregation.[21] Possessing a college degree does not mitigate employment disparities related to race. Indeed, early in the Great Recession, having a degree was observed to exaggerate racial disparities—during that time, the employment rate for African Americans with a college degree was consistently nearly twice the rate of that of whites.[22]

Education and Training Opportunities

The reasons for employment disparities among college-educated minorities are similar to those who do not have college degrees (movement of

Box 6.1. *Representing:* Jack Kemp

Born in Los Angeles during the Great Depression, John French "Jack" Kemp Jr. was a public servant who had deep concerns about racial and economic inequality in the United States. A Republican, he wished for his party to work harder to reach out to racial minorities, and he sought tax reform and market-based incentive programs to encourage economic development in majority-minority communities.

Kemp was a strong advocate for supply-side economics, which is the theory that keeping taxes low on those who supply goods (businesses and investors) will stimulate economic growth by encouraging reinvestment and job creation. As a member of Congress from Buffalo, New York (where he played professional football for the Buffalo Bills), he advocated for tax reform and passed his ideas along to Ronald Reagan during Reagan's 1980 bid for the White House.

As founder and president of the American Football League Players Association, Kemp supported black players boycotting New Orleans as a site for an all-star game because nightclubs and cabs in that city had been refusing to serve them. Kemp said on a number of occasions that his participation in professional football helped to raise his consciousness about civil rights issues in the 1960s: "I can't help but care about the rights of the people I used to shower with." But Kemp understood that racism is not simply an issue of interpersonal relations. After an unsuccessful attempt at securing the Republican presidential nomination in 1988, Kemp was appointed by President George H. W. Bush to be secretary of Housing and Urban Development (HUD). In his four years of service at HUD, he argued for destruction of failed housing projects and for tax incentives called enterprise zones to offer tax incentives for business to invest in economically depressed areas.

In 1996 Kemp ran for vice president (with Kansas senator Bob Dole) and oversaw one of his organizations, Empower America, until it merged with another organization in 2004 to become FreedomWorks. He worked as a consultant and lobbyist in the early years of the twenty-first century. Kemp died from cancer complications on May 2, 2009, leaving behind a legacy of activism and advocacy for underserved Americans through fiscally conservative, innovative ideas that bridged ideological and partisan divides.[a]

a. Adam Clymer, "Jack Kemp, Star on Field and Politics, Dies at 73," *New York Times*, May 2, 2009, http://www.nytimes.com/2009/05/03/us/03kemp.html; Common Cause, "FreedomWorks," 2011, http://www.commoncause.org/site/pp.asp?b=1497377&c=dkLNK1MQIwG; James D. Gwartney, "Supply-Side Economics," in The Concise Encyclopedia of Economics, 2008, http://www.econlib.org/library/Enc/SupplySideEconomics.html; Andrew Malcolm, "Jack Kemp, All-Star Quarterback, Politician, Father, Dead of Cancer, 73," *Los Angeles Times*, May 2, 2009, http://latimesblogs.latimes.com/washington/2009/05/jack-kemp-dies.html.

Box 6.2. *What Can I Do?:* Helping Others Find Employment

During difficult economic times, there are numerous opportunities for community involvement through volunteer activities. Some positions are organized on a national level,[a] but most are local. A growing number of these opportunities are related to helping others acquire skills to improve their chances of securing (and keeping) a good job. This box provides a few possibilities, but a well-worded Google search that includes a local geographical area can quickly lead to options that fit multiple skill levels and availability.

An estimated 24 million people are functionally illiterate, which means that they do not have basic competencies in reading, writing, and mathematics. Illiteracy affects up to 50 percent of people who are chronically unemployed—defined as unemployment resulting from "deficiencies in labor demands above and beyond cyclical fluctuations."[b] The Literacy Information and Communication System (LINCS)[c] provides numerous programs designed to reduce illiteracy, many through regional resource centers that are funded by the US Department of Education's Office of Vocational and Adult Education. Although there are no opportunities to volunteer through LINCS directly, it provides a gateway resource to connect individuals seeking services, as well as volunteers, with local opportunities. The not-for-profit advocacy group ProLiteracy[d] maintains a database with user-friendly searchable features to find local programs. Simply choose "Find a U.S. Program" and type in your zip code for a list of programs (most with websites) in your area.

Other organizations are dedicated to skills training (often in addition to literacy work). The San Francisco–based Idealist[e] offers classes on basic computer skills, for instance, run by volunteers. Literacy Chicago[f] helps

jobs away from urban centers, subconscious bias, etc.),[23] and it would be foolish to suggest that young African Americans and Latinos should forgo college to increase their employment chances over the long term. National labor projections demonstrate that most of the jobs expected to be plentiful in the coming decades are service producing, many of which require schooling beyond high school (see Figure 6.1). But a four-year college is not an option for every American, because of either inadequate preparation in K–12 schooling, lack of interest or aptitude, or cost. In this section, we consider alternate forms of job training and preparation.[24]

connect volunteers to community members who wish to learn such skills as bookkeeping, filing, or data entry. Also in Chicago, Growing Home[g] "provides transitional employment and training for individuals facing multiple barriers to securing permanent and unsubsidized employment through a social enterprise business based on organic agriculture." The organization works with volunteers to offer job training in a variety of areas on both long-term and short-term bases.

It is important to remember that the pluralist model of democracy features group involvement to solve common problems. Sometimes that involvement comes in the form of lobbying policymakers or contributing to campaigns, but often it involves public education and direct advocacy in the community. Being a part of a volunteer group that works to make one's community more vibrant, safe, and engaged can be a rewarding experience that does not require financial resources or even a burdensome time commitment. The key is to connect those who have skills and those who seek to gain them.[h]

---

a. See http://usa.gov for a list.

b. Michael W. Sherraden, "Chronic Unemployment: A Social Work Perspective," *Social Work* 30 no. 5 (1985): 403–408, at 403.

c. http://lincs.ed.gov.

d. https://proliteracy.org.

e. http://www.idealist.org.

f. http://literacychicago.org.

g. http://www.growinghomeinc.org.

h. Sandra Bynum, "Promote Adult Literacy by Teaching Reading Skills," Volunteer Guide, 2011, http://volunteerguide.org/volunteer/fewhours/adult-literacy.htm; Ronald Nash, "Three Kinds of Illiteracy," Center for Reformed Theology and Apologetics, 1996, http://www.reformed.org/webfiles/antithesis/index.html?mainframe=/webfiles/antithesis/v1n5/ant_v1n5_illiteracy.html; Sherraden, "Chronic Unemployment: A Social Work Perspective."

Community colleges offer affordable alternatives to four-year institutions. Many students attend community colleges expecting to transfer to a four-year college after two years,[25] but others attend for skills that can lead directly to employment. Miami Dade College in Florida is the largest brick-and-mortar college in the nation, with an enrollment of 170,000, 90 percent of whom are racial minorities. The college has an open admissions policy and graduates more African American and Hispanic students than any other institution.[26] The president, Dr. Eduardo J. Padrón, believes that his school is working to combat systemic disadvantage: "If

FIGURE 6.1. Projections for Employment, 2008–2018

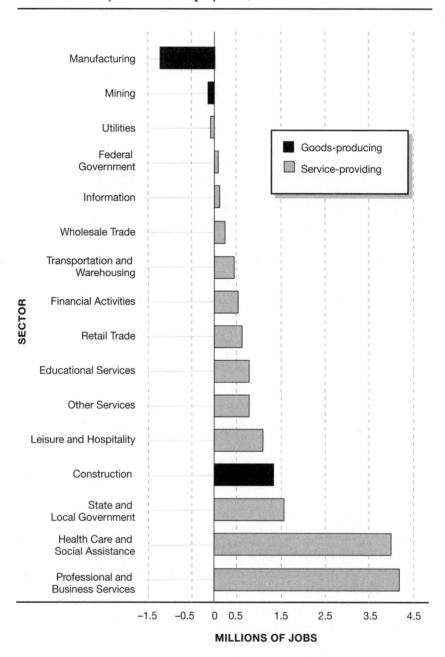

Source: US Bureau of Labor Statistics, "Employment Projections for Major Industries, 2008–18," January 4, 2010, http://www.bls.gov/opub/ted/images/2010/ted_20100104.png.

we say, 'You are not prepared. We won't admit you,' thousands and thousands would not be able to come to college. The cycle of poverty would continue."[27]

Trade schools—sometimes referred to as vocational schools or technical schools—are another alternative to four-year colleges. Rather than preparing students to transfer to a four-year institution, these schools focus solely on the skills and knowledge related to a particular area of employment. While traditional programs such as carpentry, electronics, and auto mechanics are still offered, emerging programs in computer engineering, culinary fields, and graphic arts have become increasingly popular. Business and health-care fields have dominated the occupational training landscape over the past two decades.[28] Training for skills that will help candidates compete for jobs is also available through many public libraries and faith-based organizations. All of these are related to government in one way or another. For instance, community colleges and four-year state institutions are heavily subsidized by public funds, and even private schools benefit from government support through grants and financial aid awarded to students who attend. Public libraries are funded by local municipalities and government grants, and faith-based organizations operate tax-free, which can be considered to be a type of government subsidy.

One unique approach to helping Americans secure employment that is sponsored by the federal government was Project GATE (Growing America Through Entrepreneurship) which ran in three states from 2003 to 2005. Sponsored by the US Department of Labor, in cooperation with the US Small Business Administration, Project GATE was designed to help "emerging entrepreneurs in rural and urban communities achieve the American dream of owning their own business."[29] By providing community outreach, training, and technical assistance to individuals who wish to own their own business, the project instituted a controlled experiment to determine whether the strategies were effective.[30] Innovative approaches to employment for underserved communities, such as Project GATE, offer new ways to think about persistent problems.

Immigrants and Employment

The demographic makeup of the United States has always shifted along with trends in immigration. From the earliest settlers who displaced

Box 6.3. *Representing:* Isa Noyola

Isa Noyola, a self-identified translatina activist, exemplifies the importance of intersectional approaches to social justice issues. As director of programs at the Transgender Law Center (https://transgenderlaw center.org), Noyola is charged with "raising awareness of the conditions affecting transgender people detained in immigration facilities."[a] Her efforts to call attention to the unique struggles of transgender immigrants effectively pulls together activists from a number of causes. Most immigration-rights workers tend to ignore the ways that gender identity might complicate the issue, and LGBTQ activists are not always focused on the unique challenges faced by transgender individuals who are in the country without documentation.

There are an estimated quarter-million undocumented transgender immigrants in the United States, but Noyola is quick to note that the numbers are challenging because of the ways that the Immigration and Customs Enforcement Department collects information.[b] Transgender women are often placed with cisgender men in detention centers, which constitutes a danger to their physical safety, not to mention their emotional well-being.[c] Many of these immigrants are fleeing persecution due to their gender identity in their home country,[d] which renders their mistreatment in the United States all the more tragic.

You can follow Isa Noyola on Twitter at @IsaNoyola and keep up with her work through the #Not1More (deportation) hashtag.

---

a. Brian Latimer, "Isa Noyola, the Translatina Activist Fighting for Immigrant Rights," NBC News, June 30, 2016, http://www.nbcnews.com/news/latino/translatina -activist-isa-noyola-translatina-activist-fighting-immigrant-rights-n601641.

b. Raquel Reichard, "Woman Crush(ing the Patriarchy) Wednesday: Isa Noyola," *Latina*, January 13, 2016, http://www.latina.com/lifestyle/our-issues/wcw-isa-noyola.

c. Ibid.

d. Ibid.

Native Americans, to waves of eager migrants from Europe at the turn of the twentieth century, to our current wave of newcomers from Asia and Central and South America, the United States has always been a destination for those seeking to better their opportunities. At each stage, however, resistance to immigration has come on a number of fronts, not the least of which is the perceived increased competition for employment. In this section, we turn our attention to the recent issues surrounding immigration and employment as a way to more fully understand the challenges that face citizens, immigrants who are in the country legally, and those who are here without papers.

America has been and still is widely known as a "nation of immigrants," but the past two decades have seen an increase in the number of individuals entering the United States without proper authorization. The number is believed to have decreased over the past few years, but there are still an estimated 11.1 million persons in the United States without documentation, compared to 8.4 million in 2000.[31] Those who favor policies that would imprison or deport undocumented people refer to them as "illegal aliens" or simply "illegals," while those who favor policies rooted in amnesty and paths to citizenship usually refer to them as "undocumented workers" or "undocumented immigrants," noting that a person's *actions* might be illegal but that a person cannot be "illegal." The difference in language choice echoes the interaction between race and criminal justice that we explored in the previous chapter.

While space does not permit a thorough treatment of how illegal immigration affects job prospects for black and Latino Americans, it is important to consider both the rhetoric of the contemporary immigration debate as well as the effects illegal immigration has on job prospects for American citizens. This issue is racialized today because the focus is on immigration from Mexico and other parts of South and Central America. Migrant workers from this region form an important part of several sectors of the US economy, and dire economic conditions tend to highlight competition for jobs among new arrivals and persons who have been in the United States for generations.

Whether or not a person enters the United States legally, the presence of additional potential competitors for scarce jobs can be seen as threatening. In the early years of the twentieth century, immigrants from eastern and southern Europe came in great waves looking for economic prosperity. Although they faced many obstacles such as unfamiliarity with the language and culture as well as overt bigotry, their European background allowed them to eventually assimilate into American culture and simply become classified as white.[32] In contrast, Latinos and Latinas face persistent stereotypes and discrimination to a degree that their very presence reflects illegality or criminality to many.[33] They are not incarcerated at the same rate as African Americans but at higher rates than whites, and they are burdened by a stereotype of untrustworthiness and dishonesty.

It is often argued that illegal immigrants from Central and South America take jobs that other Americans do not want.[34] While there may be some truth to the claim that second-, third-, or fourth-generation Americans would balk at working for substandard wages in jobs that are dangerous and or require grueling physical labor (such as housekeeping or working in agriculture fields), such sentiment has the potential to perpetuate race-based assumptions about Latinos generally. In contrast to the assumption that African Americans are lazy and seek public assistance (recall the welfare queen stereotype discussed in Chapter 2), Latinos are often perceived to be hard workers but undeserving of their jobs because they are presumed to be in the country illegally. As the Great Recession has worn on, arguments have been increasing that US citizens would in fact perform some of the jobs that are now regularly performed by undocumented workers.[35] Some of the most vocal advocates of this position are African Americans,[36] who, as noted in the beginning of this chapter, face unemployment rates that are twice as high as whites.

Deciding what to do with children of undocumented immigrants is particularly complicated. It is difficult to argue that they (as opposed to their parents) did anything wrong. On the other hand, those who oppose leniency in such circumstances argue that a policy that provides a path to citizenship for immigrants who entered the country illegally at a young age would serve as an incentive to illegal crossing for parents who wish to help their children become US citizens. In 2011, California—one of the states with the highest number of illegal immigrants—passed the Development, Relief, and Education for Alien Minors Act (DREAM Act), a state version of a federal proposition that creates a path to citizenship for children who entered the country illegally but are attending college or serving in the US military. The California bill allows undocumented college students to secure private funding to attend school.[37] By the summer of 2012, Congress had refused to pass a federal version of the DREAM Act, so President Obama signed an executive order halting deportations of approximately 800,000 students who would be covered under the measure.[38] Fifteen states currently have some form of the DREAM Act;[39] Maryland is the only state where voters approved such legislation through a ballot initiative.[40]

Such efforts reflect the widely held proposition (discussed in Chapter 4) that education is the most important equalizing element in American culture. Even some policymakers who are perceived to be tough on illegal immigration support the notion that those who are here ought to be educated and have a chance to contribute meaningfully to their community. Consider the case of Asian Americans. While they face numerous difficulties resulting from stereotypes and hostility (some of which can be traced back to World War II), the presence of immigrants and US-born South and Southeast Asians in high-skill fields that require advanced education (e.g., medicine, engineering) illustrates the power of education to help clear barriers of prejudice and systemic discrimination. However, significant numbers of Asians in the United States work at low-wage jobs without access to education as well; the proportion of Asians in manual service jobs is generally higher than that of whites but lower than African Americans and significantly lower (with the exception of those hailing from the Pacific Islands or Vietnam) than Latinos.[41] Further, the tendency for many Americans to not differentiate between South Asian and Middle Eastern individuals, as well as the problematic conflation of those regional origins with Islam (not to mention the association of Muslims with acts of terror), leads to an often-challenging daily life for many individuals from these backgrounds.

Conclusion

Conscious or subconscious perceptions of criminality, untrustworthiness, and laziness among employers and the mass public interact with systemic barriers to employment in ways that make it difficult for lawmakers to support meaningful reform without facing electoral consequences. If Americans generally believe that the economic system in the United States is fundamentally fair, then disparities in unemployment will be viewed as resulting from individual behavioral flaws that do not merit government-based solutions. Only a minority of Americans believe that the economic system is fair,[42] yet the unresponsiveness of elected leaders to the perceived injustice reflects the lack of saliency of the issue. While 60 percent of Americans indicated in August 2011 that the economy was the "most important problem facing America,"[43] that broad category is usually interpreted by policymakers to refer to rates of unemployment or the performance of the stock market, rather than fundamental flaws with capitalism.[44] Such beliefs are not surprising, as polls asking Americans how they feel about increasing government regulation in the free market vary greatly depending on the timing or the ideology of the polling organization.[45] Consequently the status quo persists, and generation after generation of poorer Americans, particularly persons of color, have difficulty overcoming systemic barriers to advancement.

Besides the obvious disadvantages that have been addressed to this point (inability to save money for the future or investment, difficulty in securing desirable housing, and inability to provide educational opportunities for their children), poorer Americans face unique health challenges that affect each of these other elements. In the next chapter, we turn to a consideration of those factors and the ways that they are rooted in systemic racism.

Discussion Questions

1. Is such legislation as the Civil Rights Act and the Lilly Ledbetter Fair Pay Act useful and/or necessary in contemporary America? Why or why not? Does such legislation have an effect on explicit or implicit prejudices?

2. How does the issue of immigration complicate employment-related inequality? How is immigration different from other issues presented in this chapter? In particular, consider how the issue contributes to political discourse about employment.

3. What do you make of the idea that capitalism itself is responsible for some of the inequality that exists with respect to employment? How does such consideration differ from most discussions of employment that you have experienced?

7

. . . .

Health

IT IS COMMONLY UNDERSTOOD THAT POOR HEALTH IS OFTEN A symptom of economic inequality. However, nutrition, access to preventative health care, and environmental factors also play a role in perpetuating inequality. The connection centers on the ability to afford healthful food and health-care services, but also includes awareness and education about the importance of such care. In this chapter, we consider an aspect of inequality that is not a distinct part of the cycle of advantage and disadvantage (recall Figure 2.3 on page 69) but is related to a number of elements in that cycle.

We start once again with some broad normative questions about the importance and value of health in a wealthy democratic society. In the 1940s, psychologist Abraham Maslow proposed a theory of human motivation that is often depicted as a pyramid;[1] we must satisfy the lower levels before addressing the higher ones. At the base of the pyramid are immediate physiological needs, such as food and water that we need to physically survive. Until we have satisfied those needs, we will not be able to move forward to the next level, which is safety. When we feel safe (so long as we remain nourished), we can consider satisfying other desires—one at a time—such as love and affection, esteem, and finally self-actualization.[2] To what is every individual entitled? Most of us would agree that a person bleeding profusely on a hospital sidewalk should be taken inside and treated, irrespective of ability to pay. But should that person receive follow-up treatment after the life-saving surgery? Should an obese person be provided access to nutritional consulting to regain a healthy weight and avoid illnesses (such as diabetes) that can result from excess weight? Does it matter how the person became overweight in the first place? What about someone who smoked for fifty years and developed lung cancer but has no insurance? To what extent should that person be treated? Who should pay for it? Should all people have the opportunity to purchase

141

fresh produce and healthful foods, no matter where they live? If parents cannot afford such food, should it be provided to children?

Much of the debate about health in the United States over the past two generations has focused on health care—how individuals and health-care providers are connected to one another and who pays the bills. A host of private, for-profit insurance companies offer health insurance that individuals can purchase directly or receive as compensation through their employer. As the costs of these plans have increased, health-care providers have complained about increasing restrictions, consumers have complained about being denied treatment, and public officials have argued over how to resolve the problems while continuing to encourage innovation in the medical field and provide a high quality of care. Yet evidence shows that having access to preventative care is directly related to overall health.[3]

There have been two major efforts for meaningful (if not fundamental) reform of the health-care system in the modern era. The first, in 1993, failed; the second, in 2010, resulted in a bill that President Obama believed would usher in meaningful reform but progressives dismissed as too timid and conservatives criticized as a "hostile government takeover" of the health-care system.[4] Between 2010 (when the law was passed) and 2016, an estimated 20 million more Americans obtained health insurance.[5] Still, the program was an issue in both the 2012 and 2016 presidential elections, with Donald Trump vowing to dismantle it early in his presidency.[6]

In most industrialized democracies, access to preventative health care is considered a basic human right and thus is provided at no charge to citizens, either by the government or by private providers who are paid by the government. In the United States, we have considered access to health care (with the exception of emergency care) to be a privilege, which means that social inequality is strongly related to disparities in not just health care but also in health. Those inequalities, as we will see, have a powerful effect on the ability of individuals and families to break the cycle of disadvantage.

Access to Health Care

The number of Americans who lack health insurance at any given time fluctuates and is the subject of some debate[7] but it hovered around the 40 to 50 million mark prior to the full implementation of the aforementioned Patient Protection and Affordable Care Act (hereafter, ACA), a law

sometimes referred to as Obamacare.[8] This means that, with
of emergency care, about one in six Americans went without
ical consultation and treatment. Unlike most of the examples that we have
considered to this point, however, it was not generally the poorest Americans who were uninsured.

American citizens who participate in governmental cash assistance
programs, such as Social Security Supplemental Income or those who
have limited income may be eligible for Medicaid.[9] Senior citizens (citizens over the age of sixty-five) and others with certain disabilities are eligible for Medicare, which can cover hospitalization, outpatient treatment,
and prescriptions.[10] Those without insurance were often middle-class
working people whose employers did not provide it as a benefit and who
did not make enough money to purchase it independently.

About 30 percent of Americans between the ages of nineteen and
twenty-nine were without health insurance in 2007, compared to 23 percent of those in the next largest uninsured group (ages thirty to thirty-
five).[11] Most of the uninsured were Hispanic or African American.[12] Some
young people choose not to buy insurance, using their disposable income
for other things because they do not get sick very often. This, however,
creates some problems for attempts at reform.

One of the most controversial provisions of the ACA is the requirement that individuals purchase insurance from private health insurance
companies. Some policymakers and pundits argued that the requirement
is an unconstitutional mandate by the federal government, but the US
Supreme Court upheld it in 2012.[13] Most agree that it is ethically and even
morally questionable for health insurance companies to deny individuals
the right to purchase coverage if they have a preexisting health condition.
Yet it would be financially unsustainable for the insurers if people were
allowed to wait until they got sick to purchase coverage. One of the least
controversial provisions of the ACA mandates that parents can keep their
children on their health insurance plan until the age of twenty-six. This
provision, which went into effect before some of the other provisions,
resulted in 2.3 million young people gaining coverage prior to full implementation of the act. Nearly 4 million other young Americans gained
coverage between 2013 and 2016, which resulted in a nearly 50 percent
drop in the rate of uninsured within that age group.[14]

Further, most medical professionals acknowledge that preventative
care is essential not only for promotion of long-term health but also for

saving money on costly procedures that result from a lack of health maintenance. This is particularly true with respect to prenatal care.[15] As we turn our attention to health disparities, we begin with prenatal care because of the normative questions that have structured our discussion to this point. If every American deserves an equal chance at achieving the American Dream, a focus on the opportunities of children from the earliest stages of development—from education to safety to health—is appropriate. Here, as in the previous chapters, we see that all children do not begin life with an equal chance for growth and prosperity.

Disparities in Health Care Access

The evidence for the effectiveness of prenatal care in preventing birth defects, developmental problems, and infant mortality is consistent. There are expected disparities in prenatal treatment for low-income women,[16] and there is ample evidence of racial disparities, as well. For instance, a recent study found that Asian and white mothers were more likely to take prenatal vitamins in the month prior to delivery than are African American, American Indian, or Hispanic women (see Figure 7.1). In addition, scholarly research has shown historically that

- African American women are more likely to report not receiving advice about the importance of quitting smoking and avoiding alcohol during pregnancy.[17]

- African American infants are born with a low or very low birth weight at twice the rate of whites.[18]

- African American and Hispanic expectant mothers experienced a higher rate of such conditions as intrauterine growth restriction, preeclampsia, preterm premature rupture of membranes, gestational diabetes, placenta previa, preterm or very preterm birth, cesarean delivery, and vaginal bleeding compared to white expectant mothers.[19]

While at least one study found racial disparities slightly reduced at the turn of the twenty-first century,[20] their persistence[21] reflects the types of systemic disadvantages discussed in previous chapters.

FIGURE 7.1. Mothers Who Took Multivitamins/Folic Acid in the Month Prior to Pregnancy, by Race/Ethnicity, 2011

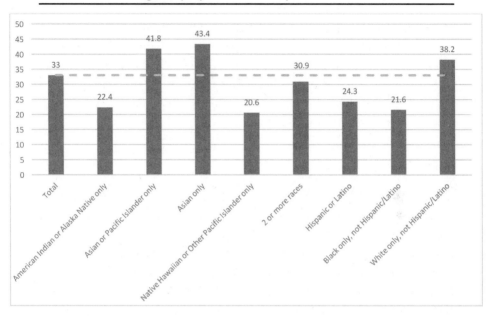

Note: 2020 target = 33.3; increase desired.

Source: Office of Disease Prevention and Health Promotion, "Maternal, Infant, and Child Health: National Snapshot," n.d., US Department of Health and Human Services, https://www.healthypeople .gov/2020/topics-objectives/topic/maternal-infant-and-child-health/national-snapshot.

Although health disparities begin before birth, they certainly do not end there. For example, the infant mortality rate has dropped in recent years, yet disparities remain. The national rate in 2013 was 6 per 1,000 live births (a historic low in the United States), but for African American infants it was 11.1 (see Figure 7.2). African American infants are nearly twice as likely to die from sudden infant death syndrome (SIDS) or unintentional injuries as are whites; American Indian or Alaskan Native infants are similarly at much higher risk for death from these causes as compared to whites.[22] Research has shown that the most effective prevention for SIDS is putting infants to sleep on their backs;[23] only 54.9 percent of African American babies and 67.9 percent of Hispanic babies were put to sleep on their backs, compared to 80.4 percent of white babies (see Figure 7.3).

FIGURE 7.2. All Infant Deaths (per 1000 Live Births, <1 Year), by Race/Ethnicity of the Mother, 1998–2013

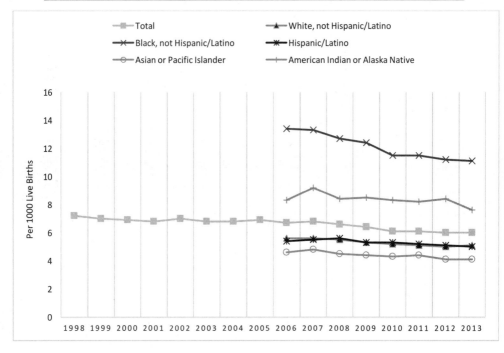

Note: 2020 target = 6.0; decrease desired.

Source: Office of Disease Prevention and Health Promotion, "Maternal, Infant, and Child Health: National Snapshot," n.d., US Department of Health and Human Services, https://www.healthypeople .gov/2020/topics-objectives/topic/maternal-infant-and-child-health/national-snapshot.

On a host of indicators—including levels of lead in the blood, incidence of asthma, obesity, and hunger, as well as treatments (such as receiving cranial CT scans)[24]—children of color are at a distinct disadvantage when compared to whites.[25] Not surprisingly, disparities based on income[26] and race and ethnicity[27] persist into adulthood. For example, even though breast cancer is more prevalent among white women,[28] African American women have the disease diagnosed later, so the size and stage at which a tumor is detected puts black women at much greater risk for not receiving potentially life-saving treatment.[29] White women between the ages of fifty and seventy-four are slightly less likely than African American women

FIGURE 7.3. Infants Put to Sleep on Their Backs (Percent, <8 months), by Race/Ethnicity, 2011

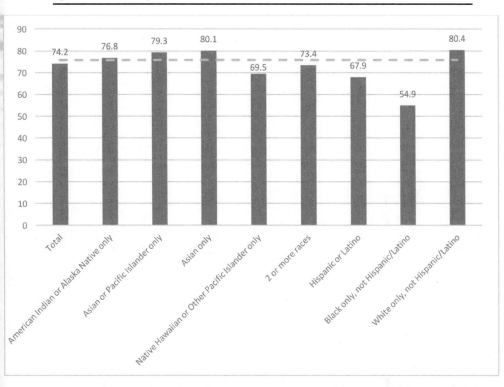

Note: *2020 target = 75.8; increase desired.*

Source: Office of Disease Prevention and Health Promotion, "Maternal, Infant, and Child Health: National Snapshot," n.d., US Department of Health and Human Services, https://www.healthypeople.gov/2020/topics-objectives/topic/maternal-infant-and-child-health/national-snapshot.

(but more likely than Hispanic women) to have received a mammogram in the past two years and a Pap smear in the past three years.[30] In fact, black women are much more likely to die from breast cancer than are white women, though Hispanic, Asian, and American Indian women die at a lower rate than white women do.[31] Even adjusting for socioeconomic status and a number of other factors (such as body mass index), older African Americans have significantly higher levels of cardiovascular disease than do older whites.[32] There are also racial disparities with respect to kidney disease,[33] HIV/AIDS,[34] rate and severity of strokes,[35] diabetes,[36] and prostate cancer,[37] as well as high blood pressure, high cholesterol, and

FIGURE 7.4. Age-Adjusted Death Rates for Selected Populations in
the US, 2011–2012

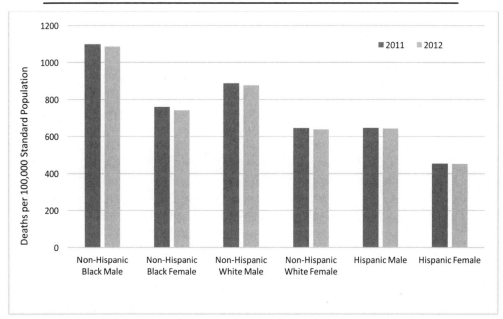

Source: Centers for Disease Control and Prevention, "Mortality in the United States, 2012," October 8,
2014, http://www.cdc.gov/nchs/products/databriefs/db168.htm.

even car crashes.[38] As illustrated in Figure 7.4, age-adjusted death rates[39]
reveal racial disparities as well.[40]

Some disparities are rooted in behavioral differences, although in ways
that are clearly related to systemic disadvantages. For example, children
who grow up in poverty are more likely to be obese and to have diabetes, and are "less likely to graduate high school and more likely to engage in risky sexual behavior as teens."[41] Although eating too much (or
eating unhealthy food), not studying, and engaging in risky sexual acts
are behavioral, they are related to external pressures that center on economic factors (such as access to healthful food). Research demonstrates
that brain development is significantly impacted by the stress related to
poverty during formative years, which can affect behavior.[42]

Ostensibly behavior-related health disparities can be racial as well as
economic. Although whites smoke more cigarettes than African Americans, the latter are more susceptible to health consequences related to

smoking.[43] While the rates of alcohol consumption vary by age, as well as race and ethnicity,[44] African Americans and Hispanics are less likely to complete treatment programs than are whites.[45] A similar pattern exists with respect to illicit drugs.[46] Although low-income Americans are generally more likely to rate their oral health as poor, the discrepancy is greater among African Americans.[47]

In addition to access to health providers, affordability, and levels of education in poorer communities, there is some evidence that a distrust of whites and medical institutions may also contribute to racial disparities.[48] Such attitudes may or may not be conscious, but they nonetheless interfere with a person's ability to have access to care.

As we saw in Chapter 3, housing has a lot to do with perpetuating disadvantage. In addition to the issues already noted, there are health-related concerns with substandard housing. The term *environmental racism* refers to institutional factors and public policy outputs that result in people of color being disproportionately at risk for illness as a result of proximity to pollution and other types of environmental irresponsibility.[49] This aspect of inequality in America is traceable directly to the nation's representative system of government. Hazardous waste facilities tend to be sited in neighborhoods where people are poor, have less education, and have little political power; wealthier and politically savvy citizens are able to pressure public officials to keep such facilities away from them and their children. People of color (over 5 million) compose the majority of those who live within 1.8 miles of a hazardous waste facility.[50] One study revealed that African Americans are more than twice as likely to live in areas where air pollution poses the greatest health threat in nineteen states,[51] while another showed that individuals who lived in neighborhoods that were more than 60 percent white were significantly less likely to be exposed to air pollution than those in neighborhoods that were less than 25 percent white.[52]

In 2016, President Obama and Governor Rick Snyder declared a state of emergency in Genesee County, Michigan, because of the unusually high levels of lead found in the drinking water.[53] This crisis began when officials in Flint (a town that is majority African American and in which 40 percent of residents live in poverty), looking for a cost-saving measure, shifted residents' water supply from the Detroit Water and Sewage Department to the Flint River. The result: Flint residents were provided with water that, because of pollution in the river, improper treatment of

---

Box 7.1. *Representing:* National Partnership for Action to End Health Disparities

The US Department of Health and Human Services (HHS) sets the nation's agenda and goals related to health and provides essential services to those in need. One HHS program, National Partnership for Action
to End Health Disparities (NPA; see http://minorityhealth.hhs.gov/npa), has
a mission to "increase the effectiveness of programs that target the elimina-
tion of health disparities through the coordination of partners, leaders, and
stakeholders committed to action." Related goals include raising awareness
of health disparities and their impact, providing leadership to address those
disparities, improving health and health care for underserved populations,
improving cultural and linguistic competency and diversity in the health-care
workforce, and providing resources and data about these issues. These
goals are codified, contextualized, and expanded on in a report entitled
National Stakeholder Strategy for Achieving Health Equity.

The NPA's work is spelled out in a document titled "HHS Action Plan
to Reduce Racial and Ethnic Disparities," which lays out five clear (though
broad) goals, along with specific strategies and policy recommendations to
achieve those goals. The plan is designed to complement the Patient Protection and Affordable Care Act with the purpose of reforming the nation's

---

the water, and resulting corrosion to the pipes delivering the water, contained nearly three times the level of lead considered to be hazardous.[54]
A switch was made back to the Detroit provider, but the long-term consequences to residents, particularly to children, who drank the water will
not be known for some time.

Because of their developmental physiology, children are particularly
susceptible to the effects of contaminants in the environment.[55] Schools
with lower levels of funding are less able to safely remove asbestos from
facilities, appropriately remove lead paint, or replace lead pipes that carry
water to cafeterias and water fountains. These conditions are also linked
to learning disabilities,[56] which in turn interfere with the potential of educational opportunities to break the cycle of disadvantage, as students with
learning disabilities in underfunded schools are less likely to receive additional resources to overcome their challenges.[57] This is further complicated by the fact that students of color are also more likely to be labeled as

health care system. Fourteen separate measures of disparity (clustered into three groups) that can serve as precise points of comparison in the future to determine the effectiveness of policies designed to increase health equality are identified in an appendix. For instance, narrowing (or eliminating) the gap in the percentage of infants born at low birth weight, the percentage of people who report difficulty seeing a specialist, or the percentage of practicing physicians, nurses, and dentists, then the policies (and the health care reform plan overall) are successful with respect to these goals.

In addition to NPA, there are separate offices of minority health in many governmental health-related agencies, such as the Centers for Disease Control and Prevention, the Food and Drug Administration, and the National Institutes of Health, as well as in each of the fifty states. These executive agencies represent the interests of all Americans by advocating and promoting health equality through education and policy action.[a]

a. US Department of Health and Human Services, "National Stakeholder Strategy for Achieving Health Equity," Office of Minority Health, 2011, http://minorityhealth.hhs.gov/npa /templates/content.aspx?lvl=1&lvlid=33&ID=286; US Department of Health and Human +Services, "HHS Action Plan to Reduce Racial and Ethnic Health Disparities: A Nation Free of Disparities in Health and Health Care," 2011, http://minorityhealth.hhs.gov/npa/files/Plans /HHS/HHS_Plan_complete.pdf.

having a learning disability, which may be related to cultural misunderstandings or lack of trained professionals in underfunded schools.[58]

Adults also face disparities with respect to mental health.[59] Racial and ethnic minorities have less access to mental health services than do white Americans, are disproportionately more likely to perceive shame or stigma in relation to mental health disorders, and consequently shoulder a disproportionately high burden from unmet mental health needs.[60] Environmental factors have been attributed to this aspect of inequality as well. For example, a connection between proximity to industrial centers and mental health has been documented.[61]

It is difficult to firmly establish links between health problems and environmental factors on such a wide scale, particularly given the geographic variability in the United States. Part of the problem for researchers is trying to figure out the interrelated factors of race and socioeconomic status,[62] but varying levels of environmental racial inequality has been found in the nation's largest metropolitan areas,[63] which renders insignificant simplistic answers to questions of representation and advocacy.[64]

Disparities in Nutrition and Access to Healthy Foods

Preventing health problems requires maintaining a healthy body weight (by eating healthy food and exercising) and getting enough rest. There are disparities with respect to both factors.

A recent study found that whites sleep longer (average of 7.4 hours per day compared to 6.9 hours for African Americans and 6.8 hours for Hispanics) and more soundly than persons of color.[65] The interrelationship between sleep and exercise,[66] as well as findings that sleep enhances athletic and academic performance and overall health, are well documented.[67] Sixty-three percent of American adults are overweight or obese.[68] While adult obesity more than doubled (from 15 percent to 34 percent) between 1980 and 2008, childhood obesity rates have tripled. Today, nearly 32 percent of children are overweight or obese.[69] Rates of obesity and overweight among African Americans and Latinos are significantly higher than for whites. Obesity rates are inversely related to income and education, which means that higher levels of each generally correspond to lower levels of obesity.[70]

It may seem counterintuitive that those who have the least money tend to weigh the most, but nutrition is as much about the quality of food as the quantity. It is true, of course, that millions of Americans are hungry. The US Department of Agriculture separates food insecurity into two broad categories: low food security, which is defined as "reduced quality, variety, or desirability of diet" with little or no indication of reduced food intake, and very low food security, which includes "multiple indications of disrupted eating patterns and reduced food intake."[71] In 2015, approximately 29 million Americans adults and 13.1 million American children lived in 15.8 million "food insecure" households.[72] Some 30 million schoolchildren participate in the federal government's National School Lunch and School Breakfast programs[73] that provide free or reduced-price meals; in some cases, that is the only meal participants are certain to receive. Subsequently children go hungry or eat unhealthily on weekends and during the summer months. Adults are not eligible for school meals and often rely on food banks or soup kitchens for sustenance (see Box 7.2).

Box 7.2. *What Can I Do?:* Food Banks, Soup Kitchens, and Community Work

Food banks (sometimes called food pantries) and soup kitchens are among the most popular, visible, and accessible volunteer opportunities in the United States. Food banks generally collect and redistribute unprepared food, whereas soup kitchens serve prepared meals. Food banks and soup kitchens are often run by faith-based organizations, such as churches, mosques, and synagogues.

Although many people volunteer at food banks and soup kitchens over the holidays—particularly Thanksgiving—large numbers of families and individuals count on these organizations on a weekly or daily basis for sustenance. Volunteers need not travel far to find a soup kitchen or food bank. Feeding America (previously known as Second Harvest), a network of some 200 food pantries and 60,000 food pantries and meal programs, provides help to nearly 50 million Americans each year.[a] Many other local organizations run food banks and soup kitchens independently, and they are always grateful for additional help and contributions.[b]

You can combine your love of learning with your desire to effect meaningful change in your community by engaging with or creating initiatives on campus. One of the most creative and exciting of such programs was launched in 2016 at Trinity University in San Antonio, Texas. As part of a broader initiative to involve students, alumni, faculty, staff, and community members in initiatives through crowdsourcing (called TUgether), Dr. Carolyn Black Becker of the Psychology Department, Dr. Keesha Middlemass of the Political Science Department, and a group of students embarked on a study designed to investigate the prevalence and characteristics of eating disorders among food insecure individuals and ultimately develop policy initiatives and programs that can effectively be delivered in the community.[c]

---

a. "Hunger and Poverty Facts and Statistics," Feeding America, n.d., http://www.feedingamerica.org/hunger-in-america/impact-of-hunger/hunger-and-poverty/hunger-and-poverty-fact-sheet.html.

b. Amy Goldstein, "Hunger a Growing Problem in America, USDA Reports," *Washington Post*, November 17, 2009, http://www.washingtonpost.com/wp-dyn/content/article/2009/11/16/AR2009111601598.html; "Soup Kitchens," in *Encyclopedia of Food and Culture,* ed. Solomon H. Katz, vol. 3; Gale Cengage, eNotes.com, August 26, 2006, http://www.enotes.com/food-encyclopedia/soup-kitchens.

c. "Food Matters: Eating Disorders and Food Insecurity," TUgether, n.d., https://tugether.trinity.edu/project/3175.

As anyone who has gone grocery shopping can confirm, eating health-fully is often more expensive than eating processed, prepackaged foods. This reality helps to explain the paradox of poorer Americans being more overweight. Consider, for instance, the "dollar menu" or "value menu" in fast-food chain restaurants. Such menus have become popular over the past decade, with most major chains featuring a number of items for approximately a dollar. For about five dollars, a consumer can get two double burgers, a medium order of french fries, and a large soda. That is a bargain, and it will stave off hunger for a while, but it is quite unhealthy in terms of the number of calories and the type of nutrition it provides.[74] It is often advised that shopping around the perimeter of the grocery store will lead to more healthy choices than shopping in the aisles, but fresh produce is expensive (even if it is not organic), as are fresh meats and fish.

To add yet another layer of complexity, millions of Americans live in "food deserts," where they do not have access to fresh produce even if they can afford it. The United States Department of Agriculture (USDA) has determined, based on 2010 census data, that approximately 10 percent of the United States' population lives in a food desert.[75] While over ten thousand new supermarkets were opened by America's seventy-five top food retailers in recent years, only about 250 of those were in food deserts.[76] In urban areas, food deserts usually force residents to buy processed food to prepare at home or encourage them to eat at inexpensive fast-food restaurants. In rural areas, the "solution" is no more appealing:

> Rural residents pay up to 30 percent more for their food from local merchants who cannot offer the prices found in most major supermarkets. Pride and physical isolation coupled with lack of public transportation keep many people from applying for food stamps. In a ten-county area in southwestern Virginia, 90,197 families qualified for food stamps in February 1992; however only 51,649 received food stamp assistance.[77]

The discrepancy between those eligible for assistance and those who request and receive it is rooted in some fundamental American values. Irrespective of our position on the ideological spectrum or our political party identification, part of the American ethos involves individualism and the belief that hard work will eventually pull us out of despair. We do not like to ask for help (especially from the government, which we want to be involved in our lives as little as possible), and our pride is hurt when we are forced to do so. The result is another paradox: many Americans who qualify for assistance are not getting it, yet a majority of Americans believe that government is providing too many services.[78]

Schools are the place where government has been most active in trying to provide healthful food and instill eating habits that lead to a healthy lifestyle. In 2010, the federal National School Lunch Program requirements were rewritten; more funding was allocated to the program so that school chefs are able to make more health-conscious choices for ingredients and recipes. At the same time, public interest groups, such as the Food Research and Action Center, have been trying to force vending machine suppliers to stock more healthful products in school vending machines.[79]

Conclusion

At the intersection of nutrition and lack of access to healthcare reside tremendous health disparities for America's poor and racial and ethnic minority communities. One study about the effect of social factors in the United States resulted in the following estimates about the indirect effects of racism and poverty:

> Approximately 245,000 deaths in the United States were attributable to low education, 176,000 to racial segregation, 162,000 to low social support, 133,000 to individual-level poverty, 119,000 to income inequality, and 39,000 to area-level poverty. These mortality estimates are comparable to deaths from the leading pathophysiological causes [such as] acute myocardial infarction . . . a subset of heart disease that was the leading cause of death in the United States in 2000[,] cerebrovascular disease . . . the third leading cause of death in 2000 . . . and lung cancer.[80]

Individual government programs can mitigate the effects of this systemic disadvantage, but at least so far, they have been unable to eliminate it. For example, the food stamp program, now known as the Supplemental Nutrition Assistance Program (SNAP), has been in place since the Great Depression. To qualify for the program, an individual's gross monthly income cannot exceed $1,287 ($15,444 per year).[81] The persistently high unemployment rate combined with escalating food prices created a greater demand for the program during the Great Recession; in August 2012, the number of participants rose to a record level, with 47.1 million individuals—15 percent of the population—relying on SNAP for food.[82] In 2016, just over 45 million Americans were participating in the program.[83]

One perspective would be that it is fortunate that such a program is in place at a time when so many Americans would be hungry or malnourished without it. But in an era of increased partisanship and heightened concern about federal spending, not everyone saw it that way. In the spring of 2011, Republican presidential hopeful and former House speaker Newt Gingrich referred to President Barack Obama as a "food stamp president,"[84] a charge that several progressive bloggers, as well as *Meet the Press*'s David Gregory, believed contained racial undertones.[85] Seemingly Gingrich was trying to argue that Obama had been ineffective as a job-creating president, but the racialized reference to what many Americans consider to be welfare in connection with the first African American president was insensitive at best and racially nefarious at worst.[86] Criticism of publicly funded programs to help the needy is consistent with conservative philosophy in many ways, however, as Republicans have argued for charitable, rather than governmental, solutions to poverty and suffering.

Ultimately, it will be the interaction of government, the private sector, not-for-profit groups, and individual attitudes and behaviors that will close the health gap in the United States. As we have seen in other aspects of economic and racial disparity, individuals act within the parameters of systemic constraints, yet at the same time, in a democracy, individuals—usually working together in groups—can put pressure on those parameters to move the boundaries and make meaningful change. In the next chapter, we will examine how gender interacts with other demographic categories and social pressures to further complicate the portrait of inequality in America.

Discussion Questions

1. Consider the normative questions at the beginning of this chapter. To what extent do you agree or disagree with the ideas presented?

2. How do core American values intersect with health disparities? To what extent do these values coincide or contrast with the

issues raised in this chapter? In what ways are these issues similar to or different than the topics raised in the previous chapters?

3. Do you agree with the idea that the language used to discuss inequality is important? Or is this an example of a professor simply making much ado about nothing?

4. Recall the cycle of advantage and disadvantage in Figure 2.3 on page 69. Health inequality was not part of the dynamic presented. Where does it fit, if at all?

5. If there are behavioral elements to health that also need to be considered, does health need to be thought of as a political issue at all? Discuss your thoughts using evidence from your own experience, as well as statistics from this chapter to support your position.

6. There is evidence that some individuals abuse government-sponsored food and nutrition programs by filing fraudulent claims, finding ways to convert funds designed for food allocation for other uses, etc. These cases get great media attention, which causes fraud to be perceived as much more rampant than it is. What, if any, responsibility do media outlets have to report on examples of fraud and/or contextualize them to offer an accurate picture of the efficacy of such programs?

8

. . . .

Gender

WHILE OUR PRIMARY FOCUS IS THE SYSTEMICALLY ROOTED INTER-
section of poverty and race, it is essential to understand the powerful interactive effect of gender in this dynamic. Much more than other forms of
demographic categorization beyond race and ethnicity (e.g., sexual orientation, religious affiliation), gender has had a disproportionate impact on
poverty in the United States. How it intersects with economics, race, and
ethnicity is important to consider.

We Just Don't Get It

During the second presidential debate in 2012, a citizen asked the candidates what new proposals they had to "rectify the inequalities in the workplace, specifically regarding females making only 72 percent of what their
male counterparts earn." President Obama responded first and talked
about his upbringing (being raised by a single mother), his signing of the
Lilly Ledbetter Act,[1] and his advocacy for access to Pell Grants for college.
When it was Governor Mitt Romney's turn to answer, he provided fodder
for weeks of ridicule, as well as an excellent starting point for our exploration of gender inequality:

> Thank you. An important topic, and one which I learned a great deal about,
> particularly as I was serving as governor of my state, because I had the
> chance to pull together a cabinet and all the applicants seemed to be men.
> And I—and I went to my staff, and I said, "How come all the people
> for these jobs are—are all men." They said, "Well, these are the people that
> have the qualifications." And I said, "Well, gosh, can't we—can't we find
> some—some women that are also qualified?"

And—and so we—we took a concerted effort to go out and find women who had backgrounds that could be qualified to become members of our cabinet. I went to a number of women's groups and said, "Can you help us find folks," and they brought us whole binders full of women. I was proud of the fact that after I staffed my cabinet and my senior staff, that the University of New York in Albany did a survey of all 50 states, and concluded that mine had more women in senior leadership positions than any other state in America. Now one of the reasons I was able to get so many good women to be part of that team was because of our recruiting effort. But number two, because I recognized that if you're going to have women in the workforce that sometimes you need to be more flexible. My chief of staff, for instance, had two kids that were still in school. She said, I can't be here until 7 or 8 o'clock at night. I need to be able to get home at 5 o'clock so I can be there for making dinner for my kids and being with them when they get home from school. So we said fine. Let's have a flexible schedule so you can have hours that work for you.

We're going to have to have employers in the new economy, in the economy I'm going to bring to play, that are going to be so anxious to get good workers they're going to be anxious to hire women. In the—in the last [*sic*] women have lost 580,000 jobs. That's the net of what's happened in the last four years. We're still down 580,000 jobs. I mentioned 3½ million women, more now in poverty than four years ago.

What we can do to help young women and women of all ages is to have a strong economy, so strong that employers that are looking to find good employees and bringing them into their workforce and adapting to a flexible work schedule that gives women opportunities that they would otherwise not be able to afford.

This is what I have done. It's what I look forward to doing and I know what it takes to make an economy work, and I know what a working economy looks like. And an economy with 7.8 percent unemployment is not a real strong economy. An economy that has 23 million people looking for work is not a strong economy.[2]

The revealing aspect of this answer is not the "binders full of women" comment, which was ridiculed for sounding silly[3] (Romney meant binders full of women's résumés, not binders with actual women in them). It is illuminating because it was seen as a Freudian slip that revealed how

Governor Romney, as well as most Americans, views the issue of sexism. First, his assumption is that sexism is simply and solely about equal pay for equal work. As we have discovered with respect to racism, and as will become clear in this chapter, the complex institutional structure that undergirds sexism is far more involved than this. Second, Governor Romney invokes the common "add women and stir" approach that treats sexism with quota-like solutions (something, ironically, that conservatives have long opposed in the legal realm, as we will explore in Chapter 9). What would seem to the casual observer to be a perfectly logical answer actually reveals many limitations of individual-level treatment of structural disadvantage.

We can start with Governor Romney's immediate instinct to answer a question about systemic disadvantage with a personal story about his experience with women in the workforce. He suggests that he recognized sexism when he was presented with a list of candidates who were all men,[4] and most of his answer was about creating an economy with a lot of jobs so that women (and presumably men) have opportunities for employment. But that was not the question. The question was about the pay gap (discussed in more detail later in this chapter) among people who are already employed.

Governor Romney's multiple references to women needing flexible schedules so that they can get home to make dinner for their families is equally illustrative of his seeming inability to understand systemic sexism. In the twenty-first century, both men and women have assumed a more equal (but as yet not completely equal) share of household duties,[5] as an increasing percentage of couples are characterized by both adults working outside of the home.[6] Further, the woman is the primary breadwinner in an increasing number of households with both an adult man and an adult woman.[7] While Governor Romney's statements might have resonated with middle-aged voters, many young voters would find such an assumption curious at best and offensive at worst. Men would also benefit from a flexible work schedule so that they can get home to make dinner for the family and, if they have children, be available to pick them up from school, get them to after-school activities, and so on. Such an antiquated view of gender roles reflects not only the degree of progress that needs to be made to eliminate sexism, but the overly simplistic nature of our collective understanding of the problems that remain.

Getting Our Language Straight

Our approach to the definitional elements of this discussion should parallel our treatment of the words *racism, bigotry,* and *prejudice* in the Introduction. That is, being precise with our language is the first step toward a more sophisticated understanding of how gender works in the United States.

Sex and Gender

Many researchers hold that the term *sex* refers to anatomical and physiological differences, whereas *gender* refers to the social construct that differentiates men from women. For instance, the fact that only women can become pregnant is a function of sex; the fact that women are disproportionately expected to be child-care providers is a function of gender. Beyond breastfeeding, there is nothing inherent about a man's biology that makes him less capable of caring for infants or children than a woman, but there are significant social constraints about parental responsibilities that center on gender.[8]

Sexism and Misogyny

As with racism, the important element that is often neglected in discussions of sexism is power. False equivalency claims are common: real or perceived disadvantages for men are presented as evidence that sexism "goes both ways." As with racism, the word *sexism* is most accurately reserved for the notion that men are superior to women. This systemic hierarchy, known as patriarchy, involves largely unspoken and powerful assumptions and expectations that privilege men in our society.

The dynamic is reflected in the language that we have available for communication. For instance, we have no gender-neutral singular pronoun—we only have *he or she,* and *him or her*—so we are forced to consider gender, even when it should not matter.[9] This is important with respect to occupations, too (e.g., fireman, policeman, mailman). Even though political scientists and most journalists use the more acceptable term *member of Congress* or the clumsier *congressperson* to refer to representatives in the US Congress, most Americans continue to refer to them as congressmen. This matters for more than symbolic reasons (though they are also important). First, it does not accurately reflect the idea that it is designed to capture (i.e., there are women who are members of

Congress) and, second, it perpetuates gender inequality by setting up an abstract ideal with which women must compete (in addition to competing with their opponents) when they run for election. Because men can more easily present themselves as closer to the ideal, they are advantaged by having the vague term presented as a gendered construct.

This is an example of *sexism*. It is systemic and often subconscious. *Misogyny*, on the other hand, while it can also be subconscious, most accurately refers to individual-level resentment or even outright hatred for women. There is no question that misogyny is rooted in sexism, but it is important, as with racism, to separate the systemic from the individual so that we can adequately address both without conflating the concepts.[10] At the individual level, women can harbor resentment toward men. We might refer to that as prejudice or bigotry, but calling it sexist undermines the historic reality of male privilege in the same way that using the term *racist* to refer to animosity toward whites by persons of color does.[11]

The 2016 presidential election provided fertile ground for discussion about these constructs. As the first female candidate nominated for president by a major political party, Hillary Clinton sought to leverage her place in history through her slogans ("I'm with her.") and campaign imagery (shattering the glass ceiling). In contrast, Donald Trump was accused of both sexism[12] and misogyny[13] as a result of his behavior and statements during the campaign, as well as information that surfaced from his past.[14] Most egregious was the recording that surfaced from an appearance on the *Access Hollywood* entertainment program wherein Trump, seemingly not knowing he was being recorded, boasted about instigating unwanted sexual contact and sexually assaulting women ("I just start kissing them . . . I don't even wait") without punishment because "when you're a star, they let you do it."[15] Those comments, along with his reference to Hillary Clinton as a "nasty woman" during a debate,[16] solidified persistent concerns from some commentators that his sexism and misogyny were issues to be considered on Election Day.

Indeed, 2016 featured the largest gender gap recorded since 1976,[17] with Hillary Clinton having a 13-percentage point advantage with women and Donald Trump having an 11-percentage point advantage among men.[18] More women voted than men (53 percent),[19] which partially accounted for Secretary Clinton's popular vote victory.[20] It is important to note, however, that a gender gap in this context reflects more than just the simple fact that one candidate was male and the other was female.

Donald Trump embodied a gendered persona that was an important thread throughout his campaign:

> This was an election in which the grievances of white men—their economic upheaval, their cultural displacement—exploded. The fallout included toxic paroxysms of racism, Islamophobia, anti-Semitism and sexism. Misogyny, it appears, thrives in the corners of the United States. Donald J. Trump's hyper-masculinity—the sexual swagger, the belittling of his opponents, his need to dominate—appealed to some men who believed he could restore them to their rightful place.[21]

However, the overall gender gap in 2016 masks a powerful truth related to intersectionality: Black women and Latinas supported Hillary Clinton by 90 points and 44 points respectively, while the majority of white women (52 percent) supported Donald Trump, reflecting a gap of 9 points. The gaps for women of color are greater than the gaps for men of color—black men favored Clinton by 69 points; Latinos favored her by 31 points. None of these trends is a function of two candidates during one campaign, however; the campaign and the candidates operate as part of a larger, longer narrative that is rooted in our deeply held beliefs and expectations about how members of each gender should behave.

Socialization

The process by which we acquire beliefs, attitudes, and behaviors from previous generations is referred to as socialization. It is certainly clear by now that we absorb racist ideas throughout our lives; sexist beliefs are acquired in much the same way. There is ample anecdotal evidence to support the notion that we are socialized into accepting gender roles even earlier and more deliberately than we are with respect to racial categorizations. For gender, the work begins in utero. With ultrasound technology, it is common for parents to learn the sex of their unborn as early as the twentieth week of pregnancy, at least partially driven by a desire to buy clothes and decorate a nursery in colors that are considered appropriate. As soon as a baby is delivered, the first question most folks ask is "What is it?" Advertisements, catalogs, and websites for toy companies are clearly delineated in blue and pink tones, and stories (both in print and on film) that are directed to toddlers contain powerful messages relating to gender norms and expectations.

Box 8.1. *Representing:* Jessica Valenti

Jessica Valenti is cofounder and former managing editor of Feministing.com, "an online community for feminists and their allies." She was named one of the top 100 inspiring women in the world by the *Guardian* in 2011,[a] and she is the author or coauthor of six books: *Full Frontal Feminism: A Young Woman's Guide to Why Feminism Matters; Yes Means Yes: Visions of Female Sexual Power and a World Without Rape; He's a Stud, She's a Slut, and 49 Other Double Standards Every Woman Should Know; The Purity Myth: How America's Obsession with Virginity Is Hurting Young Women; Why Have Kids? A New Mom Explores the Truth about Parenting and Happiness;* and *Sex Object: A Memoir.* She currently writes for the *Guardian.*

Valenti started Feministing because she felt that young women's voices were not being heard. Although feminists are often considered to be politically liberal, for Valenti reaching conservatives is an important goal. She wants to make feminism accessible and says that "more people are feminists than they realize . . . they hear the word, and they don't want to identify as feminists, but they believe in feminist values [such as] equal pay for equal work, [eliminating violence against women, and] reproductive justice." Feministing is characterized by humor and insight that are consciously designed to be accessible.[b] Valenti recognizes that white, middle-class women are still disproportionately at the helm of feminist institutions; she is consistently reflecting on her own privilege and advocating for more voices to be heard.[c]

Feministing, like other online efforts, has struggled with economic viability. Feministing has advertising, but some users prefer not to see ads. Valenti notes, however, that revenue is important to sustain the site that profits are distributed equitably among staffers, and that contributors are compensated.[d]

a. Homa Khaleeli, "Jessica Valenti: Pioneering Blogger Whose Online Activism Dragged Feminism into the 21st Century," *Guardian*, March 7, 2011, http://www.guardian.co.uk/books/2011/mar/08/jessica-valenti-100-women.

b. "A Big Think Interview with Jessica Valenti," Big Think, December 21, 2009, http://bigthink.com/ideas/17880.

c. Ibid.

d. "Interview with Jessica Valenti: Feminist Writer and Founder of Feministing.com," The Daily Femme! June 16, 2010.

Fairy tales and Disney princess movies are prime carriers of sexist messages about the proper roles for men and women in society. Cinderella sings as she cleans and dreams of attending a grand ball to be chosen by the prince, and Ariel from *The Little Mermaid* literally gives up her voice so that she can be with a man, for that is how women are taught that they will find happiness.[22] Messages about standards of beauty are also prevalent in these stories, as are stereotypes about appropriate appearance, attitudes, and behavior for men and boys.[23]

Feminism

Sometimes referred to as the "f-word" by feminists,[24] the word *feminism* has been attacked for decades and saddled with much pejorative baggage. Most Americans assume that feminists are women, though many men criticize patriarchy and advocate for increasing equality between men and women.[25] Many Americans believe that feminists hate men and wish to see a world where women are superior. Feminists, however, come from many perspectives,[26] and the zero-sum mentality mirrors concerns that whites harbor with respect to increasing racial equality.

It is mostly agreed that feminism can be conceptualized historically into three waves.[27] The first wave dealt primarily with women's suffrage (late nineteenth and early twentieth centuries); the second wave (1960s through 1980s) centered on consciousness raising, equal rights more broadly, and (at least toward the end), expanding consideration of nonwhite women's voices; the third wave began in the 1990s and is concerned with a sophisticated critique of the conceptualization and construction of gender.[28]

One particularly compelling perspective emerged from the second wave and persisted into the third: the notion of the male gaze. In the 1970s, Laura Mulvey[29] put forward a critique of film that invoked the notion that there is a tendency for the world to be seen (and filmed) from the perspective of men. This notion has come to serve as a theoretical lens through which all aspects of culture can be viewed. Central to this perspective is the notion of women as objects (rather than subjects). Some third-wave theorizing and activism has involved women reclaiming their sexuality in ways that make some second-wave feminists uncomfortable.[30] Beyond content, however, third-wave feminists are using modern technology and cultural trends to engage with one another and with the world in ways that would have been impossible for their predecessors. Blogs and

Box 8.2. *What Can I Do?:* Blogging

Reading feminist blogs is a useful (and enjoyable) way to stay apprised of the way contemporary culture can be viewed through feminist lenses. Below is a list of some prominent feminist blogs, but it is important to stay alert because new outlets are being created all the time. Since blogging avoids gatekeepers, writing one's own analysis of current events, popular culture, or other interesting aspects of life can be a meaningful form of expression with a potential to reach a very wide audience. Make sure that your blog is integrated with your other social networking sites, such as Twitter and Facebook, and do not be shy about tagging more established bloggers and columnists to try to get them to read what you are writing. A well-placed retweet or share from someone with many followers can garner attention and give you a chance to interact in a meaningful and fulfilling way with others.

- Bitch Media: https://bitchmedia.org
- Black Girl Dangerous: https://bgdblog.org
- Feminist Frequency: https://feministfrequency.com
- Feministing: http://feministing.com
- Jezebel: http://jezebel.com
- TransGriot: http://transgriot.blogspot.com

social networking have afforded these writers the opportunity to express themselves without filters or editors, but they face pressures that are inherent in this type of communication, as well (see Box 8.2).

Third-wavers have been more intentional about recognizing their own privileges (when and where they exist) with respect to social class, sexual orientation, able-bodiedness, and race, as well as being inclusive of voices that previous generations of feminists have been accused of neglecting.[31] One might speculate that the more democratic nature of our communication has converged with theoretical and empirical work by scholars to create an ideology that is better positioned to consider the ways that various hegemonic forces intersect to provide advantages and disadvantages, privileges and challenges.

Intersectionality

As noted in the Introduction, we cannot simply assume that privilege (or disadvantage) is additive, as if being white has privilege and being male has privilege, then being white and male carries twice as much privilege. Sometimes that is the case,[32] but interactions among demographic elements are complex and sometimes counterintuitive. As we consider the degree to which gender intersects with economic inequality in the United States, we must also consider how race forms an interaction that will complicate our work.

Gender Inequality and Poverty

Much has been written about how patriarchy operates in the United States and globally, but here we will focus on ways that these systemic and attitudinal factors relate to economic inequality. Like each topic we have explored, this one is complicated, though it is rarely presented that way in public discourse.

Income and Wealth

The most visible element of gender inequality in the United States is the wage gap. As noted in Chapter 2, it is well documented that women earn less pay for comparable work.[33] This gap has been relatively consistent for decades—at least since women began to enter the paid workforce in high numbers.[34] One reason for such inequity could be interpersonal—women are not valued as much as men, so they are paid less. However disturbing this reason may be, it is also too simple and far too convenient. If the problem of pay equity were limited to men in power not valuing women they hire, then the solution would be to punish those who are making inequitable decisions or wait until they retire and then replace them with Americans socialized in later eras who tend to have more explicitly egalitarian views. Unfortunately, the reality is not so straightforward.

The share of women in the labor market had increased steadily since the 1980s (until 2014, when it dipped slightly),[35] but women have not yet achieved pay equity in most occupations. Women are disadvantaged for a number of reasons relating to deeply held beliefs about their proper place (in the home versus in the workplace), their abilities and intelligence, and their biology. With respect to the latter, it is important to understand the notion of the mommy track,[36] which is a result of women taking time away from workplace participation as a result of childbirth and sometimes child rearing. While biology necessitates rest and healing after childbirth, cultural pressures dictate that women function as the primary caretaker of children,[37] which results in longer periods of time away from their career. When a woman returns to the office or worksite, a man who was hired at the same time and performed comparably will have advanced, while she returns to the position that she had before her leave. A heterosexual couple with both adults working outside the home may choose to have multiple children, and with each child the woman's career may be suspended, leading to disparities in pay and rank.[38]

Further, there are deeply held beliefs in our culture about what types of jobs are appropriate for men and for women. Such occupational segregation is partially responsible for the persistent wage gap. Women are hired disproportionately into occupations that have lower pay. These so-called pink-collar occupations (most often service-oriented positions, such as cashiers, food servers, and caretakers for the sick, elderly, and children)[39] are disproportionately populated by women and pay much less than those that are populated primarily by men. Approximately 1.6 million women in the United States earn minimum wage or less, compared to just under 1 million men.[40] A glance at the ten highest-paying occupations and the ten lowest-paying occupations in Figure 8.1 reveals that men disproportionately comprise the workforce in the former, while women dominate the latter. As we have seen in other contexts, race matters here, too, with women of color faring even worse than their white female counterparts in terms of the effect of occupational segregation on earnings.[41]

A recent report attributed the persistence of the wage gap in part to an emerging trend in labor compensation overall:

> Hourly pay has risen more than twice as fast over the past three decades for men working long hours, as employers increasingly reward employees willing to work extra hours with raises or promotions. . . . Men make up a bit more than half the full-time workforce, but they account for more than 70 percent of those working 50 hours a week or more. So as wage gains have gone disproportionately to people working long hours, they have also gone disproportionately to men, widening the earnings divide between men and women overall. . . . [This] trend contributes to the wage gap because men are so much more likely than women to work those long hours. That, in turn, is the result of a confluence of factors that are deeply embedded in the

FIGURE 8.1. Gender Composition of Highest Paying Occupations

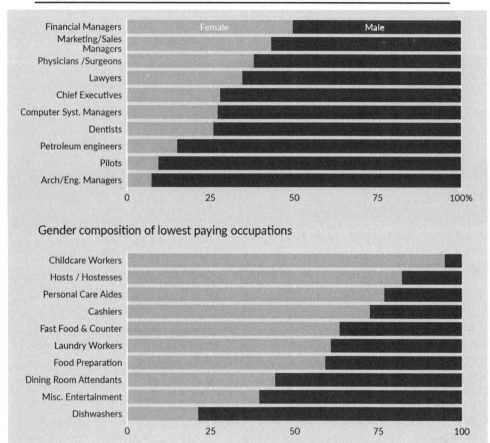

Gender composition of lowest paying occupations

Source: Author's compilation of available gender composition data for broad occupational categories with highest and lowest mean wages according to Bureau of Labor Statistics tables "May 2015 National Occupational Employment and Wage Estimates" and "Employed persons by detailed occupation, sex, race, and Hispanic or Latino ethnicity."

American economy and society: Women, on average, spend much more time than men on housework, while men . . . are expected to work as much as possible. And of course, most importantly, mothers are still far more likely than fathers to be the primary caregiver for their children.[42]

It is clear that women face systemic challenges to equality that are much more complicated than our colloquial understanding of sexism as individual-level preferences for men over women with respect to workforce participation.

FIGURE 8.2. Poverty Rates for Adult Women, 2015

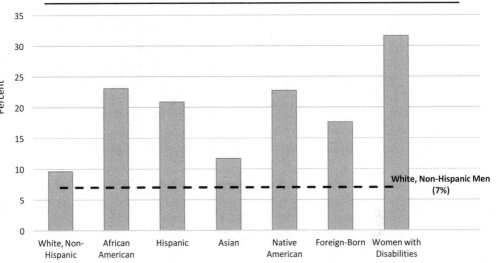

Source: National Women's Law Center, "National Snapshot: Poverty Among Women & Families, 2015," September 2016, https://nwlc.org/wp-content/uploads/2016/09/Poverty-Snapshot-Factsheet-2016.pdf.

All of this contributes to what has been termed the feminization of poverty.[43] Nearly 17 million women (about 12 percent of American women) lived in poverty in 2015; nearly half of the women who were living in poverty lived in extreme poverty (with income at or below 50 percent of the federal poverty level). More than 85 percent of the adult recipients of Temporary Assistance for Needy Families are women,[44] and females compose 58 percent of Medicaid recipients.[45] Women were 35 percent more likely to live in poverty than men. As reflected in Figure 8.2, poverty rates were higher for many women of color: 23 percent of African American women, 21 percent of Hispanic women, and 23 percent of Native American women were living in poverty in 2015.[46]

As noted in Chapter 2, however, poverty has at least as much to do with wealth as it does with income. While it is often difficult to measure wealth from the perspective of gender because wealth is measured as a function of household rather than individuals, we can gain an appreciation for the relationship between gender and poverty if we consider the case of single women. Households led by women that do not have other adult earners in the home constitute the highest levels of poverty, particularly when there are children in the home. It will be no surprise to readers at this point that race factors into these numbers in predictable ways: In 2015, nearly 40 percent of black single mothers, 42 percent of Hispanic single mothers, and 48 percent of Native American single mothers were living in poverty, as compared to 31 percent of white single mothers. The poverty rate for married couples with children (all races) was 7.5 percent.[47]

Women who are divorced are likely to have custody of children, and if they were not working outside the home while they were married, they find themselves at a competitive disadvantage for gainful employment (not to mention struggles with finding affordable child care if the children are not in school) after separation.[48] Senior women face similar challenges. Women constituted nearly two thirds of Americans who were 65 or older in 2015; the poverty rate for African American and Hispanic senior citizen women (19.6 percent and 20.1 percent, respectively) was more than two and a half times that of white senior women (7.7 percent).[49] Although women account for more than half of all Social Security beneficiaries, their benefits are smaller because their earnings, on average, were lower. In 2014, the average retired woman earned $1,167 per month in Social Security benefits compared to $1,448 for men.[50] Widows are more likely to be impoverished than widowers. Because women tend to live longer than men, widows have a longer period of time to live without their partner than widowers do. Two fifths of women experience poverty within five years of the death of their husband.[51]

Social Class

While poverty is the focus of this discussion, women in high-status occupations also face relative disadvantages that parallel the experiences of poor women. As referenced in Chapter 2, there is a stigma attached to receiving some forms of public assistance in the United States, and the correlation with racialization of the assistance is great. While few harbor animosity toward those who receive veterans' benefits, Social Security, Medicare, or even unemployment compensation, many resent Americans who participate in assistance programs, such as Temporary Assistance for Needy Families; the Women, Infants and Children (WIC) program; and the Supplemental Nutrition Assistance Program (SNAP; formerly food stamps).[52] Ronald Reagan was successful in invoking the term "welfare queen" not only because Linda Taylor was African American, but also because she was a woman.[53]

However, the notion of women being less valuable to society is a recurring narrative that stretches from the welfare line to the boardroom.

Studies of women in executive positions shed additional light on gender inequality among the highest ranked positions in corporate America. As noted in Chapter 2, women headed twenty-one Fortune 500 companies in 2016.[54] While some inequity is surely a result of issues that we have already discussed, a body of research demonstrates that socialized gender norms may be a contributing factor.[55] Further, the pattern exists in work outside of business; there is gender imbalance at the highest levels in academia, particularly in science, technology, engineering, and mathematics (STEM), because, as will be discussed in a later section, girls are not encouraged to pursue those subjects in school, and young women are discouraged from pursuing advanced degrees in those fields.[56]

Poverty, Reproductive Health, and the Struggle for Control of a Woman's Body

Mommy track norms are connected to overt attempts to exert reproductive control over a woman's body, particularly those of poor women and women of color. From decades of eugenics policies in the United States at the beginning of the twentieth century[57] (some states continued the practice of forced sterilization into the 1970s)[58] to assumptions about poor women and women of color and promiscuity, the tendency has been to ignore or remove agency from women, especially as it relates to reproductive health.

Popular assumptions hold that poverty is at least partly a result of poor individuals reproducing when they cannot afford to raise children. Because child rearing in our culture is largely presumed to be the province of women, our collective fingers are often pointed squarely at poor teens and women for not being more responsible. Ignoring for a moment that the same folks who make those accusations are often those who work to deny access to birth control or abortion (and the fact that boys and men are equally responsible for a pregnancy in consensual situations), it is important to consider the direction of the causal arrow. In other words, it is also logical to consider that poverty leads to unplanned or even unwanted pregnancy rather than the other way around. Recent research has found that to be the case with respect to teen pregnancies,[59] and our exploration here suggests that the interrelationships among such factors as education, health, and economic opportunities likely serve as constraints on the choices that poor young women make with respect to reproduction.

tween reproductive health and sexism is also not lim-
...no experience poverty. The provision in the Patient Pro-
...ordable Care Act that requires employers to provide free
...s part of their insurance coverage for employees has been
extens... ...ebated. Wheaton College, an evangelical institution in Illinois, and Catholic University in Washington, DC, both sued the Obama administration over the provision, arguing that the mandate would force them to violate core elements of their faith.[60] Debate about religious institutions and patriarchy dates back much farther than these recent policy squabbles, and reasonable people can disagree about the appropriateness of termination of pregnancies at various stages of gestation. Irrespective of one's position on those issues, however, it must be noted that women (and women's bodies) are often discussed as though they are primarily or even wholly designed to be vessels for fetal development.[61]

Gender and Housing Access

As is the case with wealth, it is difficult to discuss housing inequality with respect to gender because men and women cohabitate at far greater rates than do members of different racial and ethnic groups. As was the case with wealth, statistical analysis is largely limited to women who are heads of household, whether or not they are raising children.

In a broader sense, the notion of home has been intricately linked with women throughout the nation's history. In the nineteenth century a haven model of domestic life emerged that "emphasized the importance of sequestering women in private homes, and focused on making the home a relaxing respite from the competition of capitalist society for the husband/father and a nurturing environment for the children, maintained by the wife/mother."[62] This separate-spheres approach maintained public space as the dominion of men and reserved the private sphere for women. Government policies designed to encourage home ownership in the early part of the twentieth century often included explicit policies that disadvantaged women.[63] As divorce rates climbed or children were born out of wedlock, women were in a position to find safe, affordable housing for their family. Many of the resulting issues in this area converge with our broader discussion of housing in Chapter 3 (public housing, Section 8, etc.), but we should keep in mind that women and men often experienced these challenges differently.

Gender Inequality and Education

The existence of gender inequality in education is well documented. Data collected over the past few decades do not present a clear picture of inequity (e.g., some of the differences in achievement shift when considered at different ages, and socioeconomic status is a relevant consideration), but girls tend to have lower achievement in science and mathematics and higher scores in reading, particularly at younger ages.[64] Research demonstrates that the gender gap with respect to quantitative reasoning tends to widen during K–12 schooling and that biology interacts with environmental factors to produce such divergence.[65]

In the United States girls tend to finish high school at higher rates than boys, a trend that persists across racial and ethnic groups.[66] In the past two decades, men have been slightly less likely than women to enroll in college directly after high school,[67] which correlates positively with college enrollment (delaying enrollment tends to result in lower eventual attendance rates).[68] Boys have consistently outperformed girls on the Scholastic Aptitude Test (SAT),[69] particularly on the mathematics section, with the 2015 results revealing a 31-point gap (527 to 496).[70] The science and mathematics gap persists into college[71] and is reflected in the workforce: the pay gap for women in their first year out of college is only slightly less (82 percent of men's salaries) than the overall gender wage gap.[72]

However, women are attending college and graduating at higher rates than their male counterparts. Within the past few years, the narrowing gender gap of the portion of the US population holding a bachelor's degree resulted in women surpassing men (see Figure 8.3). This is the result of decades of women earning more bachelor's degrees than men. This pattern holds across racial groups: Since the mid-1990s, white, black, and Hispanic women were all more likely than their male counterparts to hold a bachelor's degree; by 2010, the same was true for Asian women.[73]

Women tend to drop out of college at lower rates, finish their degree more quickly, and are now more likely than men to attend graduate school and earn graduate degrees. In 2015, women earned 66.4 percent of graduate certificates, 58.4 percent of master's degrees, and 51.8 percent of doctoral degrees. These awards were not distributed evenly across fields of study, showing notable gaps in STEM fields.[74] Even so, the wage gap

FIGURE 8.3. **Percentage of US Population Holding a Bachelor's Degree**

Source: US Census Bureau, "Women Now at the Head of the Class, Lead Men in College Attainment," October 7, 2015, http://blogs.census.gov/2015/10/07/women-now-at-the-head-of-the-class-lead-men-in-college-attainment/?cid=RS23.

persists, which reflects the complexity of how advantage and disadvantage work in the United States.

Gender and Criminal Justice

Women are incarcerated much less frequently than men. Data for 2010 from the US Bureau of Justice Statistics reveal that 36 percent of women in state or federal prison have been convicted of violent crimes; most other inmates are serving sentences for property (30 percent) and drug (26 percent) offenses. Women (85 percent) are more likely than men (66 percent) to be supervised on probation or parole.[75] In 2014, men were in state or federal prison at a rate of 1,169 per 100,000 adults, while women's incarceration rate was 84 per 100,000 adults. These figures represented a decrease for men and an increase for women.[76] In fact, there was a dramatic increase in the number of women incarcerated in state and federal prisons, as well as jail—from 1980 to 2014, the number grew from 26,378 to 215,332.[77] Women are more likely than men to be incarcerated for drug or property offenses, while men are disproportionately convicted of violent offenses.[78] Half of the women who are incarcerated are the parents of minor children, in addition to 1.1 million incarcerated fathers, resulting in 2.7 million American children with at least one incarcerated parent. Approximately 10 million children have experienced the incarceration of a parent at some point in their life. Again, there is a racial component: black (11.4 percent) and Hispanic (3.5 percent) children are more likely than white children (1.8 percent) to have an incarcerated parent.[79]

Noting the historic level of incarceration for African American women, one legal scholar argues that

> African American women face challenges in reentry and reintegration that other populations do not have to face. Incarcerated African American women are mothers, care givers and heads of household before they become offenders. Once they become offenders, their children become displaced and income that is desperately needed by their families is lost. African American children languish in foster care, awaiting their parents['] release from prison or alternately become permanently severed from their families.[80]

Women of all races face these unique circumstances when they are sent to prison (and when they are released), but the disproportionate number of women of color who are incarcerated warrants increased focus on these women in particular as we seek to understand the interrelationship of crime and poverty.

Our collective narrative in this realm is familiar, as well. As is the case with public assistance (e.g., the "welfare queen" trope), there has been a tendency to blame single women (particularly women of color) for violent crime. In the early 1990s, Health and Human Services secretary Louis W. Sullivan attributed homicide figures, in part, to "the collapse of the American family," particularly in the black community.[81] Over a forty-year period, the numbers do not support such a narrative[82] (and even if they did, we would be wise to consider not only the arrow of causality but moderating and mediating factors[83] as well), but the sentiment is no less powerful for this lack of evidence. Answering a question about gun violence in the second presidential debate in 2012, Governor Mitt Romney spent time arguing for the importance of a two-parent family as a way to "make changes in the way our culture works to help bring people away from violence and give them opportunity, and bring them in the American system."[84] As we have already seen, there is certainly a correlation between crime and poverty, as well as a correlation between poverty and single-parent families. However, a sophisticated analysis is warranted; suggesting a direct relationship between single-parent households and violence provides a convenient but unfortunate opportunity for those who are less versed in the nuance of inequality to attribute the violence to poor choices made by persons of color in particular rather than larger, systemic explanations.

Gender, Reproductive Rights, and Health

While space does not permit a thorough discussion of gender disparities related to health,[85] we will look at the most politicized of women's health issues: reproductive rights. Strong moral and ethical issues are intertwined with the question of whether terminating a fetus is appropriate (including the philosophical question of whether life begins at conception, at some stage during gestation, or at birth), but few women have been part of the decision-making process. Most elected officials at all levels of government, as will be discussed in greater detail in a later section, are and have been men, as are most judges, including US Supreme Court justices, who have the last word on many aspects of this debate. In 1973 an all-male Court declared that terminating a pregnancy in the first two trimesters was a constitutionally protected right,[86] lending support for the substantive representation model of governance.

In recent years, a number of states have attempted to pass so-called personhood amendments to state constitutions, as well as the US Constitution. Such provisions would designate a fertilized human egg as a legal person, thus protecting it from termination.[87] Pro-choice advocates view such positioning as pitting the rights of a fetus against the rights of a woman.[88]

These issues are connected to broader elements of women's reproductive health and sexual violence. Georgetown University law student Sandra Fluke achieved a tremendous amount of attention[89] in 2012 when she was called a "slut" and a "prostitute" by a talk radio host for demanding that her birth control pills be covered by the Catholic institution's health-care policy. The attacks on Fluke went beyond reasonable disagreement about religious freedom or reproductive rights; she became a symbol of the collective view of women held by many Americans. Later that year, a number of candidates for public office found themselves heavily criticized for their comments about rape (as it relates to exceptions for abortion), with Missouri's Todd Akin opining that pregnancy as a result of rape is rare because if a woman is the victim of a "legitimate rape, the female body has ways to try to shut that whole thing down"[90] and Indiana's Richard Mourdock noting that if a woman does become pregnant as a result of a rape, the pregnancy (though presumably not the assault) is a "gift from God."[91] Both candidates lost their respective races.

The symbolic importance of men making statements that are factually inaccurate (Akin) and woefully insensitive (both candidates) cannot be ignored. If we revisit our consideration of symbolic and substantive representation from Chapter 1, we will be in a stronger position to examine the degree to which having more women in office might affect decisions relating not only to reproductive rights and women's health but also to core policy issues discussed throughout this chapter and book including housing, education, and crime.

Beyond reproductive rights, related issues highlight health disparities with respect to childbearing. For example, a recent study found that depression caused by discrimination leads to low birth weight in babies. Babies born to white women and Latinas are at half the risk of low birth weight as are those born to black women. The study showed, however, that even holding race constant (as well as age and type of discrimination), women who reported discrimination had higher levels of depression and babies who weighed less than those who did not report facing discrimination.[92]

Intersectional explanations for mortality and morbidity (being unhealthy) disparities over the past three decades are available as well, and this trend is not completely driven by level of education or socioeconomics; African American women with a college degree report worse health conditions than do African American men with a high school education.[93] As highlighted in the previous chapter, women of color face a variety of health disparities compared to white women. These challenges can result from disproportionate poverty and contribute to economic challenges.

Box 8.3. *Representing:* Phyllis Schlafly

One of the most vocal and visible opponents of the Equal Rights Amendment was Phyllis Schlafly, a veteran conservative writer and activist who continued her work until her passing in 2016. Schlafly, who was born in 1925, is the author of twenty books, including *The Power of the Positive Woman* and *Feminist Fantasies*.[a] She authored *The Phyllis Schlafly Report* for nearly fifty years, she wrote a syndicated column that appeared in one hundred newspapers, and she provided daily radio commentary that was broadcast on over six hundred radio stations and online.[b]

Schlafly's opposition to the ERA was centered partly on her concern about courts having too much power in the political system. She (and others) feared that a failure to narrowly define *sex* and *equality* would lead to judges, rather than elected officials, deciding how those words should be interpreted.[c] Part of that concern is rooted in opposition to LGBTQ rights. Even though she has a gay son (who works with her at her foundation, the Eagle Forum), she (and he) did not believe in LGBTQ marriage, and she believed that the courts would have legalized it years ago if the ERA had passed in the 1970s.[d]

Although Schlafly was a nemesis for feminists, she believed that she, not feminists, stood for equality. She believed that feminists "adopt [a] victimology notion" and that a "litmus test for feminists is to agree with abortion."[e] In many ways, though, Schlafly embodied feminist ideals. She graduated Phi Beta Kappa from Washington University (where she also earned a law

Women in Office

As noted in Chapter 1, the 115th Congress (2017–2019) included a record number of women (104—about 19 percent of members), a number unchanged from the 114th Congress[94] (and only three members greater than the 113th Congress).[95] For half a decade now, over one hundred women have occupied Capitol Hill offices, participating in committee work and debate and ultimately voting on national policy. Recall that from the perspective of symbolic (or "descriptive") representation, members of minority groups in particular benefit from having folks who have lived similar experiences in positions of power. The positive elements range from being visible role models for youngsters to serving as mentors to helping usher in a greater number of policy decisions that are degree and received an honorary doctorate in 2008), as well as a master's degree in political science from Harvard University;[f] she had six children and worked consistently throughout her life.[g] By her own admission, she "had it all."[h]

Into her ninth decade, she spoke out about public issues. For example, when Missouri Senate candidate Todd Akin made his controversial remarks about "legitimate rape" in 2012, Schlafly came to his defense, arguing that Republican Party leaders were "making a big thing about an unfortunate remark."[i] While she did not fit neatly into any particular ideological framework that is generally characterized as feminist, she was a vocal, strong female voice and a role model to millions.

a. "Phyllis Schlafly," Eagle Forum, http://www.eagleforum.org/about/bio.html.

b. Ibid. The direct link to the online radio broadcasts is http://www.eagleforum.org/radio/index.html.

c. Andrea Sachs, "Phyllis Schlafly at 84," *Time*, April 7, 2009, http://www.time.com/time/nation/article/0,8599,1889757,00.html.

d. Ibid.

e. "Are Conservative Women Like Sarah Palin Feminists? Phyllis Schlafly Says 'No,'" *The Daily Caller*, February 14, 2011, http://dailycaller.com/2011/02/14/are-conservative-women-like-sarah-palin-feminists-phyllis-schlafly-says-no/.

f. "Phyllis Schlafly," Eagle Forum.

g. Sachs, "Phyllis Schlafly at 84."

h. Ibid.

i. Rosalind S. Helderman, "Conservative Activist Phyllis Schlafly Defends Akin," *Washington Post*, August 20, 2012. http://www.washingtonpost.com/blogs/post-politics/wp/2012/08/20/conservative-activist-phyllis-schlafly-defends-akin/.

perceived as beneficial. On the other hand, it could be argued that so long as the interests of white women and persons of color are meaningfully considered and their voices are heard in the process, substantive benefits can be expected. At least one set of researchers, however, do not expect that the record number of women will result in more meaningful representation of issues that are of disproportionate interest to women. Their research reveals that until a deliberative body reaches at least 60 percent women, they tend to speak less frequently than do their male counterparts, and they avoid raising issues about the most vulnerable Americans.[96]

Patricia Scott Schroeder relates a story about her first term in Congress in 1973:

I recall thinking "Wow! Women are on the move. This is going to be wonderful, we are going to have women everywhere; I am going to have colleagues coming soon." . . . And with that freshman exuberance, I asked the
Library of Congress research staff how long they thought it would be before
half the House of Representatives would be female. And their answer was,
"At this rate of change, four hundred years." I was totally outraged! I was
ready to call out airstrikes on the Library of Congress, but I am now beginning to think they were right.[97]

Representative Schroeder wrote those words more than a decade ago,
and although the number of women in the Congress has increased, the
pace has not picked up enough to undermine the quip of the research
staff member. And we still have not yet elected our first female president.
Why does this matter? Because the substantive representation argument
is undermined by the reality that men's disproportionate access to power
has resulted in persistent gender inequality throughout American history.
While electoral progress is a symbolic victory for those who wish to see
gender equality, the most important results will not be realized until gender disparities are reduced or eliminated.

Conclusion

All of this calls into question Americans' commitment to women's rights
broadly. If we limit our discussion to narrow issues such as closing the pay
gap, reducing health disparities, or being attentive to the achievement gap
in education, we miss an opportunity to critique patriarchy as a powerful
systemic force that undergirds these public policy issues. The Nineteenth
Amendment became law in 1920, solidifying the status of women as full
participants in the formal democratic process. But the bulk of the work of
dismantling the systemic roots of gender inequality has taken place in the
past century, with much more work to be done.

Three years after the adoption of the Nineteenth Amendment, wom-
en's rights activist Alice Paul wrote another amendment espousing equality between men and women. The Equal Rights Amendment (ERA) states
that "equality of rights under the law shall not be denied or abridged by
the United States or by any state on account of sex," and it gives Congress
the ability to enforce the amendment through legislation.[98] A bill was

introduced in every Congress until 1972, when it was finally passed and sent to the states for ratification. To date, thirty-six states have ratified it, which is three short of the number needed for it to become an amendment.[99]

As complicated as our treatment of these issues has been to this point, the thorniest part is still ahead. Acknowledging the history and persistence of inequality is challenging enough, but finding consensus about how to rectify the situation to reduce (and eventually eliminate) disparities in these areas is far more controversial. The most comprehensive attempt to do so is referred to collectively as affirmative action, which is where we turn our attention next.

Discussion Questions

1. In your own words, define *sexism* and *misogyny*. Which term does the excerpt from Mitt Romney's response to the question in the presidential debate exemplify? Why? What about Donald Trump's boast about kissing women without their permission?

2. How is the issue of gender different from the other sources of inequality discussed in previous chapters? In what ways is it similar?

3. Discuss the concept of feminism. What are the three waves of feminism? How do they differ from one another? How does this complicate issues of public policymaking, particularly when individuals who were socialized during each of the last two waves must work together to arrive at policy solutions?

4. Consider the socialization of gender roles, particularly during the formative years, and explain what role this has in perpetuating gender inequality. Can you identify an experience from your childhood that is relevant to this discussion?

5. Recall the concepts of delegate and trustee models of representation from Chapter 1. Do the political representatives mentioned in this chapter appear to embrace one method or the other? Does this seem ideal for a democratic society? Use specific examples in your response.

6. Evidence in this chapter, as well as throughout the book, suggests that gender inequality is all the more pronounced as it intersects with economics and race/ethnicity. How would you explain this concept to someone who has not read this book? Imagine that you raise the issue at a holiday gathering. How would your parents respond? Your grandparents? Would their gender matter? Their race? Their economic situation?

9

. . . .

Affirmative Action

IN THE PRECEDING CHAPTERS, WE EXPLORED THE DEPTH, PERSISTENCE, and complexity of racial and economic inequality in the United States, as well as ways that government officials within the context of a representative democracy are able and willing to address it. The cycle of advantage and disadvantage that appears in Figure 2.3 (page 69) is at once simple and complex. It is simple in the sense that it involves three major elements: housing, education (both K–12 and postsecondary), and employment. It is complex because of the interrelationship among these elements, as well as additional considerations that affect those relationships (such as the criminal justice system and health disparities). Along the way, we have wrestled with some difficult normative questions. This chapter is no different in that respect. The most difficult questions reside here because rather than merely describing inequality, we are now forced to think about ways to reduce inequality and eliminate injustice. As noted in the Introduction, there is an assumption that inequality in America needs to be addressed. Otherwise, this chapter would be irrelevant. Those who believe that inequality is not problematic or that any existing inequality is the result of individuals making poor choices (as opposed to being systemic) need not wrestle with the issues that we consider here.

In this chapter, we explore steps that have been taken to address inequality in the twenty-first century, tracing the successes and failures over the past fifty years. While there has been a spattering of ad hoc attempts at progress, the most persistent and systematic programs fall under the umbrella term *affirmative action*.[1] The term has been heavily stigmatized, however, largely because it is misrepresented as a quota system that offers awards (jobs, admission to college and professional schools, etc.) to racial minorities at the expense of whites. Although quota programs have existed in the past, they are illegal in most respects today. Still, there are legitimate concerns over how affirmative action affects both whites and members of racial minority groups, so it is important to explore a brief history of these programs, their current practice, and the extent to which programs operating with this philosophical undercurrent are the answer to systemic inequality in the United States.

Although affirmative action programs have been codified in legislation, the most important movement on this issue has come from the courts. The US Supreme Court has issued a number of decisions that give guidance (and constraint) to institutions that wish to take race into consideration for the purposes of increasing diversity or acknowledging that historical injustices place additional burdens on persons of color. Consequently we will give disproportionate attention to the judicial branch of the US government in this chapter and focus on the potential for it to serve as a counter-majoritarian force in a representative democracy. Recall James Madison's concerns about majority tyranny and the fact that nonelected judges who serve life terms are uniquely positioned to represent those to whom the majority of citizens might deny rights. As we will see, members of racial minority groups have needed protection at times; at other times, it is whites who have claimed to be disadvantaged and have sought protection from infringement of their rights.

History of Affirmative Action in America

The legal rights of persons of color—specifically those of African descent—to avoid discrimination emanate from the Fourteenth Amendment to the US Constitution. Passed as one of the three Civil War amendments, it includes a constitutional provision that guarantees the rights of all persons to be upheld and protected by the state governments, as well as the federal government. This amendment is at the center of many legal and theoretical conflicts relating to civil rights and civil liberties in the United States. Whereas the first ten amendments to the Constitution (the Bill of Rights) were believed to apply only to the federal government for much of our nation's history, a gradual incorporation of those constitutional provisions by the courts to apply to the states through the Fourteenth Amendment has resulted in more widespread protections for citizens. With respect to racial nondiscrimination, a series of Supreme Court cases has helped to clarify these protections, including the *Brown v. Board of Education* case that halted legally mandated racial segregation of public schools. Recall

FIGURE 9.1. A Concise History of Black-White Relations in the USA

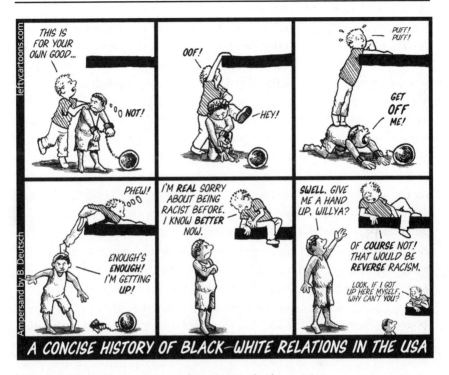

Source: Barry Deutsch, www.patreon.com/barry. Reprinted with permission.

from Chapter 4, however, that the Court's decision in *Brown* pivoted on the psychological harm that was done to students of color as a result of being segregated from whites. It left open the question of what rights whites had with respect to actions by government and private institutions to increase diversity and/or account for historical injustice when making decisions that involved the selection of individuals for various positions.

A series of executive and legislative measures have also been enacted, beginning with New Deal–era requirements for avoidance of racial discrimination by employers and in public works programs[2] in the early part of the twentieth century. The most meaningful and sweeping antidiscrimination legislation has been the Civil Rights Act of 1964. Title VI of that law prohibits discrimination on the basis of race, color, or national origin by any entity that receives federal financial assistance; Title VII has clear language indicating that employment discrimination on the basis of sex is similarly prohibited.[3]

It is important to keep in mind the substantive difference between having a policy of nondiscrimination, which can only be enforced through legal proceedings in which someone complains of and proves that discrimination occurred, and policies of preferential treatment, which are designed to proactively address systemic inequality. The latter category of policies falls under the umbrella of affirmative action. In the 1960s, during the height of the civil rights movement, President Lyndon Johnson instigated an affirmative action policy through an executive order to force federal agencies to be attentive to their practices in hiring and awarding contracts with an eye toward avoiding discrimination.[4] Similar policies were adopted at the state level, and institutions of higher education began to use a variety of mechanisms to diversify the student body and to recognize that color-blind merit admission policies were by their nature disadvantageous to students who faced barriers to achieving those ostensibly objective markers (e.g., grade point average, board exam scores, ability to write a strong essay) that other applicants did not face (see Chapter 4).[5]

The friction generated by affirmative action policies stems from the reality that positions, whether in colleges or for employment, often reflect a zero-sum game—there are a set number of openings, with more applicants than opportunities. Traditional notions of meritocracy that are key aspects of American cultural identity suggest that individuals should compete based on their abilities and hard work and that factors that lie beyond the individual's control should never be taken into consideration.[6] The assumption of meritocracy, however, requires a relatively level playing field (or equal starting line, depending on the metaphor applied), which does not reflect the reality of American racial history. As the cartoon in Figure 9.1 suggests, whites were willing to deny access and opportunity to African Americans for centuries, and though now all Americans generally agree that racial discrimination (let alone slavery) is inappropriate, we are not nearly as willing to consider the consequences of persistent disadvantage that have followed from those centuries of exclusion.

It is not difficult to understand why there is resistance. The limitation of the cartoon, of course, is that the same two characters appear in each of the six panes. Although the cartoonist needed to use this technique to be concise and convey a powerful message, he is unable to capture the important temporal dynamic that arises from current generations of whites claiming that they "never owned a slave." In the cartoon, the white racist in the first four panes is the same as the person who recognizes in the last two that racial prejudice and discrimination are wrong. Because the character equates racism (which is systemic) and prejudice (which is interpersonal), however, he refuses to take actions that would help to rectify past wrongs. He also feels that doing so would be equally improper because it relies on considerations of race. The notion that any consideration of race is racist has helped to perpetuate systems of disadvantage. Whites, who still overwhelmingly control the levers of power in the United States, have been led to believe that the real racists are those who advocate a sophisticated consideration of systemic racism in public policymaking and public discourse.

On the other hand, affirmative action programs should not be viewed as the solution to America's racist past. Various forms of affirmative action policies have been in place for half a century, and as we have discovered, the United States is far from having a society where all races and ethnicities have the same opportunities for success. However, America has made great progress in that time on a number of fronts, and while it would be improper to assume that affirmative action policies were solely responsible for that, dismissing them out of hand is also unwise. Instead, so as to appreciate the nuance and complexities of this controversial issue, let us consider three Supreme Court cases that have given shape to affirmative action policy in the United States.

From Davis to Ann Arbor to Austin

The first meaningful test of affirmative action policy in the United States came when Allan Bakke, who is white, complained about being denied admission to the University of California, Davis medical school in 1973 and again in 1974. The program, he claimed, was unconstitutional because it denied him the opportunity to compete for all of the available seats in the incoming class. Each year, the school admitted one hundred applicants but had two separate admission programs. One program, which had eighty-four seats, was open to applicants of any race, ethnicity, or educational background. The other program was reserved for applicants who identified themselves as "economically and/or educationally disadvantaged" or members of a racial minority group. The benefit of being considered under the set-aside program was that one would not be compared to applicants in the other program and that the grade point average cutoff that applied to applicants in the other program was not in effect. Bakke's

Box 9.1. *Representing:* Justice Clarence Thomas

Only the second African American to be appointed to the US Supreme Court, Clarence Thomas has opposed racial preferences and affirmative action throughout his career. While critics argue that he benefited from affirmative action policies, Thomas has consistently claimed that he was harmed by the policy because he felt that it placed a stigma on him when he graduated from Yale University.

Thomas was born in rural Georgia in 1948 and grew up in the sort of abject poverty described in Chapter 3. There was no sewage system or paved roads. Thomas's mother worked as a housekeeper and accepted church charity to make ends meet. He learned to value education from his grandfather, with whom he lived during his formative years. Thomas was not insulated from racism; he dropped out of seminary in Missouri and even supported the work of the Black Panthers while an undergraduate at Holy Cross. President Reagan appointed Thomas to a position in the Department of Education and later at the Equal Employment Opportunity Commission. After serving on the US Court of Appeals for a year, he was appointed by President George H. W. Bush to replace Justice Thurgood Marshall, who successfully argued the *Brown v. Board of Education* school desegregation case before the Supreme Court as a lawyer and who was the first African American to serve on the Court.

While Thomas clearly benefited from racial preferences on a number of occasions throughout his career, the humiliation he felt when he applied for

scores were higher than several of the students who were admitted under the second program, which meant that if he would have been permitted to compete for those seats, he would have been admitted. Although whites who were economically or educationally disadvantaged were eligible for consideration (Bakke was neither), none had been admitted in the four years that the program was in place. On this basis, Bakke argued that he was being denied equal protection under the Fourteenth Amendment by the state of California because of his race.

In *Regents of the University of California v. Bakke*,[7] the Supreme Court agreed with Bakke and ruled that such quota programs were unfair to whites (and unconstitutional), but the Court was clear that other types of programs that took race or other systemic disadvantage (including gender) into consideration were permissible. Specifically, the Court pointed jobs after graduating from Yale Law School stuck with him. That experience has affected his attitudes about affirmative action generally, as well as his ruling on racial preferences cases, such as *Grutter v. Bollinger* and *Gratz v. Bollinger*. Besides the stigmatization argument, Thomas believes that affirmative action programs in education are not effective because they do not guarantee assistance for minority students who may not be prepared to compete. Further, he agrees with those who argue that racial integration may not necessarily be beneficial to students of color. In fact, he has noted that forced integration suggests an underlying racism that "anything that is predominantly black must be inferior."

Opponents of racial preferences celebrate Thomas as a champion with credibility on the subject, while proponents dismiss him as a hypocrite and an opportunist. What is clear, however, is that Thomas's ideas about affirmative action have been shaped by his life experiences, and his justifications do not fall neatly in line with most of the people who agree with him on the issue. In many ways, Thomas embodies the complexity of an issue that has been oversimplified in American public discourse.[a]

a. "Clarence Thomas," The Oyez Project, http://www.oyez.org/justices/clarence_thomas; Ariane de Vogue, "'Silent' Justice Outspoken on Affirmative Action," *ABC News*, September 30, 2007, http://abcnews.go.com/TheLaw/story?id=3667079; Maureen Dowd, "Could Thomas Be Right?" *New York Times*, June 25, 2003, http://www.nytimes.com/2003/06/25/opinion/could-thomas-be-right.html?src=pm.

to the plan that Harvard University used in admission, which considered racial minority status as a plus factor as part of a formula that contains a number of criteria for consideration. Justice Lewis Powell, who wrote the opinion for the Court, noted that race, as well as other characteristics, was part of the diversity that is valued in higher education. This established race as a factor that many institutions of higher education still use in admissions decisions.[8] It was precisely this type of plan that was challenged twenty-five years later when the Court heard the next case dealing with affirmative action in higher education.

In 2003 the Court considered two cases simultaneously, both relating to the University of Michigan. In *Gratz v. Bollinger*,[9] the Court struck down the policy that the university used for undergraduate admissions, but in *Grutter v. Bollinger*,[10] it upheld the policy being used by the law school. In essence, the Court felt that awarding twenty points to under-represented racial and ethnic groups in the undergraduate program was disproportionate[11] and that institutions should take a more holistic approach to admissions decisions with respect to diversity. In the law school case, however, the Court found that the policy invoked a narrowly tailored approach to consider race in admissions decisions in a way that was consistent with its desire to have a diverse incoming class in order to enrich the educational experience. Because the law school did not define diversity solely in terms of race or ethnicity and could award weight to an applicant's rating based on other factors that would enhance diversity, the Court, in a 5–4 decision, upheld the program. Justice Sandra Day O'Connor, who wrote the opinion, indicated that she hoped and expected that such policies would not be necessary in another twenty-five years (see Box 8.2). It is difficult to look into the future to determine the degree to which such policies will be necessary. Although rates of college graduation for African Americans are slowly increasing, the gaps between white student graduation rates and those of African Americans and Latinos still exist.[12] More relevant to this issue, however, is the degree to which students of color would be granted admission to colleges if affirmative action plans were not in place.

It did not take twenty-five years for the Court to come back to the issue. On October 10, 2012, the Supreme Court first heard oral arguments in *Fisher v. University of Texas at Austin*.[13] Abigail Fisher, a white woman who was rejected by the University of Texas at Austin, complained that she had been denied equal treatment under the law as a result of the university's affirmative action policy. The Obama administration, as well as fourteen states, urged the Court to uphold racial preferences in college admissions.[14] At central issue in *Fisher* was whether colleges and universities had taken the Court's advice from *Grutter*, narrowing their use of racial preferences, or whether, as one scholar speculated, they have taken the *Grutter* decision "as a signal that court supervision of preferences would be lax."[15] After vacating (setting aside) the lower court's decision and ordering it to reconsider the case, the Supreme Court heard *Fisher* again in 2015, and a final decision was handed down in early 2016. The 4–3 decision[16] was authored by Justice Anthony Kennedy, who had not typically been viewed as a supporter of affirmative action programs. But Justice Kennedy invoked the *Sweatt* (and, by implication, *Brown*) case, noting that "a university is in large part defined by those intangible 'qualities which are incapable of objective measurement but which make for greatness.'" He argued that there must be considerable, though not exclusive, deference given to institutions of higher learning to define those intangible characteristics, which include the diversity of the student body. As a result of this decision, colleges and universities are free to continue to invoke carefully crafted affirmative action programs to achieve a diverse student body. We, then, are left with two important and interrelated considerations.

First, affirmative action in college (or graduate/professional school) admissions is not a guarantee of a degree or a job. Once a student is admitted, he or she needs to do the same work as any other student to be successful. Given the tremendous disparities in K–12 education, many students of color who are admitted under affirmative action programs are not as well prepared for college as their white counterparts. In this way, such programs are not an effective interruption of the cycle of disadvantage, as they are essentially setting up those students for failure. Second, white students who attend underfunded schools are at a disadvantage if colleges do not consider economic or educational disadvantage in their admission process.[17] It has been argued that middle-class students of color who attend strong high schools also gain entrance under affirmative action programs, and while that is not the intent of such programs (because those students can compete in a color-blind system), we must be careful not to extrapolate these few cases too broadly. As we have seen, race and poverty are still closely related in the United States, and even minority students from financially secure families face subconscious prejudice in schools in the form of tracking.[18] One study estimated that admission of racial minority students to the most selective colleges would be reduced by more than half without racially conscious affirmative action programs.[19]

Affirmative Action Beyond the Classroom

Affirmative action receives the most attention as it pertains to college and graduate/professional school admission, but it is important to consider its effect on employment and housing separately. Neither of these areas presupposes that individuals have a college education, so even if affirmative action programs are effective in higher education, they do not always lead to equality in housing opportunities or employment (the other two primary elements of the cycle of disadvantage). Further, even if a person who

Box 9.2. *Representing:* Justice Sandra Day O'Connor

Three years before she retired from the US Supreme Court, Sandra Day O'Connor wrote one of the most relevant opinions regarding affirmative action in a generation. A Republican state legislator from Arizona, O'Connor was the first woman in the United States to be minority leader of a state senate and the first woman to serve on the Court.

O'Connor was born to rancher parents in southeastern Arizona during the Great Depression. The ranch had no electricity or running water until she was seven years old. O'Connor was sent to boarding school so that she had a chance for a quality education. She attended Stanford for her undergraduate degree and law school. She was appointed to the Arizona Court of Appeals for two years prior to taking her seat on the Supreme Court in 1981.

In *Grutter v. Bollinger*, O'Connor wrote for a 5–4 majority that the University of Michigan's law school admissions program, which takes racial minority status into account when making decisions, was constitutional and advanced the cause of providing for a better education through a diverse student body. She added that in twenty-five years, hopefully, racial preferences in higher education would be unnecessary. Seven years after that ruling, O'Connor wrote an essay clarifying that her "twenty-five years" remark was not meant to be a deadline, as many opponents of affirmative action inferred (and promised to hold the Court to that mark). What she meant was that social scientists should reexamine the educational benefits of diverse student bodies at that time.

faced systemic disadvantage early in life obtains a college degree, subconscious (if not overt) racial prejudice is still a relevant factor in housing, as well as in hiring (see Chapters 3 and 6, respectively).

Affirmative action policies in employment work a bit differently than they do in higher education. Employers do not necessarily have a battery of comparable items to judge applicants by, as college admissions officials do, nor do employers usually have a set number of openings with all applicants submitting by a deadline. Consequently the sort of rankings and comparisons that are part of college admissions are not appropriate or possible for employers. Instead, employers monitor diversity in terms of hiring and promotion and, where necessary, develop policies to address deficiencies.[20] Most of the time such policies are voluntary, but occasionally a court orders a business to use affirmative action as a result of

While the Court has the opportunity to be counter-majoritarian (and thus protect minority rights), research has demonstrated that it rarely makes decisions that run contrary to public opinion on salient issues. George Washington University law professor Jeffrey Rosen notes that when the Court decided the *Bakke* case in 1978, public opinion was against affirmative action, so it was not surprising that the decision constrained efforts to increase racial minority enrollments in higher education. By 2003, however, when the University of Michigan cases were decided, the public was much more divided on the issue, which is consistent with the 5–4 decision in *Grutter*, as well as the decision in the companion case, *Gratz*, that limited affirmative action programs. We may never know the degree to which O'Connor or the other justices took public opinion into consideration as they reviewed the cases (and they may not know themselves), but such nuance in decisions reminds us that judges and justices, though they are not directly accountable to the people, are important aspects of representation in the United States.[a]

a. Thomas R. Marshall, *Public Opinion and the Supreme Court* (Boston: Unwin Hyman, 1989); Jeffrey Rosen, "Affirmative Action and Public Opinion," New York Times, May 23, 2011, http://www.nytimes.com/roomfordebate/2011/05/22/is-anti-white-bias-a-problem/affirmative-action-and-public-opinion; "Sandra Day O'Connor," Oyez Project, http://www.oyez.org/justices/sandra_day_oconnor; Peter Schmidt, "Sandra Day O'Connor Revisits and Revives Affirmative-Action Controversy," *Chronicle of Higher Education*, January 14, 2010, http://chronicle.com/article/Sandra-Day-OConnor-Revisit/63523/.

a lawsuit.[21] Hiring quotas based on race are illegal, yet many Americans (particularly whites) are suspicious about their use and have a personal story about someone in their family who was denied employment (or perceived that he or she was denied employment) for being white.

This disconnect is partially psychological in the sense that whites often have a nagging suspicion that they are being discriminated against in favor of persons of color, but it is also warranted in the sense that many companies have aggressive targets or goals in terms of diversity that tread dangerously close to the quota line (or at least feel that way to white applicants). Title VII of the Civil Rights Act of 1964[22] was designed to prohibit discrimination against persons of color in the workforce. The bill, as well as subsequent Court decisions (such as *Griggs v. Duke Power Company* 1971),[23] is clear that it is not enough for employers not to *intend* to discriminate (which would be a difficult measure to prove); they must proactively avoid discrimination. Proactively avoiding discrimination, however, is not the same as affirmative action. That standard merely represents a call for equal opportunity that is intentionally protected. Affirmative action programs, such as that which was at issue in the Court's 2009 *Ricci v. DeStefano*[24] decision, go farther by instituting procedures that actively seek racial and ethnic (or gender) diversity.[25]

With respect to housing, there are few formal affirmative action policies.[26] Most of the effort in housing has been to ensure that persons of color are not discriminated against, but with respect to sales and rentals, there is no clear governmental mandate or widespread practice of ensuring diversity in neighborhoods. As noted in Chapter 3, there were efforts to increase homeownership among African Americans and Latinos through the mortgage agencies Fannie Mae and Freddie Mac (these nicknames refer to the Federal National Mortgage Association and the Federal Home Loan Mortgage Corporation, respectively), but those agencies were placed into conservatorship due to the housing crisis in 2008, meaning that the federal government took control of them. As a result, there is uncertainty as to the effect on minority borrowers if they must rely on private banks to lend without the backing of the US government.[27]

Affirmative Action Ballot Initiatives and Referendums

Measuring public opinion about affirmative action can be difficult, as is capturing public sentiment on any issue relating to race. Americans are sensitive to accusations of being racially prejudiced, and white Americans in particular tend to be concerned with being accused of being racist when they are not conscious of harboring any racial animosity. As late as 2013, a slim majority of Americans favored affirmative action programs when asked directly and in the abstract, but when asked whether it is worth paying a price of disadvantaging whites to help minorities, a majority respond that it is not. Further, when asked specifically about "programs that give preferences in hiring, promotions and college admission," only preferences for the handicapped had a majority of support.[28] After *Fisher* was decided in 2016, poll results revealed that 65 percent of Americans disagreed with the decision. Seventy-six percent of whites believed that college applicants should be admitted solely on the basis of merit (compared to 50 percent of African Americans and 61 percent of Hispanics), and 67 percent of whites indicated that race should not be taken into consideration at all (with 29 percent indicating it could be a minor factor).[29] Other research has found that support for women receiving preferential treatment for affirmative action is greater than that for racial and ethnic minorities[30] and that white women have benefited most from affirmative action programs.[31] As reflected in the post-*Fisher* data, there is sometimes an interest effect such that women[32] and racial minorities[33] are more likely than men and whites, respectively, to prefer affirmative action programs. Further, whites who oppose affirmative action with respect to racial minorities often support it when it is alternately framed as a benefit to women. As might be expected, attitudes toward both types of affirmative action are related to prejudices toward women and racial minorities.[34]

When voters have had the opportunity to weigh in on affirmative action through ballot initiative or referendum, they have mostly supported bans on race-conscious policies in hiring and school admission. The first state to adopt such a ban was California, which won approval of Proposition 209 in 1996. Prop 209, as it is known, is an amendment to Article I of the California constitution and reads as follows: "The state shall not discriminate against, or grant preferential treatment to, any individual or group on the basis of race, sex, color, ethnicity, or national origin in the operation of public employment, public education, or public contracting."[35] On its face, of course, the language is entirely race neutral and protects persons of all races and ethnicities from discrimination. The measure, though, was explicitly a response to California's affirmative action policies, and it ignores historical, systemic disadvantage for women and persons of color, assuming that each Californian starts at roughly the same point and therefore can be assured fair, unbiased competition for open positions.

As expected, Prop 209 started a trend. In 1997, Washington State passed Initiative 200; in 2006, the Michigan Civil Rights Initiative passed; in 2008, Nebraska voters passed Initiative 424; and in 2010, the Arizona Civil Rights Initiative was approved by voters. All of these measures were pushed and supported by California businessman Ward Connerly, who is multiracial. While three of his anti–affirmative action initiatives failed to be approved for ballots in 2008, the only one to fail that year was in Colorado (in an extremely close vote).[36]

To more clearly understand the dynamic of increased support for affirmative action programs that benefit women versus those that benefit persons of color, it is useful to consider some of the difference between legal challenges to affirmative action policies and ballot-based efforts to eliminate the practice. The plebiscite language almost always includes gender, as well as race, color, ethnicity, and national origin, but legal challenges are almost always narrowly targeted at advantages to persons of color (even though, as noted above, white women have benefited disproportionately from these programs). For example, the language for the Michigan measure in 2006 banned "affirmative action programs that give preferential treatment to groups or individuals based on their race, gender, color, ethnicity or national origin for public employment, education or contradicting purposes."[37] In the landmark University of Michigan cases that went before the US Supreme Court, though, whites brought the suits, alleging that the policies were unfairly beneficial to persons of color.[38] In cases that involve alleged discrimination, courts have different standards in determining whether a law relating to sex is constitutional as compared with a law relating to race. Sex-related issues are subjected to intermediate scrutiny, while race-related issues must pass strict scrutiny. This means that government policies that result in preferences or discrimination based on race are very difficult to sustain because the government must demonstrate that it has a compelling interest in having a law that on its face (i.e., without taking historical factors into consideration) discriminates and that the policy in place is narrowly tailored to achieve that interest. With respect to sex, however, government must only show that the law "further[s] an important government interest by means that are substantially related to that interest."[39] Accordingly, affirmative action policies that benefit women specifically are more likely to withstand legal scrutiny than those that specifically aim to address racial discrimination.[40]

Perhaps this is not surprising. Americans want to live in a race-neutral meritocracy and believe that we do. Many of us have friends (or at least friendly acquaintances) of different races and ethnicities. Most of us do not recognize racial resentment in ourselves, we celebrate Martin Luther King Day, and we do not use racial epithets, even when we are angry. Absent a purposeful recognition and consideration of the complexities described in this book, the language of these ballot proposals fits neatly with our core values and beliefs about what America *should* be.

The primary difference between proponents of bans on affirmative action policies and supporters of affirmative action is the degree to which they are willing to acknowledge the systemic effects of historical

Box 9.3. *Representing:* Ed Blum

A former stockbroker is responsible for shepherding many of the recent affirmative action cases through the legal system to reach the United States Supreme Court. Edward Blum (pronounced "bloom") has, since he founded it in 2005, led the Project on Fair Representation,[a] which seeks to "support litigation that challenges racial and ethnic classifications and preferences in state and federal courts."[b] Blum has been successful in getting the Court to hear a number of high-profile cases relating to issues from voting rights (*Shelby County v. Holder*) to race-based gerrymandering (*Bush v. Vera*) to, perhaps most famously, affirmative action (*Fisher v. Texas*).[c]

Mr. Blum does not have a law degree, but his experience running for office and his deep desire to see America abandon racial classifications, combined with his appreciation that such issues often are resolved through the judicial branch, have compelled him to work tirelessly and in many cases, effectively, to realize his goals. Although the *Fisher* case was not decided in his favor, he was victorious in overturning the racially drawn congressional districts in Texas in *Bush v. Vera*, and the decision in *Shelby* invalidated a portion of the Civil Rights Act of 1964 that he perceived to be reinforcing racial distinctions.

---

a. Morgan Smith, "One Man Standing Against Race-Based Laws," *New York Times*, February 23, 2012, http://www.nytimes.com/2012/02/24/us/edward-blum-and-the-project-on-fair-representation-head-to-the-supreme-court-to-fight-race-based-laws.html.

b. https://www.projectonfairrepresentation.org.

c. Stephanie Mencimer, "Meet the Brains Behind the Effort to Get the Supreme Court to Rethink Civil Rights," *Mother Jones*, March/April 2016, http://www.motherjones.com/politics/2016/04/edward-blum-supreme-court-affirmative-action-civil-rights; "Meet the Supreme Court Matchmaker: Edward Blum," *NBC News*, June 11, 2013, http://usnews.nbcnews.com/_news/2013/06/11/18750240-meet-the-supreme-court-matchmaker-edward-blum; and Morgan Smith, "One Man Standing Against Race-Based Laws," *New York Times*, February 23, 2012, http://www.nytimes.com/2012/02/24/us/edward-blum-and-the-project-on-fair-representation-head-to-the-supreme-court-to-fight-race-based-laws.html

---

discrimination and prejudice. Neither Ward Connerly, nor Ed Blum (see Box 9.3), nor Jesse Jackson[41] hates America or is trying to leverage personal gain from the policies they champion. These men may disagree about the degree to which discrimination persists, the potential stigmatizing effect on minorities as a result of the programs, the value of racial diversity in the workplace and schools, and the degree to which whites are harmed by racially conscious policies, but it would be difficult to argue that they do not all have the best interest of the country at heart.

Reasonable people can (and do) disagree about the ability of affirmative action programs to appropriately rectify systemic disadvantages or lead to more racial equality. To be considered to be reasonable, however, each of us must seriously and honestly reflect on the various ways that we may be advantaged or disadvantaged by a system that is rooted in fundamental inequality. Most Americans would agree that a color-blind—or at least color-neutral—society would be preferable, but we are unable to wish away the realities of the lingering racism that continues to characterize American society.

Conclusion

Legal rights aside, most Americans (not just whites) do not really understand how affirmative action programs are designed, what they are intended to do, or whether they are effective. An honest, holistic appraisal reveals that the evidence of the effectiveness of such programs is inconclusive. Anecdotally, we can point to individuals who were provided opportunities (and were able to capitalize on them). It is more difficult to measure the long-term psychological effects on whites, many of whom feel as if they are at a disadvantage for college admission and employment, and minorities, some of whom might interpret acceptance under these programs as a tacit indicator of their unworthiness[42] (see Box 9.1, for example). Under these circumstances, we need to decide whether affirmative action programs do more harm than good or, put another way, whether America would be a more just and equitable nation if we did not have them.

Ultimately, affirmative action programs serve more as a bandage than a cure, with most proponents believing that removing such programs would exacerbate the inequality that still exists.[43] Others believe that affirmative action programs will lead to a color-blind, gender-neutral society.[44] Opponents, however, believe that the bandage is keeping the wound from healing properly. From any perspective, it is clear that a permanent solution to America's persistent racial and economic inequality must be found elsewhere.

Discussion Questions

1. Is your opinion about affirmative action the same now as before you read this chapter? What about before you began reading this book? If you changed your mind, what caused the shift?

2. Have you heard stories about white Americans being passed over for a job or promotion because of affirmative action programs? Can you recall the context in which the story was told? How do such anecdotes work to reinforce or challenge existing ideas about affirmative action in the United States?

3. Does your college or university have an affirmative action program? Do you know how it works? How diverse is your campus with respect to race and ethnicity? What about socioeconomic status? How does the diversity on your campus (or lack thereof) affect the learning environment? Identify specific instances, if you can, where the issue of diversity on campus has been discussed.

4. What do you think about the suggestion of switching from race-based affirmative action to programs based on socioeconomic status? If you favor such a shift, what should be the criteria? Income? If so, how many years' worth of tax returns should be considered? Wealth? If so, how would that be measured? What about the idea of using zip code as a surrogate for socioeconomic status? Do your preferences change depending on the type of program (e.g., college admission, employment)? What potential benefits and drawbacks might be associated with each approach?

5. If you support affirmative action, how do you answer the critics who charge that it is unfair to both whites and persons of color? If you oppose affirmative action, how do you propose to address issues of inequality in America?

Conclusion:
The Space Between
Power and Powerlessness

In August 2016, San Francisco 49rs quarterback Colin Kaepernick refused to stand for the national anthem during a preseason National Football League game. He did not hold a sign, gesture, or even turn his back. Rather, he lowered himself to one knee and waited silently until the song had ended. After the game, he told a reporter:

> I am not going to stand up to show pride in a flag for a country that op-presses black people and people of color. To me, this is bigger than football and it would be selfish on my part to look the other way. There are bodies in the street and people getting paid leave and getting away with murder.[1]

Reaction to his protest was predictably mixed. Over the next few weeks, dozens of NFL players followed suit, some simply kneeling, others raising fists in the air to replicate the black power salute that was com-mon in the height of the civil rights movement.[2] Other athletes also chose to kneel during the anthem, bringing increased attention to Kaepernick's actions.[3] Many fans (and others) were furious.[4] As with the controversy over flag burning, some could not understand how refusing to acknowl-edge what is widely perceived to be a unifying national symbol helped advance a cause. Even some noted progressives criticized the move: US Supreme Court Justice Ruth Bader Ginsburg said that while she did not believe his actions were criminal, she found them to be "dumb and dis-respectful."[5] Kaepernick expressed his disappointment, and Ginsburg walked back the remark a few days later, noting that she was "inappro-priately dismissive and harsh" in her response,[6] but her initial reaction spoke volumes about how viscerally affected Americans are by such sym-bols of patriotism. From a very early age, Americans—like citizens of all nations—are taught to love their country and have deep faith in its goodness. From the childhood expectation onward that they will pledge allegiance to the flag, learn patriotic songs, and celebrate historically significant holidays, to their being taught primarily (or solely) positive information about the nation's history, it is no wonder that college stu-dents are often disturbed and frustrated to learn the complex truth of Americans' struggle for equality.

We may feel powerless to right the great wrongs that we observe around us, particularly with respect to recognizing power differences. Af-ter all, these problems are centuries old, and millions of people just like us have worked very hard for many years—some dedicating their entire lives to the cause—to dismantle systems of inequality. It is also easy to feel frus-trated, as a small but vocal group of political figures (officials and pundits) seek to confuse the issues with platitudes about meritocracy, anecdotes used to disprove systematically collected data, and emotional appeals (of-ten rooted in core values such as patriotism) that make us feel like traitors if we are critical of the system. These folks ignore systems altogether so that each success and failure is solely the responsibility of the individual. If someone is wealthy, it was his or her hard work, natural ability, and persistence that led to the success; if someone is poor, he or she must have made bad choices, failed to take advantage of opportunities (however lim-ited), or simply chose to be poor out of laziness.

It is difficult to argue against these positions because explaining sys-tems is complicated and takes time. There is no way to explain the concept of hegemony in a sound bite. As cognitive scientists explain, appeals to reason are easily supplanted with contrasting appeals to emotion.[7] Such issues as abortion, LGBTQ marriage, and sex education in schools are considered values issues in the United States, but racial inequality and poverty are generally not. So, if we care about these issues, how do we make a difference?

The theoretical foundations of representation date back before the nation's founding, with James Madison, drawing from seventeenth-century philosophers, famously warning about the "violence of faction" in

Federalist 10. Madison understood that a representative democratic system would be endangered by groups that had power (whether they constituted the numerical majority or not) to run over the wishes of those who did not. Pluralist models of democracy predict that ordinary individuals will have power over elites through the pressure exerted by organized interests. But the powerful also organize. Political scientist Dara Strolovitch concludes:

> interest group politics reinforce as much as they rectify the bias against marginalized groups. . . . the relative power of organizations that speak for marginalized groups remains far less than that of the multitude of other organizations that represent more advantaged constituencies.[8]

It is daunting indeed to consider what can be done when the mechanisms of democracy seem stacked against the realization of its ultimate promise.

One important improvement would be the use of sharper conceptual and rhetorical tools to adequately discuss these complex issues. For example, a recent study of attitudes about poverty in the United Kingdom found that most respondents thought about global poverty in terms of providing charity, which reinforces a power dynamic where wealthy nations are in a position to give, and poor nations are in a position to take (and to be grateful for the assistance). The study's authors argue that such a disempowering rhetorical and cognitive model is problematic and that one solution is for antipoverty actors and groups to address the roots of global poverty so that there is a creation story. An appreciation of what caused poverty, the authors argue, will be more effective in helping individuals to have a more sophisticated understanding of the issue, which will likely translate into more support for solutions.[9]

Conversations designed to improve inequality often stall when the language used in the discussion becomes muddled. For some, *racism* refers to the systemic advantages that whites have over persons of color (as the term is used in this book), while for others, it means a personal distaste or resentment for someone of a race other than one's own. For some, *equality* means that all citizens have similar opportunities to achieve financial success and political power, while for others, it means that the discrepancy of income and/or wealth between those who have the most and those who have the least should be drastically reduced.

Box C.1. *What Can I Do?:* Own Your Privilege

Privilege is a confusing term. Often it is used as an absolute: "Bill Gates is privileged." However, privilege is a relative construct. While it is difficult to identify ways in which Bill Gates does not have privilege, most of us have characteristics that, in our cultural context, confer privilege on us, as well as others that do not. If we embrace the absolute construction, we lose the ability to understand privilege as a meaningful concept—if there is always someone who is more privileged in one way or another, privilege does not mean anything at all.

Whites, on the whole, have privilege compared to persons of color, all other things being equal. Of course, all other things are rarely equal, so white women may have some advantages over women of color, but are relatively disadvantaged compared to white men. Heterosexuals are privileged compared to those who are LGBTQ, but a heterosexual Latina can hardly be considered privileged in any absolute sense. Accordingly, it is useful for us to be mindful of the ways in which we are privileged and the ways we may be disadvantaged. Owning our privilege is one way of coming to terms with the complicated realities of living in a pluralistic society with a history of discrimination based on a number of characteristics. That puts us in a much better position to evaluate policy options or select candidates who will represent our interests with respect to our views on diversity and equality.

As ordinary individuals, we are not in a position to control the way language is used in mainstream public discourse. We can, however, choose to be more precise in the ways we think about and subsequently talk about issues relating to inequality in all of its forms. If we are talking about individual-level prejudice, we should avoid using the term *racism*. If we are talking about systemic disadvantages for those who are not heterosexual (heterosexism), we should not call it homophobia. If we are talking about systemic disadvantages for women, we should call it sexism, but if we are talking about individuals who harbor resentment toward others on the basis of sex or gender, we should call it prejudice or bigotry. The idea is not to control what others say, but to ensure that what we say is reflective of our understanding of the complexities of these issues so that we model a more sophisticated approach to dealing with issues that are far more complex than colloquial, blunt language reflects.

Are you able-bodied? If so, you have privilege with respect to physical ability. Even if disabled persons are not overtly discriminated against due to conscious hostility, fear, or discomfort, the world is designed and mostly inhabited by able-bodied persons. This leads to a host of disadvantages that most able-bodied people do not even notice. Are you handsome or pretty (by some commonly accepted standards, however problematic they may be)? While there are some disadvantages to being perceived as conventionally attractive (particularly for women, as our sexist culture often reduces women to their appearance), being conventionally attractive often comes with some privilege. Are you right-handed? Of average height and weight? Do you have full vision and hearing? What other privileges can you identify? Take a day or even a couple of hours and, as you move about, try to be attentive to the ways that these characteristics give you an advantage over someone who does not possess them.

Far from being a count-your-blessings exercise, the point of reflecting on and owning privilege is to become aware of how advantages and disadvantages are perpetuated on a daily basis. It reminds us that if we limit our critique of inequality to the intent of persons or groups of persons who are racist, sexist, homophobic, and so on, we are overlooking most of the inequality and disadvantage that exists.

We need to remember too that progress, while worthy of celebration, is not the same as equality. Those who wish to preserve the status quo with respect to inequality often point to the fact that things were worse in previous times. Such a position is inarguable, of course, but satisfaction with our current state of racial and economic progress is not a necessary component to appreciating that some of our worst abuses are in the past. When Booker T. Washington and W. E. B. Du Bois were advocating for racial equality at the turn of the twentieth century, many wondered why they were so interested in pushing for it—after all, things were much worse for African Americans during times of slavery. During the civil rights movement of the 1950s, opponents of racial progress had difficulty understanding why blacks and others sympathetic to the cause were so upset—things were worse fifty years earlier. Today, those who agitate and advocate for racial and economic justice often hear similar criticisms—things were so much worse during Jim Crow. It is imperative that we consider what future generations will be saying about us. How will we be evaluated?

There was a time when the smartest people believed that the world was flat, that the sun revolved around the earth, and that people of African descent were not human (and could be owned as property). In those times, it would have been very difficult to convince people that they were wrong. Only a few generations ago, most Americans found it perfectly acceptable that children—particularly poor children—worked in harsh and sometimes dangerous conditions. Child labor laws are not controversial today, but they were when they were first proposed and passed. Factory owners argued that business would be hurt by such legislation (they would lose a valuable and inexpensive part of their labor force),[10] much as businesses argue today that a rise in the minimum wage or requirements to provide health insurance would force them to close their doors.[11] The point here is not to advocate for one policy position over another, but to point out that there is a certain amount of inertia at work in American political culture. Every social movement in history has faced resistance. Success came because of constant agitation by individuals and groups. Margaret Mead is credited with reminding us to "never doubt that a small group of thoughtful, committed citizens can change the world. Indeed, it is the only thing that ever has." There is no consensus on the answers to many of the normative questions we have considered in this book, but each reader should work toward becoming comfortable with his or her own positions and the degree to which they correspond with core values and beliefs, as well as being open to adjusting those beliefs when new evidence is presented. It can be an uncomfortable process, but it is ultimately rewarding and absolutely necessary if the next generation will move us closer to the goal of a truly equitable and just society.

Notes

Introduction

1. "Full Text: Donald Trump Announces Presidential Bid," *Washington Post*, June 16, 2015, https://www.washingtonpost.com/news/post-politics/wp/2015/06/16/full-text-donald-trump-announces-a-presidential-bid/.

2. Aaron Blake, "The First Trump-Clinton Presidential Debate Transcript, Annotated," *The Washington Post*, September 26, 2016, https://www.washingtonpost.com/news/the-fix/wp/2016/09/26/the-first-trump-clinton-presidential-debate-transcript-annotated/.

3. "Transcript of the Democratic Presidential Debate in Flint, Michigan," *New York Times*, March 6, 2016, https://www.nytimes.com/2016/03/07/us/politics/transcript-democratic-presidential-debate.html.

4. The speech can be viewed at http://youtu.be/pWe7wTVbLUU.

5. Tavis Smiley and Cornel West, *The Rich and the Rest of Us: A Poverty Manifesto* (New York: Smiley Books, 2012).

6. Ibid., 173–175.

7. For a thoughtful treatment of the notion of meritocracy, see Kenneth Arrow, Samuel Bowles, and Steven Durlauf, eds., *Meritocracy and Economic Inequality* (Princeton: Princeton University Press, 2000).

8. Meghan McCain, "Who You Calling a Blue Blood, Sarah?" The Daily Beast, November 30, 2010, http://www.thedailybeast.com/articles/2010/11/30/meghan-mccain-sarah-palins-blue-blood-comment.html.

9. Mitt Romney similarly invoked this formulation during his 2012 presidential campaign. He framed the Obama administration's desire to allow tax reductions for the wealthiest Americans to expire as "punishing success," which suggests that the wealthy have worked harder and out-competed others.

10. Joseph P. Williams, "Penthouse Populist: Why the Rural Poor Love Donald Trump," *U.S. News and World Report*, September 22, 2016, http://www.usnews.com/news/articles/2016-09-22/penthouse-populist-why-the-rural-poor-love-donald-trump.

11. See Ruby K. Payne, *A Framework for Understanding Poverty: A Cognitive Approach* (5th ed.). Highlands, TX: aha! Process, Inc. (2013). For a brief table summarizing Payne's theory, see http://kathyescobar.com/wp-content/uploads/2013/12/Hidden-Rules-Among-Classes.pdf.

12. Donald Trump earned 57 percent of the white vote in the 2016 election (compared to Hillary Clinton's 37 percent). He was particularly successful with white

men: his 62 percent win in that demographic was double his opponent's. However, he also won amongst white women (52 percent to 43 percent). He captured the rural vote 61 percent to 34 percent. "Exit Polls," CNN.com, November 23, 2016, http://www.cnn.com/election/results/exit-polls.

13. For a discussion of the state of the class system in Great Britain, see Caroline Gammell, "Britain's Class System 'Alive and Well' Claims Research," *Telegraph*, April 17, 2009, http://www.telegraph.co.uk/news/uknews/5165594/Britains-class-system-alive-and-well-claims-research.html.

14. For a brief overview of the Indian caste system, see Allison Elliott, "Caste and *The God of Small Things*," 1997, http://english.emory.edu/Bahri/caste.html.

15. Alexander Chancellor, "The Class Menagerie," *Guardian*, March 9, 2005, http://www.guardian.co.uk/uk/2002/mar/09/britishidentity.comment.

16. In 2007, a CBS News poll found that only 2 percent of Americans indicated that they were "upper class," and 1 percent said that they were "lower class." Lori Robertson, "Defining the 'Middle Class,'" Factcheck.org, January 24, 2008, http://factcheck.org/2008/01/defining-the-middle-class.

17. This site was no longer operational as of the writing of this edition. For similar content, navigate to http://occupywallst.org, http://www.occupy.com, or http://occupywallstreet.net, or visit their Facebook page at https://www.facebook.com/OccupyWallSt.

18. "2016 Delegate Count and Primary Results." *New York Times*, July 5, 2016, http://www.nytimes.com/interactive/2016/us/elections/primary-calendar-and-results.html.

19. There is ongoing debate about whether the words *white* and *black* should be capitalized when referring to race. Because Westview Press follows the *Chicago Manual of Style*, which recommends lowercase, I have followed that convention in this book. For a more detailed discussion of this issue, see the following blog entry that I coauthored: http://raceproject.org/?p=613.

20. The 2010 census revealed that white babies (under the age of two) are already a numerical minority. Dara Sharif, "White Babies Now a Minority in the U.S.," TheRoot.com, June 24, 2011, http://www.theroot.com/articles/culture/2011/06/census_black_and_brown_babies_outnumber_white_babies/.

21. See, for instance, Ta-Nehisi Coates, "Fear of a Black President," *Atlantic*, September 2012, http://www.theatlantic.com/magazine/archive/2012/09/fear-of-a-black-president/309064/; Ron Rosenbaum, "Is the Republican Party Racist?," Slate, October 8, 2012, http://www.slate.com/articles/news_and_politics/the_spectator/2012/10/is_the_republican_party_racist_how_the_racial_attitudes_of_southern_voters_bolster_its_chances_.html; "A Map of Racist Tweets About President Obama's Re-election," AlterNet, November 9, 2012, http://www.alternet.org/election-2012/map-racist-tweets-about-president-obamas-re-election-mississippi-alabama-lead-pack.

22. Sara Sidner, "The Rise of Black Lives Matter: Trying to Break the Cycle of Violence and Silence," CNN, December 28, 2015, http://www.cnn.com/2015/12/28/us/black-lives-matter-evolution/.

23. Donald Nieman, "Donald Trump's Campaign Is an Echo of Reconstruction-Era Racism," *New Republic*, October 12, 2016, https://newrepublic.com/article/137741/donald-trumps-campaign-echo-reconstruction-era-racism.

24. This phrase was made famous in recent history by Democratic US senator and 2004 presidential candidate John Edwards. Chuck Raasch, "Edwards Brings 'Two Americas' to Center Stage," *USA Today*, July 28, 2004, http://www.usatoday.com /news/opinion/columnist/raasch/2004-07-28-raasch_x.htm.

25. The first slave ships arrived in North America roughly four hundred years ago, though the earliest settlers perpetuated injustices on Native Americans for more than a century prior to the arrival of Africans. Lisa Rein, "Mystery of Va.'s First Slaves Is Unlocked 400 Years Later," *Washington Post*, September 3, 2006, http://www .washingtonpost.com/wp-dyn/content/article/2006/09/02/AR2006090201097.html.

26. A recent poll revealed that 88 percent of Americans identify themselves with the term *middle class*. Peter Moore, "Poll Results: Middle Class," YouGov, May 28, 2015, https://today.yougov.com/news/2015/05/28/poll-results-middle-class/.

27. In 2014, 14.8 percent of Americans lived in poverty, as defined by the US Bureau of the Census. National Poverty Center, "Poverty in the United States: Frequently Asked Questions," 2016, http://www.npc.umich.edu/poverty/.

28. *Bigotry* is actually a broader term referring to resentment toward others who are different from the person who is exhibiting bigoted attitudes and behaviors. Besides race-based bigotry, bigotry may be related to gender, sexual orientation, age, religion, able-bodiedness, and so on.

29. *Crash* won the Academy Award for Best Picture in 2005.

30. A number of studies have employed designs where stereotypical white, Hispanic, and African American names were used to determine levels of racial bias. These studies have shown, for example, that Latinos are less likely than whites to receive a response from an election official about a voting-related question. Julie K. Faller, Noah L. Nathan, and Ariel R. White, "What Do I Need to Vote? Bias in Information Provision by Local Election Officials," manuscript, July 11, 2014, http:// scholar.harvard.edu/files/arwhite/files/fallernathanwhite_voteridexp_july2014_0.pdf. African Americans are significantly less likely to receive calls for jobs than whites with identical credentials. Marianne Bertrand and Sendhil Mullainathan, "Are Emily and Greg More Employable Than Lakisha and Jamal? A Field Experiment on Labor Market Discrimination," *American Economic Review* 94, no. 4 (2004): 991–1013. African American elected officials are more likely to respond to African Americans who write with questions, even if the person writing is not a constituent. David E. Broockman, "Black Politicians Are More Intrinsically Motivated to Advance Blacks' Interests: A Field Experiment Manipulating Political Incentives," *American Journal of Political Science* 57, no. 3 (2013): 521–536.

31. See, for instance, Anthony G. Greenwald, Debbie E. McGhee, and Jordan L. K. Schwartz, "Measuring Individual Differences in Implicit Cognition: The Implicit Association Test," *Journal of Personality and Social Psychology* 74, no. 6 (1998): 1464–1480; Allen R. McConnell and Jill M. Leibold, "Relations Among the Implicit Association Test, Descriminatory Behavior, and Explicit Measures of Racial Attitudes," *Journal of Experimental Social Psychology* 37, no. 5 (2001): 435–442; Andrew Karpinski and James L. Hilton, "Attitudes and the Implicit Association Test,"*Journal of Personality and Social Psychology* 81, no. 5 (2001): 774–788; Bertram Gawronski, "What Does the Implicit Association Test Measure? A Test of the Convergent and Discriminant Validity of Prejudice-Related IATs," *Experimental Psychology* 49, no. 3 (2002): 171–180.

32. See, for instance, P. J. Henry and David O. Sears, "The Symbolic Racism 2000 Scale," *Political Psychology* 23, no. 2 (2002): 253–283; David O. Sears and P. J. Henry, "Over Thirty Years Later: A Contemporary Look at Symbolic Racism," *Advances in Experimental Psychology* 37 (2005): 95–150; Christopher Tarman and David O. Sears, "The Conceptualization and Measurement of Symbolic Racism," *Journal of Politics* 67, no. 3 (2005): 731–761; Brad T. Gomez and J. Matthew Wilson, "Rethinking Symbolic Racism: Evidence of Attribution Bias," *Journal of Politics* 68, no. 3 (2006): 611–625; Joshua L. Rabinowitz et al., "Why Do White Americans Oppose Race-Targeted Policies? Clarifying the Impact of Symbolic Racism," *Political Psychology* 30, no. 5 (2009): 805–828; Anthony G. Greenwald et al., "Implicit Race Attitudes Predicted Vote in the 2008 U.S. Presidential Election," *Analyses of Social Issues and Public Policy* 9, no. 1 (2009): 241–253.

33. https://implicit.harvard.edu.

34. One recent study suggests that implicit bias may not be as closely related to electoral outcomes as explicit prejudice. Nathan P. Kalmoe and Spencer Piston, "Is Implicit Prejudice Against Blacks Politically Consequential?" *Public Opinion Quarterly* 77, no. 1 (2013): 305–322.

35. Jeremy Hogeveen, Michael Inzlicht, and Sukhvinder S. Obhi, "Power Changes How the Brain Responds to Others," *Journal of Experimental Psychology: General*, 2013; Susanne Quadflieg et al., "Exploring the Neural Correlates of Social Stereotyping," *Journal of Cognitive Neuroscience* 21, no. 8 (2008): 1560–1570; Jennifer A. Richeson et al., "An fMRI Investigation of the Impact of Interracial Contact on Executive Function," *Nature Neuroscience* 6, no. 2 (2003): 1323–1328; David M. Amodio et al., "Alternate Mechanisms for Regulating Racial Responses According to Internal vs External Cues," *SCAN* 1 (2006): 26–36; David M. Amodio et al., "Neural Signals for the Detection of Unintentional Race Bias," *Psychological Science* 15, no. 2 (2004): 88–93; David M. Amodio, "Can Neuroscience Advance Social Psychological Theory? Social Neuroscience for the Behavioral Social Psychologist," *Social Cognition* 28, no. 6 (2010): 695–716.

36. US Constitution, Article I, Section 2, paragraph 3.

37. A host of celebrities being caught (or admitting to) using the n-word has been the source of much media attention over the past decade. From Michael Richards to Dog the Bounty Hunter to Paula Deen, this attention serves to reinforce the belief that the primary (or only) evidence of (or concern about) white racial prejudice is the use of this word.

38. See, for instance, Patricia Hill Collins, *Fighting Words: Black Women and the Search for Justice* (Minneapolis: University of Minnesota Press, 1998); Patricia Hill Collins, *Black Feminist Thought: Knowledge, Consciousness, and the Politics of Empowerment* (New York: Routledge, 2000); Kimberlé Crenshaw, "Demarginalizing the Intersection of Race and Sex: A Black Feminist Critique of Antidiscrimination Doctrine, Feminist Theory, and Antiracist Politics," *University of Chicago Legal Forum*, 1989, 139–167; Kimberlé Crenshaw, "Intersectionality, Identity Politics, and Violence Against Women of Color," *Stanford Law Review* 43 (1991): 1241–1299; bell hooks, *Ain't I a Woman: Black Women and Feminism* (Cambridge: South End Press, 1981); bell hooks, *Feminism Is for Everybody: Passionate Politics* (Cambridge: South

End Press, 2000); Audre Lorde, *Sister Outsider: Essays and Speeches* (Berkeley, CA: Crossing Press, 1984).

39. C. Wright Mills, *The Power Elite* (New York: Oxford University Press, 2000).

40. All URLs were active as of this writing.

Chapter 1: Representation and the Roots of Inequality

1. See, for instance, Arnaud Lefranc, Nicholas Pistolesi, and Alain Trannoy, "Equality of Opportunities vs. Inequality of Outcomes: Are Western Societies All Alike?" *Review of Income and Wealth* 54, no. 4 (2008): 513–546.

2. Anne Phillips, "Defending Equality of Outcome," *Journal of Political Philosophy* 12, no. 1 (2004): 1–19.

3. James Madison [Publius], "The Federalist 10: The Utility of the Union as a Safeguard Against Domestic Faction and Insurrection (continued)," *(New York) Daily Advertiser*, November 22, 1787, http://www.constitution.org/fed/federa10.htm.

4. Donald J. McCrone and James H. Kuklinski, "The Delegate Theory of Representation," *American Journal of Political Science* 23 (1979): 278–300.

5. George Sadowsky, Raul Zambrano, and Pierre Dandjinou, "Internet Governance: A Discussion Document" (paper presented to the United Nations ICT Task Force, 2004), https://www.internetsociety.org/sites/default/files/Internet%20Governance%20A%20Discussion%20Document%20%28George%20Sadowsky%29.pdf.

6. Herbert Asher, *Polling and the Public: What Every Citizen Should Know*, 8th ed. (Washington, DC: CQ Press, 2010).

7. The median net worth of members of the 113th Congress (2013–2015) was $1,029,505 (compared with the national average of about $56,355). Russ Choma, "One Member of Congress = 18 American Households: Lawmakers' Personal Finances Far from Average," Center for Responsive Politics, January 12, 2015, https://www.opensecrets.org/news/2015/01/one-member-of-congress-18-american-households-lawmakers-personal-finances-far-from-average/. While only 20 of the 535 members of the 114th Congress had no degree beyond a high school diploma, 98 held a master's degree as their highest degree, and 262 members held terminal degrees, including 213 law degrees. Jennifer E. Manning, "Membership of the 114th Congress: A Profile," November 15, 2016, Congressional Research Service, https://www.fas.org/sgp/crs/misc/R43869.pdf.

8. Hanna Fenichel Pitkin, *The Concept of Representation* (Berkeley: University of California Press, 1972).

9. More than half of the members of the 113th Congress were millionaires. Choma, "One Member of Congress = 18 American Households."

10. Of the ten African Americans to serve in the US Senate, six were elected by the people. The first two black senators were elected by the Mississippi state legislature (prior to the passage of the Seventeenth Amendment to the Constitution in 1913), and three others were appointed to fill vacancies. (One of those three, Tim Scott, Republican of South Carolina, was appointed in 2013 but won a special election in 2014.)

11. At the start of the 115th Congress (2017–2019), there were 104 women (19 percent), including twenty-one in the Senate; forty-nine African Americans (9 percent), including three in the Senate; thirty-eight Hispanics or Latinos (7 percent), including four in the Senate; and fifteen members (3 percent), including one in the Senate, who identify as Asian American, Native American, or Pacific Islander. Cristina Marcos, "115th Congress Will Be the Most Racially Diverse in History," *The Hill*, November 17, 2016, http://thehill.com/homenews/house/306480-115th-congress-will-be-most-racially-diverse-in-history. There were seven openly LGBTQ members serving in the 113th Congress, which was a record (there are six in the 115th Congress). Jennifer E. Manning, "Membership of the 113th Congress: A Profile," Congressional Research Service, July 1, 2013. (Numbers and percentages include six territorial nonvoting delegates and the resident commissioner for Puerto Rico.)

12. For example, despite the legal gains African Americans made with respect to voting in the 1960s, only six black Americans have been elected to the US Senate and only two black governors have been elected since Reconstruction. (In addition, one African American—David Patterson of New York—was appointed to fill a vacant governorship but did not seek election for an additional term.)

13. Alexander Hamilton [as Publius], "The Federalist 79: The Judiciary Department," [New York] *Independent Journal*, June 14, 1788, http://www.constitution.org/fed/federa78.htm.

14. This, too deserves a bit of clarification. Because the Electoral College chooses the president and its members are awarded based on state allocations, five US presidents, including Donald Trump, were elected while having lost even a plurality of the popular vote.

15. 531 US 98 (2000), http://www.law.cornell.edu/supct/html/00-949.ZPC.html.

16. 369 US 186 (1962), http://www.law.cornell.edu/supct/html/historics/USSC_CR_0369_0186_ZS.html.

17. 377 US 533 (1964), http://www.law.cornell.edu/supct/html/historics/USSC_CR_0377_0533_ZS.html.

18. This principle is not a universal truism. For instance, both the US Senate and the Electoral College are structural examples of the ways that the Framers devised a system that would be attentive to minority preferences. In the former example, states with small populations have the same voting power as states with large populations; and in the latter example, small states have disproportionate power in selecting the president because of the formula that is used to determine electoral votes. Both of these mechanisms are consistent with Madison's concern with majority factions, but they also violate the one person, one vote standard that characterizes most other aspects of political life in the United States.

19. D'Vera Cohn, "Imputation: Adding People to the Census," Pew Research Center, May 4, 2011, http://pewresearch.org/pubs/1981/census-imputation-missing-housing-units-people-number-type.

20. *Utah v. Evans*, 536 US 452 (2002), http://www.law.cornell.edu/supct/html/01-714.ZS.html.

21. Cohn, "Imputation."

22. Joshua Tucker, "Turnout Rates Among the Rich and Poor," The Monkey Cage, July 5, 2013, http://themonkeycage.org/2013/07/05/turnout-rates-among -the-rich-and-poor/?utm_source=feedburner&utm_medium=feed&utm_campaign =Feed%3A+themonkeycagefeed+%28The+Monkey+Cage%29. Tucker cites evidence from Kimuli Kasara and Pavithra Suryanarayan, "When the Rich Vote Less Than the Poor and Why? Explaining Turnout Inequality Across the World" (paper prepared for the International Society for New Institutional Economics Annual Conference, March 15, 2013), http://pavisuridotcom.files.wordpress.com/2012/08 /kasarasuyanarayan_turnout20131210.pdf.

23. Data from the 2010 census reveal that women comprise 50.9 percent of the US population. Lindsay M. Howden and Julie A. Meyer, "2010 Census Briefs: Age and Sex Composition: 2010," US Bureau of the Census, May 2011, http://www.census .gov/prod/cen2010/briefs/c2010br-03.pdf.

24. While the election of Barack Obama to the presidency in 2008 and 2012 seems to serve as a counterfactual, a closer examination reveals otherwise. Although he garnered a plurality of votes in enough states to win Electoral College victories both years (and no state is majority-minority), he won only 43 percent of the white vote in 2008 and 39 percent in 2012. Paul Steinhauser, "Five Things We Learned on Election Night," CNN.com, November 8, 2012, http://www.cnn.com/2012/11/07/politics/5-things -election-night/index.html.

25. *Shaw v. Reno*, 509 US 630 (1993), http://www.law.cornell.edu/supct/html/92 -357.ZO.html. See also Linda Greenhouse, "The Supreme Court: Reapportionment; Court Questions Districts Drawn to Aid Minorities," *New York Times*, June 29, 1993. A1. A number of subsequent Court cases have also constrained the process of drawing of majority-minority districts. See, for instance, *Miller v. Johnson*, 515 US 900 (1995) and *Georgia v. Ashcroft*, 539 US 461 (2003).

26. See also Carol M. Swain, *Black Faces, Black Interests: The Representation of African Americans in Congress* (Cambridge: Harvard University Press, 1993).

27. In 2016, for instance, 89 percent of African Americans and 74 percent of nonwhites overall voted for Hillary Clinton, the Democratic candidate for president. Latinos preferred the Democratic candidate as well, but by a far slimmer margin—66 percent to 28 percent. CNN Politics, "Exit Polls," 2016, http://www.cnn.com/election /results/exit-polls/elections/National?ep=hou_na. While Latinos collectively favor Republicans on a number of social issues, there are important ideological differences between Latinos in southern Florida, who tend to have a Cuban national background, and Latinos in the Southwest and in large northern and Midwestern cities, who tend to come from Central and South America, as well as Puerto Rico and the Dominican Republic. Oscar Corral, "Hispanics and Cuban Americans Varying Political Views Yield Surprises," *Havana Journal*, April 5, 2004, http://havanajournal.com/cuban _americans/entry/hispanics_and_cuban_americans_varying_political_views_yield _surprises/. There is evidence that this trend may be shifting, as in 2012 when President Obama won 60 percent of Cuban American voters who were born in the United States. Emily Deruy, "Cuban-Americans No Longer a Sure Bet for the GOP," ABC News, November 13, 2012, http://abcnews.go.com/ABC_Univision/Politics/cuban-voters -swinging-democratic/story?id=17700174#.ULPCI-Oe8f9.

28. Michael C. Dawson, *Black Visions: The Roots of Contemporary African-American Political Ideologies* (Chicago: University of Chicago, 2001); Karen M. Kaufmann, "Black and Latino Voters in Denver: Responses to Each Other's Political Leadership," *Political Science Quarterly* 118 (2003): 107–125.

29. C. Vann Woodward, *The Strange Career of Jim Crow* (1955; New York: Oxford University Press, 2001); Jerrold M. Packard, *American Nightmare: The History of Jim Crow* (New York: St. Martin's Griffin, 2003); Michael J. Klarman, *From Jim Crow to Civil Rights: The Supreme Court and the Struggle for Racial Equality* (New York: Oxford University Press, 2006).

30. The entire act is on the Department of Justice website: http://www.justice.gov /crt/about/vot/intro/intro_b.php.

31. Associated Press, "New Rules in These States Are Frustrating Voters," *Forbes*, November 7, 2016, http://fortune.com/2016/11/07/minority-voters-election/; Pete Williams, "Judge Says North Carolina Illegally Purged Voter Lists," NBC News, November 4, 2016, http://www.nbcnews.com/storyline/2016-election-day/judge -says-north-carolina-illegally-purged-voter-lists-n677431; "Florida's Discriminatory Voter Purge," *New York Times*, May 31, 2012, http://www.nytimes.com/2012/06/01 /opinion/floridas-discriminatory-voter-purge.html.

32. Kwame Holman, "Voting Rights," *The NewsHour with Jim Lehrer,* December 15, 2000, http://www.pbs.org/newshour/bb/election/july-dec00/voting_12-15.html.

33. Mark Joseph Stern, "America Is Already in the Midst of a Voter Suppression Crisis," Slate, October 31, 2016, http://www.slate.com/articles/news_and_politics /jurisprudence/2016/10/republicans_are_already_suppressing_minority_votes _all_over_america.html; Erika L. Wood, "Florida: How Soon We Forget," Campaign Stops, April 5, 2012, http://campaignstops.blogs.nytimes.com/2012/04/05/florida -how-quickly-we-forget/.

34. Paula D. McClain, *"Can We All Get Along?" Racial and Ethnic Minorities in American Politics* (Boulder, CO: Westview, 2010), 191; Mark Berman, William Wan, and Sari Horwitz, "Voters Encounter Some Malfunctioning Machines, Other Headaches on Election Day, *Washington Post*, November 8, 2016, https:// www.washingtonpost.com/news/post-nation/wp/2016/11/08/election-day-voters -report-long-lines-intimidation-and-confusion-in-some-parts-of-the-country/?utm _term=.4fe21f8b6fcc.

35. Jess Bravin, "Court Upends Voting Rights Act," *Wall Street Journal*, June 25, 2013, http://online.wsj.com/article/SB10001424127887323469804578521363840962032.html; Adam Liptak, "Supreme Court Invalidates Key Part of Voting Rights Act," *New York Times*, June 25, 2013, http://online.wsj.com/article/SB10001424127887323 46980457852136384096 2032.html.

36. Jasmine C. Lee, "How States Moved Toward Stricter Voter ID Laws," *New York Times*, November 3, 2016, http://www.nytimes.com/interactive /2016/11/03/us/elections/how-states-moved-toward-stricter-voter-id-laws.html. For scholarly work related to the relationship between voter identification laws and voter turnout, see R. Michael Alvarez, Delia Bailey, and Jonathan N. Katz, "The Effect of Voter Identification Laws on Turnout," Social Science Working Paper 1267, California Institute of Technology, October 2007, http://jkatz.caltech.edu /research/files/wp1267.pdf and Matt A. Barreto, Stephen A. Nuño, and Gabriel

R. Sanchez, "Voter ID Requirements and the Disenfranchisements of Latino, Black and Asian Voters," (paper prepared for presentation at the 2007 meeting of the American Political Science Association), http://citeseerx.ist.psu.edu/viewdoc /download?doi=10.1.1.175.23&rep=rep1&type=pdf.

37. Matthew Rozsa, "How Voter ID Laws Helped Donald Trump Win the Presidency," Salon.com, November 14, 2016, http://www.salon.com/2016/11/14 /how-voter-id-laws-helped-donald-trump-win-the-presidency/; Mark Joseph Stern, "Did the Republican War on Voting Rights Help Trump Win?" Slate.com, November 9, 2016, http://www.slate.com/blogs/the_slatest/2016/11/09/republican_war_on _voting_rights_may_have_helped_trump_win.html.

38. German Lopez, "Voter Suppression Didn't Cost Hillary Clinton the Election," Vox.com, November 11, 2016, http://www.vox.com/policy-and-politics /2016/11/11/13597452/voter-suppression-clinton-trump-2016.

39. The title of this section is borrowed from Raymond A. Smith, *The American Anomaly: U.S. Politics and Government in Comparative Perspective,* 2nd ed. (New York: Routledge, 2011).

40. The term *single member district plurality* reflects the process of the state drawing district lines and having one person per district represent that geographical area in the legislative body (i.e., the US House of Representatives or state legislatures). Each district has a single member chosen, who must win a plurality of the votes to take office.

41. Jennifer E. Manning, "Membership of the 112th Congress: A Profile," Congressional Research Service, August 4, 2011, http://fpc.state.gov/documents/ organization/170493.pdf.

42. Helena Bottemiller Evich, "Revenge of the Rural Voter," Politico, November 13, 2016, http://www.politico.com/story/2016/11/hillary-clinton-rural -voters-trump-231266.

43. French law mandates that in most elections an equal number of men and women must appear on ballots. It does not mandate gender parity in elected bodies, but the provision has led to an increase in women both seeking office and being elected. Janine Mossuz-Lavau, "Gender Parity in Politics," *France in the United States: Embassy of France in Washington,* November 30, 2007, http://ambafrance-us .org/spip.php?article612.

44. Lani Guinier, "The Representation of Minority Interests: The Question of Single-Member Districts," *Cordozo Law Review* 14 (1993): 1135–1174.

45. William G. Ludwin, "Strategic Voting and the Borda Method," *Public Choice* 38 (1978): 85–90.

46. Matt Gehring, "Information Brief: Instant Runoff Voting," Minnesota House of Representatives Research Department, February, 2007. http://www.house.leg.state .mn.us/hrd/pubs/irvoting.pdf.

47. C. Wright Mills, *The Power Elite* (New York: Oxford University Press).

48. See, for example, Robert Dahl, *Who Governs? Democracy and Power in an American City* (New Haven: Yale University Press, 1961).

49. The right of corporations and labor unions to participate in the electoral process was widened in 2010 with the Supreme Court's decision in *Citizens United v. the Federal Election Commission* (558 US 310). The Court ruled that the First

Amendment protects such organizations from restrictions on using their treasuries (as opposed to associated political action committees) to spend money independently (i.e., not contribute directly) to influence the outcome of an election: http://www.law .cornell.edu/supct/pdf/08–205P.ZO.

50. Cornel West, *Race Matters* (New York: Vintage, 1993), 94.

51. Patricia Ireland, "Progress Versus Equality," in *The Difference "Difference" Makes: Women and Leadership,* ed. Deborah L. Rhode (Stanford, CA: Stanford University Press, 2003), 193.

Chapter 2: Income and Wealth

1. Laurie Goodstein and Elisabetta Povoledo, "Pope Sets Down Goals for an Inclusive Church, Reaching Out 'on the Streets,'" *New York Times,* November 26, 2013, http://www.nytimes.com/2013/11/27/world/europe/in-major-document-pope -francis-present-his-vision.html.

2. Federal News Service, "Full Transcript: Obama's 2014 State of the Union Address," *Washington Post,* January 28, 2014, http://www.washingtonpost.com /politics/full-text-of-obamas-2014-state-of-the-union-address/2014/01/28/e0c93358 -887f-11e3-a5bd-844629433ba3_story.html.

3. Philip Bump, Amber Phillips, and Callum Borchers, "Donald Trump's Economic Speech, Annotated," *Washington Post,* August 8, 2016, https://www.washingtonpost .com/news/the-fix/wp/2016/08/08/donald-trumps-economic-speech-annotated/.

4. Allan Ornstein, *Class Counts: Education, Inequality, and the Shrinking Middle Class* (Lanham, MD: Rowman & Littlefield, 2007), 117, 150.

5. A quintile represents 20 percent of the population. In this case, if all households in the United States were listed from the wealthiest to the poorest and then divided equally into five groups, the top quintile would be the group that includes the wealthiest 20 percent of households.

6. Michael I. Norton and Dan Ariely, "Building a Better America—One Wealth Quintile at a Time," *Perspectives on Psychological Science,* 6, no. 1 (2011): 9–12.

7. Ibid., 10.

8. As noted in the previous chapter, more than half of the members of the 113th Congress were millionaires. The median net worth of members of the 113th Congress (2013–2015) was $1,029,505 (compared with the national average of about $56,355). Russ Choma, "One Member of Congress = 18 American Households: Lawmakers' Personal Finances Far from Average," Center for Responsive Politics, January 12, 2015, https://www.opensecrets.org/news/2015/01/one-member-of-congress-18 -american-households-lawmakers-personal-finances-far-from-average/.

9. Norton and Ariely, 12.

10. US Bureau of Labor Statistics, "Labor Force Statistics from the Current Population Survey," October 7, 2016, http://www.bls.gov/web/empsit/cpsee_e16.htm.

11. Jesse Washington, "The Disappearing Black Middle Class," *Chicago Sun-Times,* July 10, 2011, http://www.suntimes.com/6397110-417/the-disappearing -black-middle-class.html.

12. Valerie Wilson, "Black Unemployment Is Significantly Higher Than White Unemployment Regardless of Educational Attainment," Economic Policy Institute,

December17,2015,http://www.epi.org/publication/black-unemployment-educational
-attainment/.

13. Carmen DeNavas-Walt, Bernadette D. Proctor, and Jessica C. Smith, "Income, Poverty, and Health Insurance Coverage in the United States: 2011," US Census Bureau, September 2012, http://www.census.gov/prod/2012pubs/p60-243.pdf.

14. In 2008 dollars, the white-black-Hispanic medians were $58,952, $34,212, and $37,419, respectively, in 1990. US Census Bureau, Table 696, Money and Income of Families—Median Income by Race and Hispanic Origin and Constant (2008) Dollars: 1990 to 2008, *Statistical Abstract: Income, Expenditures, Poverty, and Wealth,* 2011, http://www.census.gov/compendia/statab/2011/tables/11s0696.pdf.

15. Valerie Wilson and William M. Rodgers III, "Black-White Wage Gaps Expand with Rising Wage Inequality, Economic Policy Institute, September 19, 2016, http://www.epi.org/files/pdf/101972.pdf.

16. Bernadette D. Proctor, Jessica L. Semega, and Melissa A. Kollar, "Income and Poverty in the United States: 2015," US Census Bureau, September 16, 2016, http://www.census.gov/newsroom/releases/archives/income_wealth/cb10–144.html.

17. US Census Bureau, Table H-2, Share of Aggregate Income Received by Each Fifth and Top 5 Percent of Households: 1970 to 2015, http://www2.census.gov/programs-surveys/cps/tables/time-series/historical-income-households/h02ar.xls.

18. MoveOn.org, "Something Big Happened to America in 1979," June 7, 2011, http://front.moveon.org/something-big-happened-to-america-in-1979/?rc=fb.fan; Martha Hamilton, "Is It True the Rich Are Getting Richer?" Politifact.com, July 6, 2011, http://www.politifact.com/truth-o-meter/article/2011/jul/06/it-true-rich-are-getting-richer/; William Julius Wilson, "The Great Disparity," *Nation,* July 10, 2012, http://www.thenation.com/article/168822/great-disparity. Wilson reviews two books on growing economic inequality: Timothy Noah, *The Great Divergence: America's Growing Inequality Crisis and What We Can Do About It* (New York: Bloomsbury Press, 2013) and Charles Murray, *Coming Apart: The State of White America, 1960–2010* (New York: Crown Forum, 2013).

19. The White House, "Your Right to Equal Pay, https://www.whitehouse.gov/equal-pay/myth; American Association of University Women, "The Simple Truth About the Gender Pay Gap (Fall 2016)," http://www.aauw.org/research/the-simple-truth-about-the-gender-pay-gap/.

20. American Association of University Women.

21. Ibid.

22. Hanna Rosin, "The Gender Wage Gap Lie," Slate.com, August 30, 2013, http://www.slate.com/articles/double_x/doublex/2013/08/gender_pay_gap_the_familiar_line_that_women_make_77_cents_to_every_man_s.html.

23. Alliance for Board Diversity, "Missing Pieces: Women and Minorities on Fortune 500 Boards," August 15, 2013, https://fortunedotcom.files.wordpress.com/2014/02/2012_abd_missing_pieces_final_8_15_13.pdf.

24. Ibid.

25. Gregory Wallace, "Only 5 Black CEOs at 500 Biggest Companies," CNN Money, January 29, 2015, http://money.cnn.com/2015/01/29/news/economy/mcdonalds-ceo-diversity/.

26. Ellen McGirt, "Why Race and Culture Matter in the C-Suite," *Fortune,* January 22, 2016, http://fortune.com/black-executives-men-c-suite/.

27. Chris Isidore, "African-American CEOs Still Rare," CNN Money, March 22, 2012, http://money.cnn.com/2012/03/22/news/companies/black-ceo/index.htm.

28. Valentina Zarya, "The Percentage of Female CEOs in the Fortune 500 Drops to 4%, Fortune, June 6, 2016, http://fortune.com/2016/06/06/women-ceos -fortune-500–2016/.

29. Jana Kasperkevic, "America's Top CEOs Pocket 340 Times More Than the Average Worker," *Guardian,* May 17, 2016, https://www.theguardian.com/us -news/2016/may/17/ceo-pay-ratio-average-worker-afl-cio; CNN Money, "GDP Growth Not Reaching Paychecks," CNN.com, September 5, 2007, http://money.cnn .com/2007/09/03/news/economy/epi_report/index.htm; MoveOn.org, "Something Big Happened to America in 1979."

30. Jana Kasperkevic, "America's Top CEOs Pocket 340 Times More Than the Average Worker"; Derrick Z. Jackson, "Income Gap Mentality," *Boston Globe,* April 19, 2006, http://www.boston.com/news/globe/editorial_opinion/oped/articles /2006/04/19/income_gap_mentality.

31. Kasperkevic, "America's Top CEOs."

32. Binyamin Applebaum, "U.S. Household Income Grew 5.2 Percent in 2015, Breaking Pattern of Stagnation, *New York Times,* September 13, 2016, http://mobile .nytimes.com/2016/09/14/business/economy/us-census-household-income-poverty -wealth-2015.html; Dylan Matthews, "The Middle Class's Incomes Are Finally Growing Faster Than the Rich's," Vox.com, September 13, 2016, http://www.vox .com/2016/9/13/12902218/census-income-poverty-2015-report.

33. Quoctrung Bui, "Actually, Income in Rural America Is Growing, Too," *New York Times,* September 16, 2016, http://www.nytimes.com/2016/09/17/upshot /actually-income-in-rural-america-is-growing-too.html.

34. US Internal Revenue Service, "2015 Federal Tax Rates, Personal Exemptions, and Standard Deductions," n.d., https://www.irs.com/articles/2015 -federal-tax-rates-personal-exemptions-and-standard-deductions.

35. Dave Gilson and Carolyn Perot, "It's the Inequality, Stupid," *Mother Jones,* March-April, 2011, http://www.motherjones.com/politics/2011/02 /income-inequality-in-america-chart-graph.

36. Peter G. Peterson Foundation," Who Pays Taxes?" April 15, 2016, http://www .pgpf.org/budget-basics/who-pays-taxes.

37. Ben Rooney and Julianne Pepitone, "$400 Billion in Tax Breaks Seen Favoring Wealthy," CNN Money, September 22, 2010, http://money.cnn.com/2010/09/21 /news/economy/wealth_building_tax_policy/index.htm.

38. Dan Froomkin, "The Top 10 Tax Breaks—and How They Help the Wealthy the Most," Huffington Post, April 18, 2011, http://www.huffingtonpost.com/2011/04/18 /the-top-10-tax-breaks-_n_850534.html.

39. Michael D. Shear, "Romney Releases 2011 Tax Returns," *New York Times,* September 21, 2012, http://thecaucus.blogs.nytimes.com/2012/09/21/romney-to -release-2011-tax-returns/; Brody Mullins, Patrick O'Connor, and John McKinnon, "Romney's Taxes: $3 Million," *Wall Street Journal,* January 24, 2012, http://online. wsj.com/article/SB10001424052970204624204577179740171772850.html.

40. "Buffett Slams Dividend Tax Cut," CNN Money, May 20, 2003, http://money
.cnn.com/2003/05/20/news/buffett_tax/; Steve Wamhoff, "How to Implement the
Buffet Rule," Citizens for Tax Justice, October 19, 2011, http://www.ctj.org/pdf
/buffettruleremedies.pdf.

41. Jennifer Wang, "Donald Trump's Fortune Falls $800 Million to $3.7 Billion,"
Forbes, September 28, 2016, http://www.forbes.com/sites/jenniferwang/2016/09/28
/the-definitive-look-at-donald-trumps-wealth-new/#208b7e9b7e2d.

42. David Barstow, Susanne Craig, Russ Buettner, and Megan Twohey, "Donald
Trump Tax Records Show He Could Have Avoided Taxes for Nearly Two Decades,
The Times Found," *New York Times*, October 1, 2016, http://www.nytimes
.com/2016/10/02/us/politics/donald-trump-taxes.html.

43. US Internal Revenue Service. "Topic 751. Social Security and Medicare
Withholding Rates." October 10, 2016. https://www.irs.gov/taxtopics/tc751.html.
Medicare contributions were similarly regressive until 2013, but now there is now no
wage cap.

44. Bruce D. Meyer and Dan T. Rosenbaum, "Welfare, the Earned Income Tax
Credit, and the Labor Supply of Single Mothers," *Quarterly Journal of Economics* 116,
no. 3 (2001): 1063–1114.

45. In 2016, a family of five (two adults and three children) could receive a tax
benefit of $6,269. An estimated 26 million households received the benefit in 2010.
US Internal Revenue Service, "2016 EITC Income Limits, Maximum Credit Amounts
and Tax Law Updates," November 3, 2016, https://www.irs.gov/credits-deductions
/individuals/earned-income-tax-credit/eitc-income-limits-maximum-credit
-amounts.

46. Court Smith, "Minimum Wage History," 2011, http://oregonstate.edu/instruct
/anth484/minwage.html.

47. Ibid.

48. US Department of Labor, "Wage and Hour Division: Minimum Wage Laws in
the States, August 1, 2016," 2016, https://www.dol.gov/whd/minwage/america.htm.

49. Smith, "Minimum Wage History."

50. Jessie Willis, "How We Measure Poverty: A History and Brief Overview,"
Oregon Center for Public Policy, February 2000, http://www.ocpp.org/poverty/how
.htm.

51. US Department of Health and Human Services, *2016 Poverty Guidelines,*
January 1, 2016, https://aspe.hhs.gov/poverty-guidelines.

52. National Poverty Center, "Poverty in the United States: Frequently Asked
Questions," 2016, http://www.npc.umich.edu/poverty/.

53. Ibid.

54. Ibid.

55. Jasmine Tucker and Caitlin Lowell, "National Snapshot: Poverty Among
Women & Families," National Women's Law Center, September 2016, https://nwlc
.org/wp-content/uploads/2016/09/Poverty-Snapshot-Factsheet-2016.pdf.

56. Ibid.

57. Willis, "How We Measure Poverty."

58. Ibid.

59. Jackson, "Income Gap Mentality."

60. "A Minimum Wage Increase," *New York Times*, March 26, 2011, http://www
.nytimes.com/2011/03/27/opinion/27sun2.html.

61. *Washington Post*, January 28, 2014, http://www.washingtonpost.com/politics
/full-text-of-obamas-2014-state-of-the-union-address/2014/01/28/e0c93358-887f-11
e3-a5bd-844629433ba3_story.html.

62. Candidate Trump gave a number of conflicting and sometimes confusing
responses to questions about the minimum wage, however. For a review, see
Michelle Ye Hee Lee, "A Guide to All of Donald Trump's Flip-Flops on the
Minimum Wage," *Washington Post*, October 3, 2016, https://www.washingtonpost
.com/news/fact-checker/wp/2016/08/03/a-guide-to-all-of-donald-trumps-flip-flops
-on-the-minimum-wage/.

63. Marilyn Geewax, "Does a Higher Minimum Wage Kill Jobs?" National
Public Radio, April 24, 2011, http://www.npr.org/2011/04/24/135638370/does
-a-higher-minimum-wage-kill-jobs.

64. Raymond A. Smith, *The American Anomaly: U.S. Politics and Government in
Comparative Perspective* (New York: Routledge, 2011), 165–169.

65. Social Security Administration, "Historical Background and Development of
Social Security," 2011, http://www.ssa.gov/history/briefhistory3.html.

66. For example, see Stanley Feldman and John Zaller, "The Political Culture
of Ambivalence: Ideological Responses to the Welfare State," *American Journal of
Political Science* 36, no. 1 (1992): 268–307.

67. "'Welfare Queen' Becomes Issue in Reagan Campaign," *New York Times*,
February 15, 1976, http://picofarad.info/misc/welfarequeen.pdf.

68. Although prosecutors argued that the characterization of her crimes was
accurate, she was only indicted for theft of $8,000 from public welfare and for perjury.
Dan Miller, "The Chutzpa Queen: Favorite Reagan Target as Welfare Cheat Remains
Unflappable at Trial in Chicago, *Washington Post*, March 13, 1977, A3.

69. See Frank Gilliam Jr., "The 'Welfare Queen' Experiment: How Voters
React to Images of African-American Mothers on Welfare," UCLA Center for
Communications and Community, 1999, http://escholarship.org/uc/item/17m7r1rq;
Ange-Marie Hancock, *The Politics of Disgust: The Public Identity of the Welfare Queen*
(New York: New York University Press, 2004). Reagan did not mention the woman's
race explicitly. Rather, he made references to Chicago or to the South Side of Chicago
or to the inner city, which served as code for "African American." Paul Krugman,
"Republicans and Race," *New York Times*, November 19, 2007, http://www.nytimes
.com/2007/11/19/opinion/19krugman.html. As Gilliam explains, "The implicit
racial coding is readily apparent. The woman Reagan was talking about was African-
American. Veiled references to African-American women, and African-Americans
in general, were equally transparent. In other words, while poor women of all races
get blamed for their impoverished condition, African-American women commit the
most egregious violations of American values. This story line tips into stereotypes
about both women (uncontrolled sexuality) and African-Americans (laziness)."

70. Martin Gilens, *Why Americans Hate Welfare: Race, Media, and the Politics of
Antipoverty Policy* (Chicago: University of Chicago Press, 1999), 68.

71. Ibid., 68–69.

72. Hancock, *Politics of Disgust*.

73. Marketplace, "Your State on Welfare," American Public Media, n.d., http://linkis.com/marketplace.org/EaI13.

74. Pam Fessler, "20 Years Since Welfare's Overhaul, Results Are Mixed," National Public Radio, August 22, 2016, http://www.npr.org/2016/08/22/490245470/20-years-since-welfares-overhaul-results-are-mixed.

75. Stephen Slivinsky, "The Corporate Welfare State: How the Federal Government Subsidizes U.S. Businesses," *Policy Analysis* 592 (2007): 1–21.

76. Melvin L. Oliver and Thomas M. Shapiro, *Black Wealth/White Wealth: A New Perspective on Racial Inequality*, 10th ed. (New York: Routledge, 2006).

77. Lisa A. Keister, *Wealth in America: Trends in Wealth Inequality* (New York: Cambridge University Press, 2000), 10.

78. Ibid.; Joseph E. Stiglitz, *The Price of Inequality: How Today's Divided Society Endangers Our Future* (New York: Norton, 2012).

79. Figures are expressed in 2010 dollars. Linda Levine, "An Analysis of the Distribution of Wealth Across Households, 1989–2010," Congressional Research Service, July 17, 2012, http://www.fas.org/sgp/crs/misc/RL33433.pdf. Household wealth grew faster than median wealth over that period, suggesting concentration at the upper end of the wealth distribution. As Levine notes, while both declined by 2012, the greater decline in the median reflects that the recession "affected those in the lower half of the wealth distribution more than those higher up in the distribution" (p. 3).

80. Tami Luhby, "America: More Diverse, Less Wealthy," CNN Money, July 27, 2015, http://money.cnn.com/2015/07/27/news/economy/wealth-diverse/.

81. Bonnie Kavoussi, "Nearly Half of Americans Die Without Money, Study Finds," Huffington Post, August 6, 2012, http://www.huffingtonpost.com/2012/08/06/americans-die-without-money_n_1746862.html.

82. Paul Taylor et al., "Wealth Gaps Rise to Record Highs Between Whites, Blacks and Hispanics: Twenty-to-One," Pew Research Center, July 26, 2011, http://www.pewsocialtrends.org/2011/07/26/wealth-gaps-rise-to-record-highs-between-whites-blacks-hispanics/; Dedrick Asante-Muhammad, Chuck Collins, Josh Hoxie, and Emanuel Nieves, "The Ever-Growing Gap," August, 2016, http://cfed.org/policy/federal/The_Ever_Growing_Gap-CFED_IPS-Final.pdf.

83. Jeanne Sahadi, "The Richest 10% Hold 76% of the Wealth," CNN Money, August 18, 2016, http://money.cnn.com/2016/08/18/pf/wealth-inequality/; "Census: Wealth Gap Widens Between Whites and Minorities," *USA Today*, July 26, 2011, http://www.usatoday.com/news/washington/2011-07-26-census-wealth-data_n.htm.

84. Tami Luhby, "America: More Diverse, Less Wealthy."

85. Dedrick Asante-Muhammad, et al., "The Ever-Growing Gap."

86. Ibid.

87. Karuna Jaggar, "The Race and Gender Wealth Gap," *Race and Regionalism* 15, no. 1 (2008), http://urbanhabitat.org/node/2815.

88. Megan Thibos, Danielle Lavin-Loucks, and Marcus Martin, "The Feminization of Poverty," YWCA Dallas, 2007, http://www.ywcadallas.org/PDF/womens-health/FeminizationofPoverty.pdf.

89. Bridget Lavelle and Pamela Smock, "Divorce and Women's Risk of Health Insurance Loss in the U.S.," *Population Studies Center Research Report no. 11–734*,

Institute for Social Research, University of Michigan, March, 2011, http://www.psc
.isr.umich.edu/pubs/pdf/rr11-734.pdf.

90. Jaggar, "Race and Gender Wealth Gap." For more information on gender
and race in wealth disparity, especially with respect to homeownership, see Beverlyn
Lundy Allen, "Race and Gender Inequality in Homeownership: Does Place Make a
Difference?" *Rural Sociology* 67, no. 4 (2002): 603–621.

91. Matthew Miller and Duncan Greenberg, "The Forbes 400: Almost All of
America's Wealthiest Citizens Are Poorer This Year," Forbes.com, September 30,
2009, http://www.forbes.com/2009/09/29/forbes-400-buffett-gates-ellison-rich-list
-09-intro.html.

92. For a video representation of the US wealth gap, see http://mashable
.com/2013/03/02/wealth-inequality/. For a video representation of the racial wealth
gap in the United States, see this video from the Urban Institute: https://youtu
.be/7KvCjZWS_kc.

93. During the Republican nominating contests in 2012, Mitt Romney offered that
the way to achieve economic success in America is to "take a shot, go for it. Take a risk.
Get the education. Borrow money if you have to from your parents. Start a business."
Sarah Huisenga, "Romney Suggests Young Adults Get Loans . . . from Their Parents,"
National Journal, April 27, 2012, http://www.nationaljournal.com/2012-presidential-
campaign/romney-suggests-young-adults-get-loans-from-their-parents-20120427.
Opponents seized on the statement as a reflection of some Republicans' willingness
to reduce student loan benefits, but the Romney campaign insisted that the "borrow"
comment was meant to relate to starting a business. Either way, the prospects are slim
for most young Americans. The United States has one of the strongest links between
individual and parent earnings in the industrialized world. Organisation for Economic
Cooperation and Development, *Economic Policy Reforms: Going for Growth 2010*,
chap. 5, "A Family Affair: Intergenerational Social Mobility across OECD Countries,"
http://www.oecd.org/tax/public-finance/chapter%205%20gfg%202010.pdf. For his
part, President Donald Trump has acknowledged a $1 million gift from his father in
1978 to start his first business enterprise, and though it is impossible to know the exact
amount, estimates range that he borrowed between $10 million and $200 million. Glenn
Kessler, "Fact Checker: Trump's False Claim He Built His Empire with a 'Small Loan'
from His Father," *Washington Post*, March 3, 2016, https://www.washingtonpost.com
/news/fact-checker/wp/2016/03/03/trumps-false-claim-he-built-his-empire-with-a
-small-loan-from-his-father/. For an in-depth examination and analysis of the transfer
of wealth in various forms and from a number of perspectives, see Yuval Elmelech,
Transmitting Inequality: Wealth and the American Family (Lanham, MD: Rowman
& Littlefield, 2008).

94. Maury Gittleman and Edward N. Wolff, "Racial Differences in Patterns of
Wealth Accumulation," *Journal of Human Resources* 39 (2004): 193–227.

95. Paul L. Menchik and Nancy Ammon Jianakoplos, "Black-White Wealth
Inequality: Is Inheritance the Reason?" *Economic Inquiry* 35 (2007): 428–442, quote 441.

96. Victor Tan Chen, "All Hollowed Out: The Lonely Poverty of America's White
Working Class," *Atlantic*, January 16, 2016, http://www.theatlantic.com/business
/archive/2016/01/white-working-class-poverty/424341/.

97. Federal Reserve Bank of San Francisco, "What Steps Can Be Taken to Increase Savings in the United States Economy?" February 2002, http://www.frbsf.org /education/activities/doctor-econ/2002/February/savings-disposable-personal-income.html.

98. New America Foundation, *Savings in American Households,* November 16, 2009, http://assets.newamerica.net/files/1109SavingsFacts.pdf.

99. Quentin Fottrell, "Most Americans Have Less than $1,000 in Savings," MarketWatch, December 23, 2015, http://www.marketwatch.com/story/most -americans-have-less-than-1000-in-savings-2015-10-06.

100. Laura Shin, "The Racial Wealth Gap: Why a Typical White Household Has 16 Times the Wealth of a Black One," *Forbes,* March 26, 2015, http://www.forbes.com /sites/laurashin/2015/03/26/the-racial-wealth-gap-why-a-typical-white-household -has-16-times-the-wealth-of-a-black-one/#cd5e4066c5bc.

101. U.S. Federal Deposit Insurance Corporation, "2015 FDIC National Survey of Unbanked and Underbanked Households: Executive Summary," October 20, 2016, https://www.fdic.gov/householdsurvey/2015/2015execsumm.pdf; Michael A. Fletcher, "Blacks, Hispanics Hold Few Investments, Poll Shows," *Washington Post,* February 21, 2011, http://www.washingtonpost.com/wp-dyn/content/article /2011/02/21/AR2011022104350.html.

102. Matt Fellowes, *From Poverty, Opportunity: Putting the Market to Work for Lower Income Families,* Brookings Institution, 2006, http://www.brookings.edu/reports /2006/07poverty_fellowes.aspx.

103. See David J. Hand and William E. Henley, "Statistical Classification Methods in Consumer Credit Scoring: A Review," *Journal of the Royal Statistical Society* 160, no. 3 (1997): 523–541.

104. Ibid.

105. Statistical and qualitative studies of black business owners, for example, identify unique and persistent challenges in securing loans, intrusion of larger companies into traditionally black markets, and lack of experience. See Timothy Bates, *Banking on Black Enterprise: The Potential of Emerging Firms for Revitalizing Urban Economics* (Washington, DC: Joint Center for Political and Economic Studies, 1993); Michael Bonds, "Looking Beyond the Numbers: The Struggles of Black Businesses to Survive: A Qualitative Approach," *Journal of Black Studies* 37, no. 5 (1997): 581–601; Jan E. Christopher, "Minority Business Formation and Survival: Evidence on Business Performance and Visibility," *Review of Black Political Economy* 26, no. 7 (1998): 37–72; Robert W. Fairlie and Alicia M. Robb, "Why Are Black-Owned Businesses Less Successful Than White-Owned Businesses? The Role of Families, Inheritances, and Business Human Capital," University of California–Santa Cruz, 2005, http://repositories.cdlib.org/ucscecon/618; Robert Mark Silverman, "Black Business, Group Resources, and the Economic Detour: Contemporary Black Manufacturers in Chicago's Ethnic Beauty Aids Industry," *Journal of Black Studies* 30, no. 2 (1999): 232–258; Joe William Trotter Jr., *Black Milwaukee: The Making of an Industrial Proletariat, 1915–1948* (Urbana: University of Illinois Press, 1985).

106. There is a rich literature in economics regarding conditions under which individuals tend to be risk averse as opposed to risk seeking. See, for instance, Daniel

Kahneman and Amos Tversky, "Choices, Values, and Frames," *American Psychologist* 39, no. 4 (1984): 341–350.

107. Jeffrey M. Jones, "One in Six Americans Gamble on Sports," Gallup, July 30, 2008, http://www.gallup.com/poll/104086/One-Six-Americans-Gamble-Sports.aspx.

108. Ibid.

109. "Gambling Facts and Statistics," OvercomingGambling.com, http://www.overcominggambling.com/facts.html; see also H. Roy Kaplan, "The Social and Economic Impact of State Lotteries," *Annals of the American Academy of Political and Social Science* 474 (1984): 91–106.

110. Michael A. Stegman, "Payday Lending," *Journal of Economic Perspectives* 21, no. 1 (2007): 169–190.

111. Michael A. Stegman and Robert Faris, *Welfare, Work, and Banking: The North Carolina Financial Services Survey* (Chapel Hill, NC: Center for Community Capitalism, 2001); Stegman and Faris, "Welfare, Work, and Banking: The Use of Consumer Credit by Current and Former TANF Recipients in Charlotte, North Carolina," *Journal of Urban Affairs* 27, no. 4 (2005): 379–402, cited in Stegman, "Payday Lending," 173–174.

112. Reuters, "New Rules Could Dramatically Alter the Payday Loan Market," *Fortune*, June 2, 2016, http://fortune.com/2016/06/02/cfpb-payday-loan-rules/.

113. Gillian B. White, "Payday Loans' Potentially Predatory Replacement," *Atlantic*, August 12, 2016, http://www.theatlantic.com/business/archive/2016/08/what-will-replace-payday-loans/495656/.

114. Matt Fellowes, "From Poverty, Opportunity: Putting the Market to Work for Lower Income Families," Brookings Institution, 2006, http://www.brookings.edu/reports/2006/07poverty_fellowes.aspx.

115. Ronald Paul Hill, David L. Ramp, and Linda Silver, "The Rent-to-Own Industry and Pricing Disclosure Tactics," *Journal of Public Policy and Marketing* 17, no. 1 (1998): 3–10.

116. "Consumer Protection: Reforming the 'RTO' Rip-Off," *Consumer Reports*, August 1995, 507, cited in Hill, Ramp, and Silver, "Rent-to-Own Industry and Pricing Disclosure Tactics."

117. Shankar Vedantam, "Why High-Income Households Benefit More from Product Innovations," National Public Radio, August 16, 2016, http://www.npr.org/2016/08/16/490174061/why-high-income-households-benefit-more-from-product-innovations.

118. Thomas Woods Jr., "Do Rent-to-Own Stores Hurt the Poor?" Ludwig von Mises Institute, August 3, 2006, http://mises.org/daily/2261.

119. Elizabeth T. Powers and Emilie Bagby, "Poverty and Inequality in Illinois," Institute of Government and Public Affairs, University of Illinois, 2008, http://igpa.uillinois.edu/system/files/08-ILRept08-Pov-IneqPg49–60.pdf.

120. Catherine Cozzarelli, Anna V. Wilkinson, and Michael J. Tagler, "Attitudes Toward the Poor and Attributions for Poverty," *Journal of Social Issues* 57, no. 1 (2001): 207–227, 209.

121. Powers and Bagby, "Poverty and Inequality in Illinois"; see also Matthew O. Hunt, "Race/Ethnicity and Beliefs About Wealth and Poverty," *Social Science Quarterly* 85, no. 3 (2004): 827–853.

122. Dean Preatorius, "2010 Census: Poorest Counties in America," Huffington Post, December 21, 2010, http://www.huffingtonpost.com/2010/12/21/2010-census -the-poorest-c_n_799526.html; Kenneth Stepp, "Twenty-two of the One Hundred Poorest Counties in the U.S. Are Here," *Economic Journal*, February 28, 2009, http:// steppforcongress.blogspot.com/2009/02/twenty-two-of-one-hundred-poorest.html.

123. "The Poorest Counties of America," *New York Times*, November 18, 2009, http://economix.blogs.nytimes.com/2009/11/18/the-poorest-counties-of-america/.

124. This figure, calculated after the 2010 census and reapportionment of House seats, represents an increase of approximately 60,000 persons over the average after the 2000 census.

125. Data in this paragraph are assembled from US Census data reported by ProximityOne, "Congressional District Economic Data," 2016, http://proximityone .com/cd151dp3.htm; Half in Ten, "Interactive Map: Poverty Data by Congressional District," September 30, 2010, http://halfinten.org/issues/articles/poverty-data -by-congressional-district/; "Election 08 Results by District: Presidential Results," *Congressional Quarterly*, 2010, http://innovation.cq.com/atlas/district_08; and available from the US Census Bureau, "Fast Facts for Congress," 2011, http://fastfacts .census.gov/home/cws/main.html. What was New York's Sixteenth District when this report was written is largely composed of what is now the Fifteenth District after the 2012 congressional map was adopted.

126. Richard Sisk, "South Bronx Is Poorest District in Nation, U.S. Census Bureau Finds: 38% Live Below Poverty Line," *New York Daily News*, September 29, 2010, http://www.nydailynews.com/new-york/south-bronx-poorest-disrict-nation-u-s -census-bureau-finds-38-live-poverty-line-article-1.438344.

127. Puerto Rico is the poorest congressional district with 45 percent of its residents living in poverty. While Puerto Rico has a delegate in the US House of Representatives, Pedro Pierluisi, he does not vote; because Puerto Rico is not a state, it has no representation in the US Senate.

128. Half in Ten, "Interactive Map: Poverty Data by Congressional District"; US Census Bureau, *Fast Facts for Congress*, 2011, http://fastfacts.census.gov/home/cws /main.html.

129. For a detailed analysis of voting behavior and representation in minority communities, see John D. Griffin and Brian Newman, *Minority Report: Evaluating Political Equality in America* (Chicago: University of Chicago Press, 2008), especially pt. 2.

130. Dalton Conley, *Being Black, Living in the Red: Race, Wealth, and Social Policy in America*, 10th ed. (Berkeley: University of California Press, 2010), 157.

131. Ibid.

132. Shapiro, Meschede, and Sullivan, "Racial Wealth Gap Increases Fourfold," 2.

Chapter 3: Housing

1. Rachel G. Bratt, Michael E. Stone, and Chester Hartman, "Why a Right to Housing Is Needed and Makes Sense: Editors' Introduction," in *A Right to Housing: Foundation for a New Social Agenda*, ed. Rachel G. Bratt, Michael E. Stone, and Chester Hartman (Philadelphia: Temple University Press, 2006), 1.

2. Lauren J. and Robert L. Kaufman, "Housing and Wealth Inequality: Racial-Ethnic Differences in Home Equity in the United States," *Demography* 41, no. 3 (2004): 585–605.

3. Data from the 2010 census reveal that African Americans have been moving out of urban centers at high frequencies. For example, 89 percent of the net population loss in the city of Chicago between 2000 and 2010—more than 200,000 people—is attributable to African Americans leaving. Judy Keen, "Blacks' Exodus Reshapes Cities," *USA Today,* May 19, 2011, http://www.usatoday.com/news /nation/census/2011-05-20-chicago-blacks-exodus_n.htm.

4. US Census Bureau, "FFF: Hispanic Heritage Month 2015," September 14, 2015, http://www.census.gov/newsroom/facts-for-features/2015/cb15-ff18.html.

5. Pew Hispanic Center, "Latinos by Geography: Hispanic Population by County, 2009," 2011, http://pewhispanic.org/states/population/.

6. National Alliance to End Homelessness, "The State of Homelessness in America, 2016," http://www.endhomelessness.org/page/-/files/2016%20State%20Of%20 Homelessness.pdf.

7. Ellen L. Bassuk, Carmela J. DeCandia, Corey Anne Beach, and Fred Berman, "America's Youngest Outcasts: A Report Card on Child Homelessness," 2014, http:// www.air.org/sites/default/files/downloads/report/Americas-Youngest-Outcasts -Child-Homelessness-Nov2014.pdf.

8. Ibid.

9. National Alliance to End Homelessness, "The State of Homelessness in America, 2016."

10. "Chronic homelessness" refers "to those who have been continuously homeless for a year or more, or are experiencing at least their fourth episode of homelessness in three years." Dennis Culhane, "Five Myths About America's Homeless," *Washington Post,* July 11, 2010, http://www.washingtonpost.com/wp-dyn/content /article/2010/07/09/AR2010070902357.html.

11. National Alliance to End Homelessness, "Snapshot of Homelessness," 2016, http://www.endhomelessness.org/pages/snapshot_of_homelessness.

12. "Substance Abuse and Homelessness," National Coalition for the Homeless, July 2009, http://www.nationalhomeless.org/factsheets/addiction.pdf.

13. Dennis Culhane, "Five Myths About America's Homeless."

14. The US government placed both of these publicly traded entities into conservatorship in 2008 as stock prices plummeted with news of the impending crisis. David Ellis, "U.S. Seizes Fannie and Freddie," CNN Money, September 7, 2008, http:// money.cnn.com/2008/09/07/news/companies/fannie_freddie/index.htm.

15. US Department of Housing and Urban Development, "History," 2011, http:// portal.hud.gov/hudportal/HUD?src=/about/hud_history.

16. Paul D. Ballew, "Housing Bubble Burst: More Than Just Foreclosures," CNBC, August 4, 2011, http://www.cnbc.com/id/44022473.

17. Peter Coy, "'Real' Homeownership Rate at Nearly 50-Year Low," *Businessweek,* August 29, 2012, http://www.businessweek.com/articles/2012-08-29 /real-homeownership-rate-at-nearly-50-year-low.

18. Prashant Gopal, "Homeownership Rate in the U.S. Drops to Lowest Since 1965," Bloomberg, July 28, 2016, http://www.bloomberg.com/news/articles/2016-07-28 /homeownership-rate-in-the-u-s-tumbles-to-the-lowest-since-1965.

19. Adam Shell, Paul Davidson, and John Waggoner, "Finding Blame: Crisis in Inequality Panel Calls Recession Avoidable," *USA Today*, January 28, 2011, http://www.usatoday.com/printedition/money/20110128/crisisreport27_cv.art.htm.

20. Ibid. For an accessible yet thorough examination of the housing collapse, see *This American Life*, "The Giant Pool of Money," WBEZ Public Radio, May 9, 2008, http://www.thisamericanlife.org/radio-archives/episode/355/the-giant-pool-of-money.

21. US Department of Housing and Urban Development, Section 8 Program Background Information, 2011, http://portal.hud.gov/hudportal/HUD?src=/program _offices/housing/mfh/rfp/s8bkinfo.

22. Quoted in Kenneth J. Cooper, "Loans to Minorities Did Not Cause Housing Crisis, Study Finds," *Tribuna Connecticut*, February 16, 2011, http://www.tribunact.com/news/2011-02-16/News/Loans_to_minorities_did_not_cause_housing _crisis_s.html.

23. There is considerable evidence, however, that banks preyed on African Americans in particular in the midst of the housing boom. Wells Fargo bank, for instance, pushed African Americans who could have qualified for prime mortgage loans into subprime loans and doctored records to allow nonqualifying applicants to receive subprime loans. The bank was fined a record $85 million in the summer of 2011 as a result of these activities. Michael Powell, "Bank Accused of Pushing Mortgage Deals on Blacks," *New York Times*, June 6, 2009, http://www.nytimes .com/2009/06/07/us/07baltimore.html; Ben Rooney, "Fed Hits Wells Fargo with $85 million Fine," CNN Money, July 20, 2011, http://money.cnn.com/2011/07/20/news /companies/wells_fargo_fined/index.htm.

24. National Alliance to End Homelessness, "FAQs," 2016, http://www .endhomelessness.org/pages/faqs; Carol S. North and Elizabeth M. Smith, "Comparisons of White and Nonwhite Homeless Men and Women," *Social Work* 39, no. 6 (1994): 639–647; The US Conference of Mayors–Sodexho, Hunger and Homelessness Survey, 2006, December 2006, http://usmayors.org/hunger survey/2006/report06.pdf.

25. "Black Economic Gains Reversed in Great Recession, *USA Today*, July 9, 2011, http://usatoday30.usatoday.com/money/economy/2011-07-09-black -unemployment-recession_n.htm. It is estimated that African Americans lost $71 billion to $93 billion in home wealth value as a result of subprime loans between 1998 and 2006 (before the housing crash of 2008). Barbara Ehrenreich and Dedrick Muhammad, "The Recession's Racial Divide," *New York Times*, September 12, 2009, http://www .nytimes.com/2009/09/13/opinion/13ehrenreich.html.

26. Sharmila Choudhury, "Racial and Ethnic Differences in Wealth and Asset Choices," *Social Security Bulletin* 64, no. 4 2002, http://www.ssa.gov/policy/docs/ssb /v64n4/v64n4p1.html.

27. Sanjaya DeSilva and Yuval Elmelech, "Inequality in the United States: A Decomposition Analysis of Racial and Ethnic Disparities in Homeownership," Levy Economics Institute, Working Paper no. 565 (2009), 13.

28. The Joint Center for Housing Studies of Harvard University, "America's Rental Housing: Meeting Challenges, Building on Opportunities," 2011, http://www.jchs .harvard.edu/americas-rental-housing.

29. Joint Center for Housing Studies of Harvard University, "America's Rental Housing: Expanding Options for Diverse and Growing Demand," 2015, http://

www.jchs.harvard.edu/research/publications/americas-rental-housing-expanding
-options-diverse-and-growing-demand.

30. Ibid. 26.

31. Melvin L. Oliver and Thomas M. Shapiro, *Black Wealth/White Wealth: A New Perspective on Racial Inequality,* 10th ed. (New York: Routledge, 2006), 267.

32. John Eligon and Robert Gebeloff, "Affluent and Black, and Still Trapped by Segregation, *New York Times,* August 20, 2016, http://www.nytimes.com/2016/08/21/us/milwaukee-segregation-wealthy-black-families.html.

33. Douglas S. Massey, "Origins of Economic Disparities: Historical Roles of Housing Segregation," in *Segregation: The Rising Costs for America,* ed. James H. Carr and Nandinee K. Kutty (New York: Routledge, 2008), 39–80.

34. The Fair Housing Act was passed as part of the Civil Rights Act of 1968. Administered by the Department of Housing and Urban Development, it "prohibits discrimination in the sale, rental and financing of dwellings based on race, color, religion, sex or national origin." US Department of Housing and Urban Development, "Programs Administered by [Fair Housing and Equal Opportunity]: The Fair Housing Act," 2011, http://portal.hud.gov/hudportal/HUD?src=/program_offices/fair_housing_equal_opp/progdesc/title8.

35. Nancy A. Denton, "Segregation and Discrimination in Housing," in *A Right to Housing: Foundation for a New Social Agenda,* ed. Rachel G. Bratt, Michael E. Stone, and Chester Hartman (Philadelphia: Temple University Press, 2006), 61–81; Stephen Grant Meyer, *As Long as They Don't Move Next Door: Segregation and Racial Conflict in American Neighborhoods* (Lanham, MD: Rowman & Littlefield, 2000).

36. Massey, "Origins of Economic Disparities," 44.

37. Ibid.

38. Tukufu Zuberi, *Thicker Than Blood: How Racial Statistics Lie* (Minneapolis: University of Minnesota Press, 2003); Noel Ignatiev, *How the Irish Became White* (New York: Routledge, 1996), cited in Massey, "Origins of Economic Disparities," 49.

39. The concept of redlining has been expanded to corporate behavior. So-called retail redlining refers to the practice of avoiding locating retail establishments such as restaurants and stores in middle-class communities with a significant nonwhite population as a result of preconceived notions (based primarily on anecdotal evidence) of how racial minority residents will behave. Research from the University of Illinois has recently found some evidence for retail redlining practices. Emily Badger, "Retail Redlining: One of the Most Pervasive Forms of Racism Left in America?" *Atlantic,* April 17, 2013, http://www.theatlanticcities.com/neighborhoods/2013/04/retail-redlining-one-most-pervasive-forms-racism-left-america/5311.

40. Denton, "Segregation and Discrimination in Housing"; Preston H. Smith II, *Racial Democracy and the Black Metropolis* (Minneapolis: University of Minnesota Press, 2012).

41. David M. Freund, *Colored Property: State Policy and White Racial Politics in Suburban America* (Chicago: University of Chicago Press, 2007), chap. 1; Meyer, *As Long as They Don't Move Next Door.*

42. Massey, "Origins of Economic Disparities," 53–55.

43. Catherine Silva, "Racial Restrictive Covenants: Enforcing Neighborhood Segregation in Seattle," Seattle Civil Rights and Labor History Project, 2009, http://depts.washington.edu/civilr/covenants_report.htm.

44. Massey, "Origins of Economic Disparities."

45. Elizabeth Anderson and Jeffrey Jones, "Causes of Housing Segregation," The Geography of Race in the United States, University of Michigan, 2002, http://www.umich.edu/~lawrace/causes1.htm.

46. Emily Badger, "Watch These American Cities Segregate, Even as They Diversify," *Atlantic*, June 25, 2012, http://www.theatlanticcities.com/neighborhoods/2012/06/watch-these-us-cities-segregate-even-they-diversify/2346/; Ingrid Gould Ellen, *Sharing America's Neighborhoods: The Prospects for Stable Racial Integration* (Cambridge: Harvard University Press, 2000); Metropolitan Policy Program, *State of Metropolitan America: On the Front Lines of Demographic Transformation*, Brookings Institution, 2010, http://www.brookings.edu/~/media/Files/Programs/Metro/state_of_metro_america/metro_america_report.pdf, 46–49.

47. "Chicago Closes Cabrini-Green Project," *USA Today*, December 2, 2010, http://www.usatoday.com/news/nation/2010-12-01-cabrini-green_N.htm.

48. "Cabrini-Green," BlackHistory.com, January 23, 2008, http://www.blackhistory.com/cgi-bin/blog.cgi?blog_id=62103&cid=53.

49. Mary Schmich, "Last Residents Leave Cabrini-Green High-Rise," *Chicago Tribune*, December 1, 2010, http://articles.chicagotribune.com/2010-12-01/news/ct-met-schmich-1201-20101201_1_cabrini-green-burling-building-thousands-of-cabrini-residents.

50. Brentin Mock, "A Requiem for Chicago's Cabrini Green Housing Project," *Atlantic*: CityLab, June 17, 2016, http://www.citylab.com/housing/2016/06/a-documentary-on-cabrini-green-that-was-20-years-in-the-making/487445/; Alexandra Chachkevitch, "Door Shutting on Residents of Last Unrenoved Cabrini-Green Row Houses, *Chicago Tribune*, February 12, 2012, http://articles.chicagotribune.com/2012-02-16/news/ct-met-cabrini-green-rowhouses-20120216_1_row-houses-cabrini-green-residents-public-housing.

51. Eugene Robinson, *Disintegration: The Splintering of Black America* (New York: Doubleday, 2010).

52. Massey, "Origins of Economic Disparities."

53. Erik Wesley, "Poverty in Appalachia: Third World Living Conditions in America?" USAHM-News, August 2, 2011, https://usahitman.com/piatwlcia/.

54. The Appalachian Poverty Project, "Appalachian Poverty," n.d., http://www.app-pov-proj.org/igive.html.

55. Housing Assistance Council, "Poverty in Rural America," October, 2011, http://www.ruralhome.org/storage/documents/info_sheets/povertyamerica.pdf; US Department of Agriculture, "Rural Poverty at a Glance," Rural Development Research Report 100, July 2004, http://www.ers.usda.gov/publications/rdrr100/rdrr100.pdf; Economic Research Service, *Geography of Poverty*, November 7, 2012, http://www.ers.usda.gov/topics/rural-economy-population/rural-poverty-well-being/geography-of-poverty.aspx.

56. Housing Assistance Council, "Rural Poverty Decreases, Yet Remains Higher than the U.S. Poverty Rate," September 16, 2014, http://www.ruralhome.org/sct-information/mn-hac-research/rrn/990-official-poverty-rate-2014.

57. US Department of Agriculture, "Rural Poverty at a Glance."

58. Housing Assistance Council, "Poverty in Rural America."

59. U.S. Department of Agriculture, "Child Poverty," September 13, 2016, https://www.ers.usda.gov/topics/rural-economy-population/rural-poverty-well-being/child-poverty/.

60. See George Will, "Burning Down the House," *Washington Post*, July 1, 2011, http://www.washingtonpost.com/opinions/burning-down-the-house/2011/06/30/AGeRSGuH_story.html; Gretchen Morgenson and Joshua Rosner, *Reckless Endangerment: How Outsized Ambition, Greed, and Corruption Led to Economic Armageddon* (New York: Times Books, 2011). Will blames Democratic politicians, while Morgenson and Rosner describe a complex interplay between Washington insiders and Wall Street.

Chapter 4: Education

1. Deeptha Thattai, "A History of Public Education in the United States," *Journal of Literacy and Education in Developing Societies*, November, 2001, http://www.academia.edu/5177440/A_history_of_public_education_in_the_United_States.

2. Some slaves defied the rules and learned to read and write. For a comprehensive overview, see Heather Andrea Williams, *Self-Taught: African American Education in Slavery and Freedom* (Chapel Hill: University of North Carolina Press, 2005).

3. PBS, *From Swastika to Jim Crow: Historically Black College and Universities,* 2011, http://www.psfp.com/fsjc.htm; Carol D. Lee, "The State of Knowledge About the Education of African Americans," in *Black Education: A Transformative Research Action Agenda for the New Century,* ed. Joyce E. King (New York: Routledge, 2005), 45–71; Ron, "Education Prohibited." U.S. Slave, March 4, 2011, http://usslave.blogspot.com/2011/03/education-prohibited.html.

4. Thattai, "A History of Public Education in the United States."

5. Ibid.

6. Booker T. Washington, *Up from Slavery: An Autobiography* (New York: Doubleday, 1901). Full text available free online at http://www.bartleby.com/1004/; W. E. B. Du Bois, *The Souls of Black Folk* (Chicago: A. C. McClurg, 1903). Full text available online at http://www.bartleby.com/114/.

7. 163 US 537 (1896), http://www.law.cornell.edu/supct/html/historics/USSC_CR_0163_0537_ZS.html.

8. PBS, *From Swastika to Jim Crow.*

9. *Sweatt v. Painter*, 339 US 629 (1950), http://www.law.cornell.edu/supct/html/historics/USSC_CR_0339_0629_ZO.html.

10. 347 US 483 (1954), http://www.law.cornell.edu/supct/html/historics/USSC_CR_0347_0483_ZS.html.

11. *Sweatt v. Painter*, 633–634 (emphasis added).

12. *Brown v. Board of Education*, 495 (emphasis added).

13. Half of African American Chicago public school students attend schools that are characterized by extreme segregation: 90 percent or more of the students are African American. Even though black enrollment fell by 50,000 students between 1990 and 2010, the number of schools characterized by extreme segregation increased from 276 to 287 at the same time. The number of Hispanic students in Chicago attending racially isolated schools increased from twenty-six to eighty-four in those years.

Conversely, the number of integrated schools—where no one race comprises more than 50 percent of the student body—has decreased from 106 to 66 since 1990. Linda Lutton and Becky Vevea, "Greater Segregation for Region's Black, Latino Students," WBEZ Public Radio, June 27, 2012, http://www.wbez.org/series/race-out-loud /greater-segregation-regions-black-latino-students-100452.

14. Gary Orfield, "Reviving the Goal of an Integrated Society: A 21st Century Challenge," Civil Rights Project at UCLA, 2009, http://civilrightsproject.ucla .edu/research/k-12-education/integration-and-diversity/reviving-the-goal-of-an -integrated-society-a-21st-century-challenge/orfield-reviving-the-goal-mlk-2009 .pdf; Jacob L. Vigdor and Jens Ludwig, "Segregation and the Test Score Gap," in *Steady Gains and Stalled Progress: Inequality and the Black-White Test Score Gap*, ed. Katherine Magnuson and Jane Waldfogel (New York: Russell Sage Foundation, 2008), 181–211.

15. Richard Rothstein, *Class and Schools: Using Social, Economic, and Educational Reform to Close the Black-White Achievement Gap* (Washington, DC: Economic Policy Institute, 2004), 2.

16. For example, the average spending per student in New York in 2014 was $20,610, whereas in Idaho it was $6,621. U.S. Census Bureau, "Public Education Finances, 2014," U.S. Department of Commerce, June 2016, http://census.gov /content/dam/Census/library/publications/2016/econ/g14-aspef.pdf (Table 8). While this may reflect state priorities, the cost of living varies from place to place. In 2008, two largely rural states captured the ends of the continuum: Vermont spent the highest percentage of its taxable resources on education (5.5 percent), while South Dakota spent the least (2.8 percent). Dana Epstein, *Measuring Inequality in School Funding*, Center for American Progress, 2011, https://www.americanprogress.org /issues/education/reports/2011/08/03/10122/measuring-inequity-in-school-funding/.

17. Emma Brown, "In 23 States, Richer School Districts Get More Local Funding Than Poorer Districts," *Washington Post*, March 12, 2015, https://www.washingtonpost .com/news/local/wp/2015/03/12/in-23-states-richer-school-districts-get-more -local-funding-than-poorer-districts/?utm_term=.8731d75f1367.

18. The report is available at http://www2.ed.gov/pubs/NatAtRisk/index.html.

19. George Ansalone, *Exploring Unequal Achievement in the Schools: The Social Construction of Failure* (Lanham, MD: Lexington, 2009); Katherine Magnuson and Jane Waldfogel, eds., *Steady Gains and Stalled Progress: Inequality and the Black-White Test Score Gap* (New York: Russell Sage Foundation, 2008).

20. Eric A. Hanushek, "What Matters for Student Achievement," *Education Next* 16, no. 2 (Spring 2016), http://educationnext.org/what-matters-for-student-achievement/.

21. The values in the data presented in the first three bullet points do not refer to percentages but raw scores on a standardized achievement test.

22. Trymaine Lee, "Educational Racial Gap Wide as Ever, According to NAEP," MSNBC, May 7, 2014, http://www.msnbc.com/msnbc/student-proficiency-stagnant -race-gap-wide.

23. Cadelle F. Hemphill and Alan Vanneman, "Achievement Gaps: How Hispanic and White Students in Public Schools Perform in Mathematics and Reading on the National Assessment of Educational Progress," 2011, http://nces.ed.gov /nationsreportcard/pdf/studies/2011459.pdf.

24. Alan Vanneman, Linda Hamilton, and Janet Baldwin Anderson, "Achievement Gaps: How Black and White Students in Public Schools Perform in Mathematics and Reading on the National Assessment of Educational Progress," 2009, http://nces .ed.gov/nationsreportcard/pdf/studies/2009455.pdf.

25. Center for Civil Rights Remedies, *A Summary of New Research: Closing the School Discipline Gap: Research to Policy,* Civil Rights Project at UCLA, January 10, 2013, http://civilrightsproject.ucla.edu/events/2013/summary-of-new-research -closing-the-school-discipline-gap-research-to-policy/Research_Summary_Closing _the_School_Discipline_Gap.pdf.

26. Wayne Au, *Unequal by Design: High-Stakes Testing and the Standardization of Inequality* (New York: Routledge, 2009); Ruth S. Johnson, *Using Data to Close the Achievement Gap: How to Measure Equality in Our Schools* (Thousand Oaks, CA: Corwin, 2002); Pauline Lipman, *High Stakes Education: Inequality, Globalization, and Urban School Reform* (New York: Routledge Falmer, 2004); Gary Orfield and Mindy L. Kornhaber, eds., *Raising Standards or Raising Barriers? Inequality and High-Stakes Testing in Public Education* (New York: Century Foundation Press, 2001).

27. William Hayes, *No Child Left Behind: Past, Present, and Future* (Lanham, MD: Rowman & Littlefield, 2008); Paul E. Peterson and Martin R. West, *No Child Left Behind? The Politics and Practice of School Accountability* (Washington, DC: Brookings Institution Press, 2003).

28. US Department of Education, No Child Left Behind, 2011, http://www2 .ed.gov/nclb/landing.jhtml.

29. Valerie Strauss, "No Child Left Behind: What Standardized Test Scores Reveal About Its Legacy," *Washington Post,* March 10, 2015, https://www.washingtonpost. com/news/answer-sheet/wp/2015/03/10/no-child-left-behind-what-standardized -test-scores-reveal-about-its-legacy/.

30. Alliance for Excellent Education, "Everything You Need to Know About the Every Student Succeeds Act," n.d., http://all4ed.org/essa/.

31. Linda Darling-Hammond, "New Standards and Old Inequalities: School Reform and the Education of African American Students," in *Black Education: A Transformative Research and Action Agenda for the New Century,* ed. Joyce E. King (New York: Routledge, 2005), 197–223.

32. Roy O. Freedle, "Correcting the SAT's Ethnic and Social-Class Bias: A Method for Reestimating SAT Scores," *Harvard Educational Review* 73, no. 1 (2003): 1–43; Christopher Jencks and Meredith Phillips, eds., *The Black-White Test Score Gap* (Washington, DC: Brookings Institution Press, 1998); MariaVeronica Santelices and Mark Wilson, "Unfair Treatment? The Case of Freedle, the SAT, and the Standardization Approach to Differential Item Functioning," *Harvard Educational Review* 80, no. 1 (2010): 106–134.

33. Donald C. Orlich and Glenn Gifford, "Test Scores, Poverty, and Ethnicity: The New American Dilemma" (paper presented at the annual meeting of Phi Delta Kappa, 2006), http://www.cha.wa.gov/?q=files/Highstakestesting_poverty_ethnicity.pdf.

34. Michelle Florence, Mark Asbridge, and Paul J. Veugelers, "Diet Quality and Academic Performance," *Journal of School Health* 78, no. 4 (2008): 209–215; Diana F. Jyoti, Edward A. Frongillo, and Sonya J. Jones, "Food Insecurity Affects School Children's Academic Performance, Weight Gain, and Social Skills," *Journal of*

Nutrition 135, no. 12 (2005): 2831–2839; R. E. Kleinman et al., "Diet, Breakfast, and Academic Performance in Children," *Annals of Nutrition & Metabolism* 46 suppl. 1 (2002): 24–30; Michael Murphy et al., "The Relationship of School Breakfast to Psychosocial and Academic Functioning: Cross-sectional and Longitudinal Observations in an Inner-City School Sample," *Archives of Pediatrics & Adolescent Medicine* 152, no. 9 (1998): 899–907.

35. Natasha K. Bowen and Gary L. Bowen, "Effects of Crime and Violence in Neighborhoods and Schools on the School Behavior and Performance of Adolescents," *Journal of Adolescent Research* 14, no. 3 (1999): 319–342; Camille Z. Charles, Gniesha Dinwiddle, and Douglas S. Massey, "The Continuing Consequences of Segregation: Family Stress and College Academic Performance," *Social Science Quarterly* 85, no. 5 (2004): 1353–1373; Johnnie Lassiter Dyson, "The Effect of Family Violence on Children's Academic Performance and Behavior," *Journal of the National Medical Association* 82, no. 1 (1990): 17–22; Shumow Lee, Deborah Lowe Vandell, and Jill Posner, "Risk and Resilience in the Urban Neighborhood: Predictors of Academic Performance Among Low-Income Elementary School Children," *Merrill-Palmer Quarterly* 45, no. 2 (1999): 309–331; P. David Kurtz, John S. Wodarski, and Phyllis T. Howing, "Maltreatment and the School-Aged Child: School Performance Consequences," *Child Abuse and Neglect* 17, no. 7 (1992): 581–589.

36. Michael Winerip, "In Public School Efforts, a Common Background: Private Education, *New York Times*, April 17, 2011, http://www.nytimes.com/2011/04/18 /education/18winerip.html.

37. Institute of Education Sciences, "Percentage of high school dropouts among persons 16 to 24 years old (status dropout rate), by sex and race/ethnicity: Selected years, 1960 through 2014," 2015, https://nces.ed.gov/programs/digest/d15/tables /dt15_219.70.asp. For a scholarly analysis of the converging factors that contribute to gaps in graduation rates, see Heather L. Storer et al., "Moving Beyond Dichotomies: How the Intersection of Race, Class, and Place Impacts High School Graduation Rates for African American Students," *Journal of Sociology and Social Welfare* 39, no. 1 (2012): 17–44, http://www.wmich.edu/hhs/newsletters_journals/jssw_institutional /institutional_subscribers/39.1.Storer.pdf.

38. Evan Soltas, "Intergenerational Inequality," Economics and Thought, March 21, 2013, http://esoltas.blogspot.com/2013/03/intergenerational-inequality. html, as cited in Charles Kenny, "How Did the World's Rich Get That Way? Luck," Bloomberg Businessweek, April 22, 2013, http://www.businessweek.com /articles/2013-04-22/how-did-the-worlds-rich-get-that-way-luck.

39. While this figure is important, the often repeated claim that more African American men are in prison than in college has been challenged recently by new data. Howard University psychology professor Ivory Toldson reports that there are approximately 600,000 more African American men in college than in prison. The top ten institutions enrolling black men include "three for-profit institutions [e.g., the University of Phoenix], four community colleges, and three public four-year institutions." Ivory A. Toldson, "More Black Men in Jail Than College? Wrong," The Root, February 28, 2013, http://www.theroot.com/views /more-black-men-jail-college-wrong.

40. Neil Shah, "Smaller Share of High School Grads Going to College," Real Time Economics, April 17, 2013, http://blogs.wsj.com/economics/2013/04/17/smaller-share-of-high-school-grads-going-to-college/.

41. Emily Jane Fox, "College Enrollment Rate Surges for Black High School Grads," CNN Money, April 16, 2015, http://money.cnn.com/2015/04/16/pf/college/college-enrollment-race/.

42. Sean F. Reardon, Rachel Baker, and Daniel Klasik, *Race, Income, and Enrollment Patterns in Highly Selective Colleges, 1982–2004*, Center for Education Policy Analysis, Stanford University, August 3, 2012, http://cepa.stanford.edu/sites/default/files/race%20income%20%26%20selective%20college%20enrollment%20august%203%202012.pdf.

43. V. J. Taylor and G. M. Walton, "Stereotype Threat Undermines Academic Learning," *Personal and Social Psychology Bulletin* 37, no. 8 (2011): 1055–1067, at 1055.

44. Pedro A. Noguera and Antwi Akom, "The Significance of Race in the Racial Gap in Academic Achievement," In Motion, 2000, http://www.inmotionmagazine.com/pnaa.html.

45. Daniel J. Losen and Jonathan Gillespie, *Opportunities Suspended: The Disparate Impact of Disciplinary Exclusion from School*, Civil Rights Project at UCLA, August 7, 2012, http://civilrightsproject.ucla.edu/resources/projects/center-for-civil-rights-remedies/school-to-prison-folder/federal-reports/upcoming-ccrr-research.

46. Walter S. Gilliam, Angela N. Maupin, Chin R. Reyes, Maria Accavitti, and Frederick Shic, "Do Early Educators' Implicit Biases Regarding Sex and Race Relate to Behavior Expectations and Recommendations of Preschool Expulsions and Suspensions?" Yale University Child Study Center, September 28, 2016, http://ziglercenter.yale.edu/publications/Preschool%20Implicit%20Bias%20Policy%20Brief_final_9_26_276766_5379.pdf.

47. Noguera and Akom, "The Significance of Race."

48. The gap for bachelor's degrees between whites and blacks and Latinos of both genders is larger today than in the 1960s and 1970s. American Council on Education, "College Gender Gap Appears to be Stabilizing with One Notable Exception, American Council on Education Finds," January 26, 2010, http://affirmact.blogspot.com/2010/01/college-gender-gap-appears-to-be.html; NewsOne, "The Winners and Losers in Minority Graduation Rate Gaps," August 12, 2010, http://newsone.com/nation/newsonestaff4/the-winners-and-losers-in-minority-graduation-rate-gaps/; Boyce Watkins, "Why Aren't Black Men Graduating from College?" NewsOne, April 7, 2010, http://newsone.com/nation/boycewatkins/dr-boyce-why-arent-black-men-graduating-from-college/.

49. Andrew Howard Nichols, Kimberee Eberle-Sudre, and Meredith Welch, "Rising Tide II: Do Black Students Benefit as Grad Rates Increase?" The Education Trust, March 2016, https://edtrust.org/wp-content/uploads/2014/09/RisingTide_II_EdTrust.pdf.

50. Peter Orszag, "The Diploma Gap Between Rich and Poor," Bloomberg, March 5, 2013, http://www.bloomberg.com/news/2013-03-05/the-diploma-gap-between-rich-and-poor.html, citing Martha J. Bailey and Susan M. Dynarski, "Gains and Gaps:

Changing Inequality in U.S. College Entry and Completion," National Bureau of Economic Research, NBER Working Paper no. 17633, http://www.nber.org/papers/w17633.pdf.

51. Ibid.

52. Jonathan P. Hicks, "Graduation Rates Increase at HBCUs," BET, April 22, 2013, http://www.bet.com/news/national/2013/04/22/graduation-rates-increase-at-hbcus.html.

53. Jon Valant and Daniel A. Newark, "The Politics of Achievement Gaps: U.S. Public Opinion on Race-Based and Wealth-Based Differences in Test Scores," *Educational Researcher* 46, no. 6 (2016): 1–16 (online first).

54. For a critique of this rationale, see Jonathan Kozol, *The Shame of the Nation: The Restoration of Apartheid Schooling in America* (New York: Three Rivers Press, 2005). Kozol notes that "some people who [are reluctant to throw money at failing schools], while they live in wealthy districts where schools are funded at high levels, don't send their children to these public schools but choose instead to send them to expensive private day-schools. . . . so they may be spending over $60,000 on their children's education every year. Yet here I am one night, a guest within their home, and dinner has been served and we are having coffee now; and this entirely likable, and generally sensible, and beautifully refined and thoughtful person looks me in the eyes and asks me whether you can really buy your way to better education for the children of the poor" (p. 57).

55. Dorie Turner, "School Voucher Bills Flood GOP-Led Statehouses," August 2, 2011, http://www.edchoice.org/Newsroom/News/AP-School-Voucher-Bills-Flood-GOP-led-Statehouses.aspx.

56. Kevin Huffman, "A Rosa Parks Moment for Education," *Washington Post*, January 31, 2011, http://www.washingtonpost.com/wp-dyn/content/article/2011/01/30/AR2011013003556.html.

57. Teachers unions and progressive activists, while moved by the film, feel that it represented teachers and teachers unions, rather than larger systemic pressures, as obstacles to quality education. Further, they argue that charter schools are not all successful. Dana Goldstein, "Grading 'Waiting for Superman,'" *Nation*, September 23, 2010, http://www.thenation.com/article/154986/grading-waiting-superman.

58. Kate Zernike, "Condemnation of Charter Schools Exposes a Rift Over Black Students," *New York Times*, August 20, 2016, http://www.nytimes.com/2016/08/21/us/blacks-charter-schools.html.

59. Goldstein, "Grading 'Waiting for Superman.'"

Chapter 5: Crime and Criminal Justice

1. James Madison, "Federalist 51: The Structure of the Government Must Furnish the Proper Checks and Balances Between the Different Departments," https://www.congress.gov/resources/display/content/The+Federalist+Papers#TheFederalist Papers-51.

2. Robert Costa, Lindsey Bever, J. Fredom du Lac, and Sari Horwitz, "Church Shooting Suspect Dylann Roof Captured amid Hate Crime Investigation," *Washington Post*, June 18, 2015, https://www.washingtonpost.com/news/morning

-mix/wp/2015/06/17/white-gunman-sought-in-shooting-at-historic-charleston
-african-ame-church/?postshare=2131434616717681&utm_term=.59049c4e168f.

3. Dustin Waters and Mark Berman, "Dylann Roof Found Guilty on All Counts in Charleston Church Massacre Trial," *Washington Post*, December 15, 2016, https://www.washingtonpost.com/news/post-nation/wp/2016/12/15/jurors-begin-deliberating-in-charleston-church-shooting-trial/?utm_term=.0614333c3472.

4. Jessica Lussenhop, "US Election 2016: Trump and His Central Park Five Defiance," BBC News, October 12, 2016, http://www.bbc.com/news/election-us-2016-37614095.

5. Ibid.

6. David K. Shipler, "Why Do Innocent People Confess?" *New York Times*, February 23, 2012, http://www.nytimes.com/2012/02/26/opinion/sunday/why-do-innocent-people-confess.html.

7. Herbert L. Packer, "Two Models of the Criminal Process," *University of Pennsylvania Law Review*, 113 no. 1 (1964). Available at http://scholarship.law.upenn.edu/penn_law_review/vol113/iss1/1.

8. Ibid.

9. 430 U.S. 387 (1977).

10. "What Happened in Ferguson?" *New York Times*, August 10, 2015, http://www.nytimes.com/interactive/2014/08/13/us/ferguson-missouri-town-under-siege-after-police-shooting.html.

11. Julie Bosman and Joseph Goldstein, "Timeline for a Body: 4 Hours in the Middle of a Ferguson Street," *New York Times*, August 23, 2014, https://www.nytimes.com/2014/08/24/us/michael-brown-a-bodys-timeline-4-hours-on-a-ferguson-street.html.

12. Niraj Chokshi, "How #BlackLivesMatter Came to Define a Movement," *New York Times*, August 22, 2016, https://www.nytimes.com/2016/08/23/us/how-blacklivesmatter-came-to-define-a-movement.html.

13. Daniel Victor, "Why 'All Lives Matter' Is Such a Perilous Phrase," *New York Times*, July 15, 2016, http://www.nytimes.com/2016/07/16/us/all-lives-matter-black-lives-matter.html.

14. Mark Martin, "'Blue Lives Matter' Speaks Out After Four Officers Shot in 24 Hours," CBN News, November 22, 2016, http://www1.cbn.com/cbnnews/us/2016/november/blue-lives-matter-speaks-out-after-four-officers-shot-in-24-hours.

15. Kimberly Kindy and Kimbriell Kelly, "Thousands Dead, Few Prosecuted," *Washington Post*, April 11, 2015, http://www.washingtonpost.com/sf/investigative/2015/04/11/thousands-dead-few-prosecuted/.

16. Jonah Engel Bromwich, "White and Black Police Officers Are Sharply Divided About Race, Pew Finds," *New York Times*, January 11, 2017, https://mobile.nytimes.com/2017/01/11/us/police-officers-pew-poll.html.

17. Jonah Engel Bromwich," White and Black Police Officers Are Sharply Divided About Race."

18. William T. L. Cox and Patricia G. Devine, "Experimental Research on Shooter Bias: Ready (or Relevant) Application in the Courtroom?" *Journal of Applied Research in Memory and Cognition* 5 (2016): 236–238.

19. Wesley Lowery, "Study Finds Police Fatally Shoot Unarmed Black Men at Disproportionate Rates," *Washington Post*, April 7, 2016, https://www.washingtonpost .com/national/study-finds-police-fatally-shoot-unarmed-black-men-at-dispro portionate-rates/2016/04/06/e494563e-fa74-11e5-80e4-c381214de1a3_story.html.

20. Michelle Ye Hee Lee, "Yes, U.S. Locks People Up at a Higher Rate Than Any Other Country," *Washington Post*, July 7, 2015, https://www.washingtonpost.com /news/fact-checker/wp/2015/07/07/yes-u-s-locks-people-up-at-a-higher-rate-than -any-other-country/?utm_term=.2e1cee2cbf11.

21. Danielle Kaeble and Lauren Glaze, "Correctional Populations in the United States, 2015," US Department of Justice, December 2016, https://www.bjs.gov /content/pub/pdf/cpus15.pdf.

22. Ibid.

23. Jeff Guo, "America Has Locked Up So Many Black People It Has Warped Our Sense of Reality," *Washington Post*, February 26, 2016, https://www.washingtonpost. com/news/wonk/wp/2016/02/26/america-has-locked-up-so-many-black-people-it -has-warped-our-sense-of-reality/?utm_term=.578ab93a37d1.

24. "Incarceration Rates by Race, Ethnicity, and Gender in the U.S.," WorldAtlas, July 13, 2016, http://www.worldatlas.com/articles/incarceration-rates-by-race -ethnicity-and-gender-in-the-u-s.html.

25. Ibid.

26. Snejana Farberov, "Chicago Decriminalizes Possession of Small Amounts of Pot," *Daily Mail*, June 27, 2012, http://www.dailymail.co.uk/news /article-2165805/Chicago-decriminalizes-possession-small-amounts-pot-caught -puffing-joint-arrested.html?ito=feeds-newsxml. With respect to racial disparities in misdemeanor drug arrests in New York City, see Andrew Golub, Bruce D. Johnson, and Eloise Dunlap, "The Race/Ethnicity Disparity in Misdemeanor Marijuana Arrests in New York City," *Criminology and Public Policy* 6, no. 1 (2007): 131–164.

27. Marc Mauer and David Cole, "Five Myths About Americans in Prison," *Washington Post*, June 17, 2011, http://www.washingtonpost.com/opinions/five -myths-about-incarceration/2011/06/13/AGfIWvYH_story.html. For updated data relating to this trend, see C. Eugene Emery, Jr., "Van Jones Claim on Drug Use, Imprisonment Rates for Blacks, Whites Is Mostly Accurate," Politifact, July 13, 2016, http://www.politifact.com/punditfact/statements/2016/jul/13/van-jones/van -jones-claim-drug-use-imprisonment-rates-blacks/.

28. Nearly 6 million Americans (one out of forty adults and nearly 7.7 percent of African American adults) are prohibited from voting because they have been convicted of a felony. In eleven states, individuals lose voting rights forever after being convicted. Christopher Uggen, Sarah Shannon, and Jeff Manza, "State-Level Estimates of Felon Disenfranchisement in the United States, 2010," The Sentencing Project, July 2012, http://www.sentencingproject.org/doc/publications/fd_State _Level_Estimates_of_Felon_Disen_2010.pdf. Forty-eight states and the District of Columbia prohibit voting during incarceration, thirty states prohibit those who are on parole or probation from voting, and five prohibit voting by parolees. Hatty Lee and Jamilah King, "America's Millions of Disenfranchised, Largely Black Voters,"

Colorlines, November 2, 2010, http://colorlines.com/archives/2010/11/restoring
_the_vote_for_14million_disenfranchised_black_men.html.

29. Ibid.

30. Racial disparities in pretrial release decisions for drug offenders have been found as well. Tina L. Freiburger, Catherine D. Marcum, and Mari Pierce, "The Impact of Race on the Pretrial Decision,"*American Journal of Criminal Justice* 35 (2010): 76–86.

31. US Department of Justice, Table 43A: Arrests by Race, 2015, Crime in the United States, 2015, https://ucr.fbi.gov/crime-in-the-u.s/2015/crime-in-the -u.s.-2015/tables/table-43. See also Katherine Beckett, Kris Nyrop, and Lori Pfingst, "Race, Drugs, and Policing: Understanding Disparities in Drug Delivery Arrests," *Criminology* 44 no. 1 (2006): 105–137; Gary LaFree, Eric P. Baumer, and Robert O'Brien, "Still Separate and Unequal? A City-Level Analysis of the Black-White Gap in Homicide Arrests Since 1960," *American Sociological Review* 75 (2010): 75–100.

32. See, for instance, Marisol Bello and Kevin Johnson, "Racial Profiling Debate Not Over," *USA Today*, July 23, 2009, http://www.usatoday.com/news/nation/2009 -07-22-racial_N.htm; Gene Callahan and William Anderson, "The Roots of Racial Profiling: Why Are Police Targeting Minorities for Traffic Stops?" Reason.com, August-September 2001, http://reason.com/archives/2001/08/01/the-roots-of-racial -profiling; Will Guzzardi, "Illinois State Police Racial Bias: New Studies Show Trend of Discrimination Continued Last Year," Huffington Post, July 13, 2011, http:// www.huffingtonpost.com/2011/07/13/illinois-state-police-rac_n_897551.html; University of Minnesota Law School, *Racial Profiling Data Collection Status Report,* 2000, http://www1.umn.edu/irp/publications/ARB/ARB%20.html; and the Racial Profiling Data Collection Resource Center at Northeastern University, http://www .racialprofilinganalysis.neu.edu.

33. Researchers have found that Americans disproportionately fear being subject to violent crime (or street crime), as opposed to white-collar crime, even though white-collar crime results in greater financial losses. See Randall A. Gordon et al., "Perceptions of Blue-Collar and White-Collar Crime: The Effect of Defendant Race on Simulated Juror Decisions," *Journal of Social Psychology* 128, no. 2 (1998): 191–197; Kristy Holtfreter et al., "Public Perceptions of White-Collar Crime and Punishment," *Journal of Criminal Justice* 36, no. 1 (2008): 50–60; Jeffrey Reiman and Paul Leighton, *The Rich Get Richer and the Poor Get Prison,* 9th ed. (Upper Saddle River, NJ: Prentice Hall, 2009); Robert L. Young, "Perceptions of Crime, Racial Attitudes, and Firearms Ownership," *Social Forces* 64, no. 2 (1985): 473–486. See also David O. Friedrichs, *Trusted Criminals: White Collar Crime in Contemporary Society,* 4th ed. (Belmont, CA: Wadsworth, 2010); Stuart A. Scheingold, *The Politics of Street Crime: Criminal Process and Cultural Obsession* (Philadelphia: Temple University Press, 1991). It is worth noting that there are racial disparities with respect to presidential pardons as well, with white convicts nearly four times more likely to be pardoned than persons of color. Dafina Linzer and Jennifer LaFleur, "Presidential Pardons Heavily Favor Whites," Propublica, December 3, 2011, http://www.propublica.org/article/shades -of-mercy-presidential-forgiveness-heavily-favors-whites.

34. In the winter of 2013, Supreme Court Justice Sonia Sotomayor publicly criticized a prosecutor who questioned an African American defendant as follows: "You've got African Americans, you've got Hispanics, you've got a bag full of money. Does that tell you—a light bulb doesn't go off in your head and say, this is a drug deal?" Sotomayor called the statement "pernicious in its attempt to substitute racial stereotype for evidence." Lawrence Hurley, "Sonia Sotomayor Condemns Prosecutor's Racially Charged Question," Huffington Post, February 25, 2013, http://www.huffingtonpost.com/2013/02/25/sonia-sotomayor-prosecutor_n_2759273.html.

35. Peter Dreier, "How the Media Compound Urban Problems," *Journal of Urban Affairs* 27, no. 2 (2005): 193–201; Robert Elias, "Official Stories: Media Coverage of American Crime Policy," *Humanist* 54, no. 1 (1994): 5–10; Steve Macek, *Urban Nightmares: The Media, the Right, and the Moral Panic Over the City* (Minneapolis: University of Minnesota Press, 2006).

36. Justin T. Pickett, Ted Chiricos, Kristin M. Golden, and Marc Gertz, "Reconsidering the Relationship between Perceived Neighborhood Racial Composition and Whites' Perceptions of Victimization Risk: Do Racial Stereotypes Matter?" *Criminology* 50 no. 1 (2012): 145–186.

37. Matthew Cella and Alan Neuhauser, "Race and Homicide in America, by the Numbers," *U.S. News and World Report*, September 29, 2016, http://www.usnews.com/news/articles/2016-09-29/race-and-homicide-in-america-by-the-numbers.

38. Alfred S. Regnery, "Black on Black Crime: Blame It on the System and Ignore the Evidence," Breitbart, May 24, 2016, http://www.breitbart.com/big-government/2016/05/24/black-black-crime-blame-system-ignore-evidence/.

39. In February 2012 Trayvon Martin, an African American teenager, was shot by a neighborhood watch captain who was white and Latino in Sanford, Florida. The case put racial profiling in the spotlight. Research related to such profiling became salient because studies have demonstrated that people are more likely to assume that an object in the hand of an African American is a gun than if the same poorly seen object is held by someone who is white. Malcolm Ritter, "Trayvon Martin Case: Study Shows Holding a Gun May Make You Think Others Are Too," Huffington Post, March 20, 2012, http://www.huffingtonpost.com/2012/03/20/trayvon-martin-case-study_n_1368524.html, citing Jessica K. Witt and James R. Brockmole, "Action Alters Object Identification: Wielding a Gun Increases the Bias to See Guns," *Journal of Experimental Psychology* 38, no. 5 (2012): 1159–1167. See also Joshua Correll, Geoffrey R. Urland, and Tiffany A. Ito, "Event-Related Potentials and the Decision to Shoot: The Role of Threat Perception and Cognitive Control," *Journal of Experimental and Social Psychology* 42, no. 1 (2006): 120–128; Anthony G. Greenwald, Mark A. Oakes, and Hunter G. Hoffman, "Targets of Discrimination: Effects of Race on Responses to Weapons Holders," *Journal of Experimental and Social Psychology* 39, no. 4 (2003): 399–405; Keith B. Payne, "Prejudice and Perception: The Role of Automatic and Controlled Processes in Misperceiving a Weapon," *Journal of Personality and Social Psychology* 81, no. 2 (2001): 181–192.

40. Devah Pager, *Marked: Race, Crime, and Finding Work in an Era of Mass Incarceration* (Chicago: University of Chicago Press, 2007), cited in Seth Wessler, "Race and Recession: How Inequality Rigged the Economy and How to Change the

Rules," Applied Research Center, May 2009, http://arc.org/downloads/2009_race _recession_0909.pdf, 23.

41. Devah Pager, "The Mark of a Criminal Record," *American Journal of Sociology* 108, no. 5 (2003): 937–975.

42. Groups include Temporary Assistance for Needy Families (TANF) recipients, veterans, food stamp recipients, individuals living in a designated empowerment zone or rural renewal county, sixteen- and seventeen-year-olds working during the summer, disabled persons working with vocational rehabilitation referral agencies, former felons, and individuals who have recently received Supplemental Social Security Income benefits. US Department of Labor, *The Work Opportunity Tax Credit (WOTC) $olution*, 2011, http://www.doleta.gov/business/incentives/opptax/PDF /WOTC_Program_ARRA_Brochure.pdf. Some credits are a flat rate and vary from $1,200 per hire (for summer youth) to $9,000 per hire for long-term TANF recipients. Others, such as the credit for hiring ex-felons, are a percentage of wages on a sliding scale; if the employee works more than four hundred hours in a year, the employer receives a 40 percent credit (capped at $6,000). US Department of Labor, "Employers: 8 Ways to Earn Income Tax Credits for Your Company," 2011, http://www.doleta .gov/business/incentives/opptax/PDF/WOTC_Fact_Sheet_new.pdf.

43. US Department of Labor, Federal Bonding Program, 2011, http://www .bonds4jobs.com/.

44. US Department of Labor, Workforce Professionals, 2011, http://www.doleta .gov/usworkforce/.

45. "Marijuana Legalization and Decriminalization Overview," FindLaw.com, n.d., http://criminal.findlaw.com/criminal-charges/marijuana-legalization-and -decriminalization-overview.html.

46. For a thoughtful overview, see Jonathan Rothwell, "Drug Offenders in American Prisons: The Critical Distinction between Stock and Flow," The Brookings Institution, November 25, 2015, https://www.brookings.edu/blog/social-mobility -memos/2015/11/25/drug-offenders-in-american-prisons-the-critical-distinction -between-stock-and-flow/.

Chapter 6: Immigration and Employment

1. US Bureau of Labor Statistics, Employment Status of the Civilian Noninstitutional Population by Race, Hispanic or Latino Ethnicity, Sex, and Age (Table A-15), 2009, http://www.bls.gov/web/empsit.supp.toc.htm.

2. US Bureau of Labor Statistics, "Employment Situation Summary," 2011, http:// www.bls.gov/news.release/empsit.nr0.htm.

3. Corey Dade, "Government Job Cuts Threaten Black Middle Class," National Public Radio, May 9, 2012, http://www.npr.org/2012/05/09/152297370 /government-job-cuts-threaten-black-middle-class.

4. US Bureau of Labor Statistics, "Labor Force Statistics from the Current Population Survey," October 7, 2016, http://www.bls.gov/web/empsit/cpsee_e16.htm.

5. Sylvia Allegretto and Devon Lynch, "The Composition of the Unemployed and Long-Term Unemployed in Tough Labor Markets," October, 2010, http://www.bls .gov/opub/mlr/2010/10/art1full.pdf.

6. Ibid.

7. In 2002, as a result of a suit brought by the Equal Employment Opportunity Commission, Target employees responsible for screening applicants at job fairs in the Milwaukee area admitted to routinely destroying applications from African Americans. Devah Pager, "The Use of Field Experiments for Studies of Employment Discrimination: Contributions, Critiques, and Directions for the Future," *Annals of the American Academy of Political and Social Science* 609 (2007): 104–133, at 104–105.

8. Ibid.

9. For an accessible overview of recent studies about unconscious biases that complements the scholarly articles found in the endnotes from the Introduction, see Keith Payne, "What Your Brain Won't Let You See," Salon.com, June 13, 2013, http://www.salon.com/2013/06/13/what_your_mind_wont_let_you_see_partner/.

10. See, for instance, Marianne Bertrand and Sendhil Mullainathan, "Are Emily and Greg More Employable than Lakisha and Jamal? A Field Experiment on Labor Market Discrimination," *American Economic Review* 94, no. 4 (2004): 991–1013.

11. Ibid., 992.

12. Laura Giuliano, David I. Levine, and Jonathan Leonard, "Manager Race and the Race of New Hires," *Journal of Labor Economics* 27, no. 4 (2009): 589–631.

13. John J. Beggs, Wayne J. Villemez, and Ruth Arnold, "Black Population Concentration and Black-White Inequality: Expanding the Consideration of Place and Space Effects," *Social Forces* 76 (1997): 65–91.

14. Matt L. Huffman and Philip N. Cohen, "Racial Wage Inequality: Job Segregation and Devaluation across U.S. Labor Markets," *American Journal of Sociology* 109, no. 4 (2004): 902–936, at 928–929.

15. See Hurbert M. Blalock, *Towards a Theory of Minority Group Relations* (New York: Wiley, 1967); Mark A. Fossett and K. J. Kiecolt., "The Relative Size of Minority Populations and White Racial Attitudes," *Social Science Research* 70 (1989): 820–835.

16. Tricia McTague, Kevin Stainback, and Donald Tomaskovic-Devey, "An Organizational Approach to Understanding Sex and Race Segregation in U.S. Workplaces," *Social Forces* 87, no. 3 (2009): 1499–1527; Kevin Stainback, Corre L. Robinson, and Donald Tomaskovic-Devey, "Race and Workplace Integration," *American Behavioral Scientist* 48, no. 9 (2005): 1200–1228; Donald Tomaskovic-Devey, *Gender and Racial Inequality at Work: The Sources and Consequences of Job Segregation* (New York: ILR Press, 1993).

17. Douglas S. Massey, "Origins of Economic Disparities: Historical Roles of Housing Segregation," in *Segregation: The Rising Costs for America*, ed. James H. Carr and Nandinee K. Kutty (New York: Routledge, 2008), 39–80.

18. On the surface, this is not an issue of race or ethnicity but of poverty. However, racial and ethnic housing segregation once again challenges us to consider the disproportionate effect on African Americans and Latinos.

19. Don Hirasuna and Joel Michael, "Enterprise Zones: A Review of the Economic Theory and Empirical Evidence," January 2005, http://www.house.leg.state.mn.us/hrd/pubs/entzones.pdf.

20. Steve McDonald, Nan Lin, and Dan Ao, "Networks of Opportunity: Gender, Race, and Job Leads," *Social Problems* 56, no. 3 (2009): 385–402.

21. Niki T. Dickerson, "Black Employment, Segregation, and the Social Organization of Metropolitan Labor Markets," *Economic Geography* 83, no. 3 (2007): 283–307.

22. Jean McGianni Celestin, "The Jobless Rate Among Black College Graduates Is Nearly Double That of Whites. Why?" TheRoot.com, March 5, 2011, http://www.theroot.com/views/college-degrees-won-t-shield-blacks-unemployment; Michael Luo, "In Job Hunt, College Degree Can't Close Racial Gap," *New York Times*, November 30, 2009, http://www.nytimes.com/2009/12/01/us/01race.html.

23. Less educated Americans, however, particularly young African American men, are more likely to be burdened with additional factors that contribute to unemployment, such as incarceration and enforcement of child support laws. Harry J. Holzer, Paul Offner, and Elaine Sorensen, "Declining Employment Among Young Black Less-Educated Men: The Role of Incarceration and Child Support," *Journal of Policy Analysis and Management* 24, no. 2 (2005): 329–350.

24. The California-based not-for-profit group Strive for College is geared toward ensuring that "every qualified, low-income high school student has the information and support necessary to enroll in their best-fit college." http://www.striveforcollege.org/about/mission.html.

25. The American Association of Community Colleges notes that half of the students who receive a baccalaureate degree in the United States have also attended a community college along the way. "Students at Community Colleges," American Association of Community Colleges, 2011, http://www.aacc.nche.edu/AboutCC/Trends/Pages/studentsatcommunitycolleges.aspx.

26. Lizettte Alvarez, "A Community College in Florida Works to Attract the Poor and the Presidential," *New York Times*, April 29. 2011, http://www.nytimes.com/2011/04/30/us/30dade.html.

27. Ibid.

28. Karen Levesque et al., "Career and Technical Education in the United States: 1990 to 2005," National Center for Education Statistics, July 2008, http://nces.ed.gov/pubs2008/2008035.pdf, 86–94.

29. US Department of Labor, "Project GATE: Growing America Through Entrepreneurship," January 25, 2010, https://www.doleta.gov/reports/projectgate/.

30. The initial sites included three cities in Maine, one in Philadelphia, and two (one urban and one rural) in Minnesota. In 2008 the program was expanded to sites in Alabama, North Carolina, and Virginia.

31. Alan Gomez, "Number of Undocumented Immigrants in U.S. Stays Same for 6th Year," *USA Today*, September 20, 2016, http://www.usatoday.com/story/news/world/2016/09/20/illegal-immigration-united-states-mexico-asia-africa/90735292/; Jeffrey Passel and D'Vera Cohn, "Unauthorized Immigrant Population: National and State Trends, 2010," Pew Hispanic Center, 2011, http://www.pewhispanic.org/2011/02/01/unauthorized-immigrant-population-brnational-and-state-trends-2010/; Julia Preston, "Illegal Immigrants Number 11.5 Million," *New York Times*, March 24, 2012, http://www.nytimes.com/2012/03/24/us/illegal-immigrants-number-11-5-million.html.

32. Jennifer Guglielmo and Salvatore Salerno, eds., *Are Italians White? How Race Is Made in America* (New York: Routledge, 2003); Noel Ignatiev, *How the Irish Became White* (New York: Routledge, 2009).

33. José Luis Morin, "Latinas/os and US Prisons: Trends and Challenges," *Latino Studies* 6 (2008): 11–34.

34. An August 2011 poll revealed that 40 percent of Americans believe that illegal immigrants take jobs away from US citizens, but 49 percent believe that they perform jobs that US citizens will not do. Rasmussen, "49% Say Illegal Immigrants Perform Jobs U.S. Citizens Won't Do," Rasmussen Reports, August 25, 2011, http://www.rasmussenreports.com/public_content/politics/current_events/immigration/49_say_illegal_immigrants_perform_jobs_u_s_citizens_won_t_do.

35. "Jobs That Americans Won't Do," *Christian Science Monitor*, September 1, 2009, http://www.csmonitor.com/Commentary/the-monitors-view/2009/0901/p08s01-comv.html.

36. Cord Jefferson, "How Illegal Immigration Hurts Black America," TheRoot.com, February 10, 2010, http://www.theroot.com/views/how-illegal-immigration-hurts-black-america.

37. Maeve Reston, "Brown Signs California Dream Act," *Los Angeles Times*, July 26, 2011, http://articles.latimes.com/2011/jul/26/local/la-me-brown-dream-act-20110726.

38. Kevin Loria, "DREAM Act Stalled, Obama Halts Deportations for Young Illegal Immigrants," *Christian Science Monitor*, June 15, 2012, http://www.csmonitor.com/USA/Politics/2012/0615/DREAM-Act-stalled-Obama-halts-deportations-for-young-illegal-immigrants-video.

39. "Federal and State DREAM Acts," Legalmatch.com, October 3, 2016, http://www.legalmatch.com/law-library/article/dream-act-lawyers.html.

40. "Election 2012: Maryland Passes Version of DREAM Act," Fox News Latino, November 7, 2012, http://latino.foxnews.com/latino/politics/2012/11/07/election-2012-maryland-passes-version-dream-act/.

41. C. N. Le, "Employment and Occupational Patterns," Asian-Nation: The Landscape of Asian America, August 25, 2011, http://www.asian-nation.org/employment.shtml.

42. "What We Love and Hate about America," Harris Interactive, June 8, 2010, http://www.harrisinteractive.com/NewsRoom/HarrisPolls/tabid/447/mid/1508/articleId/405/ctl/ReadCustom%20Default/Default.aspx.

43. "Problems and Priorities," PollingReport.com, 2011, http://www.pollingreport.com/prioriti.htm.

44. By November 2016, in the heat of a presidential election, only 14 percent of Americans named the economy as the most important problem facing America. It was, however, the most frequently mentioned item in the open-ended question. "Economy, Elections Top Problems Facing U.S.," Gallup, November 17, 2016, http://www.gallup.com/poll/197786/economy-elections-top-problems-facing.aspx?g_source=Politics.

45. Daniel Halper, "Poll: Workers Want Less Regulation," *Weekly Standard*, March 30, 2011, http://www.weeklystandard.com/blogs/poll-workers-want-less-regulation_556014.html; John McCormick and Alison Vekshin, "Wall Street Despised in Poll Showing Most Want Regulation (Update 1)," Bloomberg, March 24, 2010, http://www.bloomberg.com/apps/news?pid=newsarchive&sid=a4nQoiYaj2ag.

Chapter 7: Health

1. Maslow's hierarchy of needs has been updated to reflect changes in psychology over the past fifty years. "Self-actualization" has been replaced at the top of the pyramid along with mate acquisition, mate retention, and parenting. Tom Jacobs, "Maslow's Pyramid Gets a Makeover," *Miller-McCune,* June 22, 2010, http://www .miller-mccune.com/culture/maslows-pyramid-gets-a-makeover-20682/; Douglas T. Kenrick et al.,"Renovating the Pyramid of Needs: Contemporary Extensions Built upon Ancient Foundations," *Perspectives on Psychological Science* 5, no. 3 (2010): 292–314; Rick Nauert,"Updated Maslow's Pyramid of Needs," PsychCentral, August 23, 2010, http://psychcentral.com/news/2010/08/23/updated-maslows-pyramid-of -needs/17144.html.

2. Nauert, "Updated Maslow's Pyramid of Needs."

3. For instance, two recent studies showed that individuals who are diagnosed with cancer have a better chance of survival if they have private health insurance than those who do not. They are diagnosed earlier and lived longer than those who had no insurance, or even those who were covered by Medicaid. Michelle Andrews, "Studies Link Cancer Patients' Survival Time to Insurance Status," National Public Radio, September 16, 2016, http://www.npr.org/sections/health-shots/2016/09/16/494139538 /studies-link-cancer-patients-survival-time-to-insurance-status.

4. Uwe E. Reinhardt, "A 'Government Takeover' of Health Care?" *New York Times,* February 26, 2010, http://economix.blogs.nytimes.com/2010/02/26/a-government -takeover-of-health-care/. While remaining neutral on the value of the bill, the nonpartisan organization PolitiFact called the "government takeover" language the "lie of the year" in 2010, since the government is only minimally involved and private insurers will gain millions of new customers. Bill Adair and Angie Drobnic Holan, "PolitiFact's Lie of the Year: 'A Government Takeover of Health Care,'" PolitiFact .com, December 16, 2010, http://www.politifact.com/truth-o-meter/article/2010 /dec/16/lie-year-government-takeover-health-care/.

5. US Department of Health and Human Services, "20 Million People Have Gained Health Insurance Coverage Because of the Affordable Care Act, New Estimates Show," March 3, 2016, http://www.hhs.gov/about/news/2016/03/03/20-million-people-have -gained-health-insurance-coverage-because-affordable-care-act-new-estimates.

6. Eunice Lee, "Donald Trump Vows Again to Repeal Obamacare," *U.S. News & World Report,* November 2, 2016, http://www.usnews.com/news/politics/ articles/2016-11-02/donald-trump-vows-again-to-repeal-obamacare.

7. For example, see Philip Klein, "The Myth of the 46 Million," *American Spectator,* March 20, 2009, http://spectator.org/archives/2009/03/20/the-myth-of-the -46-million.

8. Andy Miller, "Census Bureau Report Shows Slight Increase in Uninsured in 2008," WebMD, September 10, 2009, http://www.webmd.com/healthy-aging /news/20090910/more-americans-have-no-health-insurance; Joshua Norman, "Report: 59 Million Americans Lack Health Care," CBSNews.com, November 10, 2010, http://www.cbsnews.com/stories/2010/11/10/health/main7040408.shtml; Jennifer Pifer-Bixler, "Study: 86.8 Million Americans Uninsured over Last Two Years," CNN, March 4, 2009, http://articles.cnn.com/2009-03-04/health/uninsured .epidemic.obama_1_families-usa-health-insurance-health-coverage.

9. US Department of Health and Human Services, "Medicaid Eligibility: Overview," Centers for Medicare and Medicaid Services, http://www.medicaid.gov /AffordableCareAct/Provisions/Eligibility.html.

10. Medicare.gov, "Medicare Basics," 2008, http://www.medicare.gov/Pubs /pdf/11034.pdf.

11. Kate Bolduan, "The Plight of Young, Uninsured Americans," CNN, March 7, 2009, http://www.cnn.com/2009/POLITICS/03/07/young.uninsured/.

12. Rachel Garfield, Rachel Licata, and Katherine Young, "The Uninsured at the Starting Line: Findings from the 2013 Kaiser Survey of Low-Income Americans and the ACA," The Henry J. Kaiser Family Foundation, February 6, 2014, http://kff.org /uninsured/report/the-uninsured-at-the-starting-line-findings-from-the-2013 -kaiser-survey-of-low-income-americans-and-the-aca/.

13. David B. Rivkin and Lee A. Casey, "Mandatory Insurance Is Unconstitutional," *Wall Street Journal*, September 18, 2009, http://online.wsj.com/article/SB1000 14240529702045185045744166231093624 80.html; Kevin Sack, "Federal Judge Rules That Health Law Violates Constitution," *New York Times*, January 31, 2011, http://www.nytimes.com/2011/02/01/us/01ruling.html; Adam Liptak, "Supreme Court Upholds Health Care Law, 5-4, in Victory for Obama," *New York Times*, June 28, 2012, http://www.nytimes.com/2012/06/29/us/supreme-court-lets -health-law-largely-stand.html.

14. CHIRP Los Angeles, "20 Million People Have Gained Health Insurance Coverage Because of the Affordable Care Act, New Estimates Show," http://www .chirpla.org/news/20-million-people-have-gained-health-insurance-coverage -because-affordable-care-act-new.

15. Greg R. Alexander and Carol C. Korenbrot, "The Role of Prenatal Care in Preventing Low Birth Weight," *Future of Children* 5, no. 1 (1995): 103–120; Jane Huntington and Frederick A. Connell, "For Every Dollar Spent: The Cost-Savings Argument for Prenatal Care," *New England Journal of Medicine* 331 (1994): 1303–1307.

16. Maria G. Gonzalez, "Factors Affecting Prenatal Care in Rural, Low-Income Neighborhoods," Poster presented at the SUNY Undergraduate Research Conference, 2015, http://digitalcommons.brockport.edu/surc/2015/schedule/297/. Julie A. Gaz-mararian et al., "Prenatal Care for Low-Income Women Enrolled in a Managed-Care Organization," *Obstetrics & Gynecology* 94, no. 2 (1999): 177–184.

17. Michael D. Kogan et al., "Racial Disparities in Reported Prenatal Care Advice from Health Care Providers," *American Journal of Public Health* 84, no. 1 (1994): 82–88.

18. Jann L. Murray and Merton Bernfield, "The Differential Effect of Prenatal Care on the Incidence of Low Birth Weight Among Blacks and Whites in a Prepaid Health Care Plan," *New England Journal of Medicine* 319 (1988): 1385–1391.

19. Andrew J. Healy et al., "Early Access to Prenatal Care: Implications for Racial Disparity in Perinatal Mortality," *Obstetrics & Gynecology* 107, no. 3 (2006): 625–631.

20. Greg R. Alexander, Michael D. Kogan, and Sara Nabukera, "Racial Differences in Prenatal Care Use in the United States: Are Disparities Decreasing?" *American Journal of Public Health* 92, no. 12 (2002): 1970–1975.

21. More recent studies continue to reflect racial and ethnic disparities. For instance, one study in a California high-risk clinic found such differences in expectant

mothers with respect to such factors as appointment attendance, diabetes, illicit drug use, smoking, and psychiatric diagnosis. Melanie Thomas, Anna Spielvogel, Frances Cohen, Susan Fisher-Owens, Naomi Stotland, Betsy Wolfe, and Martha Shumway, "Maternal Differences and Birth Outcome Disparities: Diversity within a High-Risk Prenatal Clinic," *Journal of Racial and Ethnic Health Disparities* 1, no. 1 (2014): 12–20. A separate focus group study found that structural barriers to accessing prenatal care included access to transportation, insurance, negative attitudes about prenatal care, and overall psychosocial stress. Mary C. Mazul, Trina C. Salm Ward, and Emmanuel M. Ngui, "Anatomy of Good Prenatal Care: Perspectives of Low Income African-American Women on Barriers and Facilitators to Prenatal Care," *Journal of Racial and Ethnic Health Disparities* (2016): 1–8 (online first).

22. T. J. Matthews and Marian F. MacDorman, *Infant Mortality Statistics from the 2008 Period Linked Birth/Infant Death Data Set,* National Vital Statistics Reports 60, no. 5 (2012), http://www.cdc.gov/nchs/data/nvsr/nvsr60/nvsr60_05.pdf.

23. Eunice Kennedy Shriver National Institute of Child Health and Human Development, "Research on Back Sleeping and SIDS," n.d., https://www.nichd.nih.gov/sts/campaign/science/Pages/backsleeping.aspx.

24. "White Children More Likely to Receive CT Scans Than Hispanic or African-American Children," Science Codex, August 6, 2012, http://www.sciencecodex.com/white_children_more_likely_to_receive_ct_scans_than_hispanic_or_african american_children-96136.

25. David Seith and Courtney Kalof, "Who Are America's Poor Children? Examining Health Disparities by Race and Ethnicity," National Center for Children in Poverty, Columbia University, 2011, http://www.nccp.org/publications/pdf/text_1032.pdf.

26. Michael Marmot, "The Influence of Income on Health: Views of an Epidemiologist," *Health Affairs* 21, no. 2 (2002): 31–46.

27. David R. Williams and Pamela Braboy Jackson, "Social Sources of Racial Disparities in Health," *Health Affairs* 24, no. 2 (2005): 325–334.

28. Centers for Disease Control and Prevention, "Breast Cancer Rates by Race and Ethnicity," September 28, 2010, http://www.cdc.gov/cancer/breast/statistics/race.htm.

29. Roxanne Nelson, "Racial Disparities in Breast Cancer Survival Are Most Apparent in Advanced Stages," Medscape Medical News, August 14, 2007, http://www.medscape.com/viewarticle/561377; "Disparities in Healthcare Quality Among Minority Women: Findings from the 2011 National Healthcare Quality and Disparities Reports," Agency for Healthcare Research and Quality, October 2012, http://www.ahrq.gov/qual/nhqrdr11/nhqrminoritywomen11.pdf.

30. "Disparities in Healthcare Quality Among Minority Women."

31. Centers for Disease Control and Prevention, "Breast Cancer Rates by Race and Ethnicity."

32. Ronica N. Rooks et al., "Racial Disparities in Health Care Access and Cardiovascular Disease Indicators in Black and White Older Adults in the Health ABC Study," *Journal of Aging and Health* 20, no. 6 (2008): 599–614.

33. Keith C. Norris and Lawrence Y. Agodoa, "Unraveling the Racial Disparities Associated with Kidney Disease," *Kidney International* 68 (2005): 914–924.

34. Sarah Bounse and Debra Miller, "Racial Disparities Among AIDS Diagnoses: A Regional Analysis," Council of State Governments, August 17, 2011, http://knowledgecenter.csg.org/drupal/content/racial-disparities-among-aids-diagnoses-regional-analysis.

35. Dawn M. Bravata et al., "Racial Disparities in Stroke Risk Factors: The Impact of Socioeconomic Factors," *Stroke* 36 (2005): 1507–1511.

36. Agency for Healthcare Research and Quality, "Diabetes Disparities Among Racial and Ethnic Minorities," November 2001, http://www.ahrq.gov/research/diabdisp.pdf; Luisa N. Borrell et al., "Perception of General and Oral Health in White and African American Adults: Assessing the Effect of Neighborhood Socioeconomic Conditions," *Community Dentistry and Oral Epidemiology* 32, no. 5 (2004): 363–373.

37. Carrie N. Klabunde et al., "Trends and Black/White Differences in Treatment for Nonmetastatic Prostate Cancer," *Medical Care* 36, no. 9 (1998): 1337–1348; Kathryn E. Richert-Boe et al., "Racial Differences in Treatment of Early-Stage Prostate Cancer," *Urology* 71, no. 6 (2007): 1172–1176.

38. Centers for Disease Control and Prevention, *CDC Health Disparities and Inequalities Report: United States, 2011,* Morbidity and Mortality Weekly Report, January 14, 2011, http://www.cdc.gov/mmwr/pdf/other/su6001.pdf.

39. An age-adjusted death rate provides for a more accurate comparison because it controls for variance in age within populations. Missouri Department of Health and Human Services, "Age-Adjusted Rate," http://health.mo.gov/data/mica/CDP_MICA/AARate.html.

40. For a comprehensive overview of health disparities, see "Health, United States, 2011: With Special Feature on Socioeconomic Status and Health," National Center for Health Statistics, May 2012, http://www.cdc.gov/nchs/data/hus/hus11.pdf.

41. Ibby Caputo, "Poverty Impacts Developing Brains," WGBH News, April 4, 2013, http://www.wgbhnews.org/post/poverty-impacts-developing-brains.

42. Ibid.

43. Rachel Ann Reimer, Meg Gerrard, and Frederick X. Gibbons, "Racial Disparities in Smoking Knowledge Among Current Smokers: Data from the Health Information National Trends Surveys," *Psychology Health* 25, no. 8 (2010): 943–959. Further, recent research suggests that African Americans who live in more segregated communities are more likely to die from lung cancer than are African Americans who live in more integrated communities. Sabrina Tavernise, "Segregation Linked in Study with Lung Cancer Deaths," *New York Times*, January 16, 2013, http://www.nytimes.com/2013/01/17/health/study-links-segregation-and-lung-cancer-deaths-in-blacks.html.

44. Kellie E. Barr et al., "Race, Class, and Gender Differences in Substance Abuse: Evidence of Middle-Class/Underclass Polarization Among black Males," *Social Problems* 40, no. 3 (2003): 314–327.

45. Ricky N. Bluthenall, Jerry O. Jacobson, and Paul L. Robinson, "Are Racial Differences in Alcohol Treatment Completion Associated with Racial Differences in Treatment Modality Entry? Comparison of Outpatient Treatment and Residential Treatment in Los Angeles County, 1998 to 2000," *Alcoholism: Clinical and Experimental Research* 31, no. 11 (2007): 1920–1926.

46. Barr et al., "Race, Class, and Gender Differences in Substance Abuse"; National Institute on Drug Abuse, "Strategic Plan on Reducing Health Disparities," July 2004, http://www.nida.nih.gov/PDF/HealthDispPlan.pdf.

47. Borrell et al., "Perception of General and Oral Health."

48. Andrew A. Zekeri, "African American College Students' Perceptions of Psychosocial Factors Influencing Racial Disparities in Health," *College Student Journal* 40, no. 4 (2006): 901–915.

49. Robert D. Bullard, ed., *Unequal Protection: Environmental Justice and Communities of Color* (San Francisco: Sierra Club Books, 1997).

50. Robert D. Bullard et al., "Toxic Wastes and Race at Twenty: 1987–2007," United Church of Christ Justice and Witness Ministries, 2007, http://www.ucc.org /assets/pdfs/toxic20.pdf.

51. David Pace, "Blacks, Poor Most Likely to Breathe Polluted Air," December 14, 2005, http://www.deseretnews.com/article/635168651/blacks-poor-most-likely -to-breathe-polluted-air.html.

52. Miranda R. Jones, Ana V. Diez-Roux, Anjum Hajat, Kiarri N. Kershaw, Marie S. O'Neill, Eliseo Guallar, Wendy S. Post, Joel D. Kaufman, and Ana Navas-Acien, "Race/Ethnicity, Residential Segregation, and Exposure to Ambient Air Pollution: The Multi-Ethnic Study of Atherosclerosis (MESA), *American Journal of Public Health* 104, no. 11 (2014): 2130–2137.

53. Merrit Kennedy, "Lead-Laced Water in Flint: A Step-by-Step Look at the Makings of a Crisis," National Public Radio, April 20, 2016, http://www.npr.org/ sections/thetwo-way/2016/04/20/465545378/lead-laced-water-in-flint-a-step-by -step-look-at-the-makings-of-a-crisis.

54. Ibid.

55. Agency for Toxic Substances and Disease Registry, ATSDR Case Studies in Environmental Medicine: Principles of Pediatric Environmental Health, U.S. Department of Health and Human Services, February 15, 2012, https://www.atsdr .cdc.gov/csem/ped_env_health/docs/ped_env_health.pdf.

56. Roman Bystrianyk, "Learning and Developmental Disabilities Linked to Environmental Toxins," Health Sentinel, September 25, 2008, http://www .healthsentinel.com/joomla/index.php?option=com_content&view=article&id=2442; Dan Orzech, "Chemical Kids: Environmental Toxins and Child Development," *Social Work Today* 7, no. 2 (2007): 37, http://www.socialworktoday.com/archive /marapr2007p37.shtml; JiyeonPark, Ann P. Turnbull, and H. Rutherford Turnbull, "Impacts of Poverty on Quality of Life in Families of Children with Disabilities," *Exceptional Children* 68, no. 2 (2002): 151–170.

57. Joseph Ruzich,"Special Education Programs Begin to Feel Budget Pinch," *Chicago Tribune*, March 8, 2011, http://articles.chicagotribune.com/2011-03-08 /news/ct-x-s-special-ed-cuts-0309-20110309_1_special-education-students-with -severe-disabilities-teachers-end; Ronald J. Sider, "Making Schools Work for the Rich and Poor," *Christian Century*, August 25, 1999, 802–809, http://www.religion-online .org/showarticle.asp?title=702.

58. Beth Harry and Mary G. Anderson, "The Disproportionate Placement of African American Males in Special Education Programs: A Critique of the Process," *Journal of Negro Education* 63, no. 4 (1995): 602–619; Carla O'Connor, Carla and

Sonia DeLuca Fernandez, "Race, Class, and Disproportionality: Reevaluating the Relationship Between Poverty and Special Education Placement," *Educational Researcher* 35, no. 6 (2006): 6–11.

59. Kisha Holden, Brian McGregor, Poonam Thandi, Edith Fresh, Kameron Sheats, Allyson Belton, Gail Mattox, and David Satcher, "Toward Culturally Centered Integrative Care for Addressing Mental Health Disparities Among Ethnic Minorities," *Psychological Services* 11 no. 4 (2014): 357–368.

60. The World Health Organization reports that "three-quarters of the worlds' neuropsychiatric disorders are in low-income or low-middle income countries" and that depression is significantly undertreated in poorer nations. Tina Rosenberg, "Fighting Depression, One Village at a Time," *New York Times*, July 18, 2012, http://opinionator.blogs.nytimes.com/2012/07/18/fighting-depression-one-village-at-a-time/. For the full report, see *Scaling Up Care for Mental, Neurological, and Substance Use Disorders*, World Health Organization, 2008, http://apps.who.int/iris/bitstream/10665/43809/1/9789241596206_eng.pdf. See also US Department of Health and Human Services. *Mental Health: Culture, Race, and Ethnicity— A Supplement to Mental Health: A Report of the Surgeon General* (Rockville, MD: Center for Mental Health Services, 2001), http://www.surgeongeneral.gov/library/mentalhealth/cre/sma-01-3613.pdf.

61. Liam Downey and Marieke Van Willigen, "Environmental Stressors: The Mental Health Impacts of Living Near Industrial Activity," *Journal of Health and Science Behavior* 46, no. 3 (2005): 289–305.

62. Norm Oliver, "Understanding Health Disparities: Race, Class, or Both?" Oliver's Twist, 2009, http://healthdisparities.virginia.edu/2009/05/13/race_class_or_both/.

63. Liam Downey, "US Metropolitan-Area Variation in Environmental Inequality Outcomes," *Urban Studies* 44, no. 5–6 (2007): 953–977.

64. These issues are further complicated by a growing body of research that addresses health disparities through the lens of the social construction of race (rather than treating race as a biological construction as it relates to health and medicine). See, for instance, Martin Donohoe, ed., *Public Health and Social Justice Reader* (San Francisco: Jossey-Bass, 2012); Camera Phyllis Jones et al., "Using 'Socially Assigned Race' to Probe White Advantages in Health Status," *Ethnicity & Disease* 18, no. 4 (2008): 496–504; Jesse Daniels and Amy J. Schulz, "Constructing Whiteness in Health Disparities Research," in *Gender, Race, Class, and Health*, ed. Amy J. Schulz and Leith Mullings (San Francisco: Jossey-Bass, 2005), 89–127. For recent work on the broader notion of race as a social construct, see Anne Fausto-Sterling's review of books by Richard C. Francis (*Epigenetics: The Ultimate Mystery of Inheritance*), Ann Morning (*The Nature of Race: How Scientists Think and Teach about Human Difference*), and Dorothy Roberts (*Fatal Invention: How Science, Politics, and Big Business Re-create Race in the Twenty-first Century*) in the May-June 2012 issue of *Boston Review*, http://www.bostonreview.net/BR37.3/anne_fausto-sterling_biology_race.php.

65. Erin White, "Whites Tend to Sleep Better Than Asians, Blacks, and Hispanics: Study Shows Differences in Length, Quality of Sleep, and Daytime Sleepiness by Race," Northwestern University, June 13, 2012, http://www.northwestern.edu/newscenter/stories/2012/06/carnethon-sleep-race.html.

66. Serge Brand et al., "High Exercise Levels are Related to Favorable Sleep Patterns and Psychological Functioning in Adolescents: A Comparison of Athletes and Controls," *Journal of Adolescent Health* 46, no. 2 (2010): 133–141.

67. See Kathleen McCann, "Ongoing Study Continues to Show That Extra Sleep Improves Athletic Performance," American Academy of Sleep Medicine, 2008, http://www.aasmnet.org/Articles.aspx?id=954; Elizabeth K. Gray and David Watson, "General and Specific Traits of Personality and Their Relation to Sleep and Academic Performance," *Journal of Personality* 70, no. 2 (2002): 177–206; Mickey T. Trockel, Michael D. Barnes, and Dennis L. Egget, "Health-Related Variables and Academic Performance Among First-Year College Students: Implications for Sleep and Other Behaviors," *Journal of American College Health* 49, no. 3 (2000): 125–131; Harvard University Medical School, "Why Sleep Matters," http://healthysleep.med.harvard.edu/healthy/matters.

68. The Henry J. Kaiser Family Foundation, "Overweight and Obesity Rates for Adults by Race/Ethnicity: 2015," n.d., http://kff.org/other/state-indicator/adult-overweightobesity-rate-by-re/?currentTimeframe=0. The terms *overweight* and *obesity* are defined by the degree to which weight is disproportionate to height as measured by the body mass index (BMI). Adults with a BMI or 25 to 29.9 are overweight; those with a BMI over 30 are obese. Robert Wood Johnson Foundation, *Issue Report: F as in Fat: How Obesity Threatens America's Future,* 2011, http://www.rwjf.org/files/research/fasinfat2011.pdf, 15.

69. Robert Wood Johnson Foundation, *Issue Report: F as in Fat*; "Health, United States, 2011," National Center for Health Statistics, May 2012, 257–265, http://www.cdc.gov/nchs/data/hus/hus11.pdf.

70. Ibid.

71. US Department of Agriculture, "Food Security in the United States: Definitions of Hunger and Food Security," November 15, 2010, http://www.ers.usda.gov/briefing/foodsecurity/labels.htm#new_labels.

72. "Hunger and Poverty Facts and Statistics, Feeding America, n.d., http://www.feedingamerica.org/hunger-in-america/impact-of-hunger/hunger-and-poverty/hunger-and-poverty-fact-sheet.html.

73. US Department of Agriculture, "Child Nutrition Tables," Food and Nutrition Service, November 10, 2016, http://www.fns.usda.gov/pd/child-nutrition-tables.

74. "Cheap Eats for Hard Times: The Five Most Unhealthful Fast Food 'Value Menu' Items," The Cancer Project, Winter 2008, http://www.cancerproject.org/PDFs/Five%20Worst%20Value%20Menu%20Items%20Report.pdf; Mary Kane, "The Real Value of the Fast Food 'Dollar Menu' in a Recession," *Washington Independent*, May 12, 2009, http://washingtonindependent.com/42485/the-real-value-of-the-fast-food-dollar-menu-in-a-recession.

75. "If You Build It, They May Not Come," *Economist*, July 7, 2011, http://www.economist.com/node/18929190. For food deserts in the United States, visit the USDA's interactive map at http://www.ers.usda.gov/data-products/food-access-research-atlas.aspx.

76. Andrew Soergel, "Millions of Food Desert Dwellers Struggle to Get Fresh Groceries," *U.S. News & World Report*, December 7, 2015, http://www.usnews.com/news/articles/2015/12/07/millions-of-food-desert-dwellers-struggle-to-get-fresh-groceries.

77. Appalachia Service Project, *An Overview of Poverty in Appalachia*, 2009, http://asphome.org/learn_about_appalachia/overview_of_poverty.

78. Pew Research Center, "Beyond Distrust: How Americans View Their Government," November 23, 2015, http://www.people-press.org/2015/11/23/2-general-opinions-about-the-federal-government/.

79. Carolyn Lochhead, "Fat Fight Turns to a New Front: School Lunches," *Houston Chronicle*, February 10, 2010, http://www.chron.com/news/houston-texas/article/Fat-fight-turns-to-a-new-front-school-lunches-1711419.php.

80. Sandro Galea et al., "Estimated Deaths Attributable to Social Factors in the United States," *American Journal of Public Health* 101, no. 8 (2011): 1456–1465, quote 1462.

81. Supplemental Nutrition Assistance Program, Food and Nutrition Service, October 20, 2016, http://www.fns.usda.gov/snap/eligibility.

82. Supplemental Nutrition Assistance Program, Food and Nutrition Service, November 9, 2012, http://www.fns.usda.gov/pd/34SNAPmonthly.htm.

83. Supplemental Nutrition Assistance Program, Food and Nutrition Service, November 10, 2016, http://www.fns.usda.gov/pd/supplemental-nutrition-assistance-program-snap.

84. Philip Rucker, "Gingrich Promises to Slash Taxes, Calls Obama 'Food Stamp President,'" *Washington Post*, May 13, 2011, http://www.washingtonpost.com/politics/gingrich-promises-to-slash-taxes-calls-obama-food-stamp-president/2011/05/13/AF9Q602G_story.html.

85. Jessie Daniels, "Newt Gingrich Calls President Obama 'Food Stamp President,' Bristles at Charges of Racism," Racism Review, May 15, 2011, http://www.racismreview.com/blog/2011/05/15/newt-food-stamp-president/.

86. The effects of race-based political messages need not be related to any intent. See Charlton D. McIlwain and Stephen M. Caliendo, *Race Appeal: How Candidates Invoke Race in U.S. Political Campaigns* (Philadelphia: Temple University Press, 2011).

Chapter 8: Gender

1. The Lilly Ledbetter Fair Pay Act of 2009 extends the amount of time a person has to file an equal-pay discrimination lawsuit, http://www.gpo.gov/fdsys/pkg/PLAW-111publ2/html/PLAW-111publ2.htm.

2. October 16, 2012, Debate Transcript, Commission on Presidential Debates, http://www.debates.org/index.php?page=october-1-2012-the-second-obama-romney-presidential-debate.

3. Susana Schrobsdorff, "Romney's Binders: The Meme Women Love to Hate," *Time*, October 19, 2012, http://ideas.time.com/2012/10/19/romneys-binders-the-meme-women-love-to-hate/.

4. Reports immediately after the debate suggested that the story was not even accurate. A Boston-based journalist noted that a bipartisan interest group, MassGAP, which was formed before the 2002 gubernatorial election, put more women in leadership positions in the Massachusetts government. That group compiled the "binder" and presented it to Governor Romney. David S. Bernstein, "Mind the

Binder," *(Boston) Phoenix*, October 16, 2012, http://blog.thephoenix.com/BLOGS
/talkingpolitics/archive/2012/10/16/mind-the-binder.aspx.

5. There is a rich scholarly literature on the politics of housework. See, for instance,
Sampson Lee Blair and Daniel T. Lichter, "Measuring the Division of Household
Labor: Gender Segregation of Housework Among American Couples," *Journal of
Family Issues* 12, no. 1 (1991): 91–113; Mick Cunningham, "Influences of Women's
Employment on the Gendered Division of Household Labor over the Life Course:
Evidence from a 31-Year Panel Study," *Journal of Family Issues* 28, no. 3 (2007):
422–444; Roderic Beaujot and Jianye Liu, "Models of Time Use in Paid and Unpaid
Work," *Journal of Family Issues* 7 (2005): 924–946; Theodore N. Greenstein, "Gender
Ideology and Perceptions of the Fairness of the Division of Household Labor: Effects
on Marital Quality," *Social Forces* 74, no. 3 (1996): 1029–1042; Michael Braun et al.,
"Perceived Inequality in the Gendered Division of Household Labor," *Journal of
Marriage and Family* 70, no. 5 (2008): 1145–1156.

6. For a discussion of attempts in Great Britain to improve flexible time policies for
both men and women, see Amelia Gentelman, "Rebalancing Child-Care Equations,"
New York Times, November 20, 2012, http://www.nytimes.com/2012/11/21/world
/europe/21iht-letter21.html.

7. Carolyn B. Maloney and Charles E. Schumer, *Women and the Economy
2010: 25 Years of Progress but Challenges Remain*, US Congress Joint Economic
Committee, August 2010, http://www.jec.senate.gov/public/?a=Files.Serve&File
_id=8be22cb0-8ed0-4a1a-841b-aa91dc55fa81. See also Liza Mundy, "Women,
Money, and Power," *Time*, March 26, 2012, http://www.time.com/time/magazine
/article/0,9171,2109140,00.html.

8. While this conceptualization is still prevalent, there is notable criticism of its
limitations. Some writers have argued that the binary distinction relating to sex is also
socially constructed, and consequently the convenient sex-gender binary is not an
adequate tool for understanding that construction. Diane Richardson, "Conceptualizing
Gender," in *Introducing Gender and Women's Studies*, ed. Diane Richardson and
Victoria Robinson, 3rd ed. (New York: Palgrave Macmillan, 2007), 3–19.

9. There has been a movement in recent years, driven in part by activism on the part
of transgender individuals and their allies, to formalize the "singular *they*," whereby a
plural pronoun, since it is not gender specific, is permitted to be coupled with a singular
antecedent. For example, we would write, "A bookkeeper must be precise in their
work" in an effort to avoid invoking gender when it is not relevant. Benjamin Mullin,
"The Washington Post Will Allow Singular 'They,'" Poynter.org, December 1, 2015,
http://www.poynter.org/2015/the-washington-post-will-allow-singular-they/387542/.

10. Similarly, the term *heterosexism* (or *heteronormativity*) refers to the hegemonic
norm that leads individuals to assume that people are heterosexual unless they know
otherwise. For instance, sex-segregated restrooms are grounded in the premise that
everyone is heterosexual; otherwise, there is little point in ensuring that men and
women do not see one another in a state of undress. There is nothing particularly
malicious or individualistic about this tendency, or the fact that most laws centering
on couples are rooted in similar assumptions. The more common term *homophobia*
refers to resentment, animosity, or hatred of folks who are not heterosexual. Such
individual-level attitudes are rooted in heterosexism to the extent that the belief that

heterosexuals are normal and those who are not are deviant, but the constructs should be considered separately.

11. For an interesting discussion about the difference between sexism and misogyny in the context of an Australian dictionary's decision to shift the definition of the latter to include "entrenched prejudice against women" (rather than only hatred of them), see Naomi Wolf et al., "Sexism and Misogyny: What's the Difference?" *Guardian*, October 17, 2012, http://www.guardian.co.uk/commentisfree/2012/oct /17/difference-between-sexism-and-misogyny. *New York Times* columnist Nicholas Kristof has struggled with the difference between these concepts and how each contributes to violence against women in a global context. Nicholas D. Kristof, "Misogyny vs. Sexism," *New York Times*, April 7, 2008, http://kristof.blogs.nytimes .com/2008/04/07/misogyny-vs-sexism/.

12. Olga Khazan, "The Lasting Harm of Trump-Style Sexism," *Atlantic*, November 4, 2016, http://www.theatlantic.com/science/archive/2016/11/how-trump-style -words-hurt/506456/; Jia Tolentino, "Donald Trump's Unconscious, Unending Sexism," *New Yorker*, October 10, 2016, http://www.newyorker.com/culture/jia -tolentino/donald-trumps-unconscious-unending-sexism.

13. Franklin Foer, "Donald Trump Hates Women: It's the One Position He's Never Changed," Slate.com, March 24, 2016, http://www.slate.com/articles/news_and _politics/politics/2016/03/donald_trump_has_one_core_philosophy_misogyny .html; Michael Barbaro and Megan Twohey, "Crossing the Line: How Donald Trump Behaved with Women in Private," *New York Times*, May 14, 2016, http://www .nytimes.com/2016/05/15/us/politics/donald-trump-women.html.

14. For comprehensive lists of Donald Trump's sexist and misogynistic comments, see Nina Easton, "The History of Donald Trump's Insults to Women," *Fortune*, August 9, 2015, http://fortune.com/2015/08/09/trump-insult-women-history/; Claire Cohen, "Donald Trump Sexism Tracker: Every Offensive Comment in One Place," *Telegraph* (UK), November 9, 2016, http://www.telegraph.co.uk/women/politics/donald-trump -sexism-tracker-every-offensive-comment-in-one-place/; and Libby Nelson, "Donald Trump's History of Misogyny, Sexism, and Harassment: A Comprehensive Review," Vox.com, October 12, 2016, http://www.vox.com/2016/10/8/13110734/donald -trump-leaked-audio-recording-billy-bush-sexism.

15. David A. Fahrenthold, "Trump Recorded Having Extremely Lewd Conversation About Women in 2005," *Washington Post*, October 8, 2016, https:// www.washingtonpost.com/politics/trump-recorded-having-extremely-lewd -conversation-about-women-in-2005/2016/10/07/3b9ce776-8cb4-11e6-bf8a-3d26 847eeed4_story.html.

16. Lorraine Ali, "'Such a Nasty Woman': Trump's Debate Dig Becomes a Feminist Rallying Cry," *Los Angeles Times*, October 20, 2016, http://www.latimes .com/entertainment/tv/la-et-nasty-woman-trump-clinton-debate-janet-jackson -20161020-snap-story.html.

17. ABC News Analysis Desk and Paul Blake, "Election 2016 National Exit Poll Results and Analysis," ABC News, November 9, 2016, http://abcnews.go.com /Politics/election-2016-national-exit-poll-results-analysis/story?id=43368675.

18. "Exit Polls," CNN.com, November 23, 2016, http://www.cnn.com/election /results/exit-polls.

19. Ibid.

20. Although Hillary Clinton won more than 2 million more votes than Donald Trump, she fell short of an Electoral College victory, which is the mechanism by which presidents are chosen in the United States. Gabriel Debenedetti, Kyle Cheney, and Nolan D. McCaskill, "Clinton's Lead in the Popular Vote Surpasses 2 Million," Politico.com, November 23, 2016, http://www.politico.com/story/2016/11/clinton -lead-popular-vote-2016-231790.

21. Susan Chira, "Vote Highlighted a Gender Gap, with Both Sides Feeling They've Lost Ground," *New York Times*, November 9, 2016, http://www.nytimes .com/2016/11/10/us/politics/gender-gap-campaign.html.

22. The effects of such messages can be observed in (and are then reinforced by) much of reality television programming. For a thorough treatment, see Jennifer L. Pozner, *Reality Bites Back: The Troubling Truth About Guilty Pleasure TV* (Berkeley, CA: Seal Press, 2010).

23. The literature—both scholarly and popular—is extensive in this area. See, for example, Lori Baker-Sperry and Liz Grauerholz, "The Pervasiveness of the Feminine Beauty Ideal in Children's Fairy Tales," *Gender & Society* 17, no. 5 (2003): 711–726; Elizabeth Bell, Lynda Haas, and Laura Sells, eds., *From Mouse to Mermaid: The Politics of Film, Gender and Culture* (Bloomington: Indiana University Press, 2008); Donald Haase, ed., *Fairy Tales and Feminism: New Approaches* (Detroit: Wayne State University Press, 2004); U. C. Knoepflmacher, *Ventures into Childland: Victorians, Fairy Tales, and Femininity* (Chicago: University of Chicago Press, 1998); Karen E. Rowe, "Feminism and Fairy Tales," *Women's Studies: An Interdisciplinary Journal* 6, no. 3 (1979): 237–257; Ella Westland, "Cinderella in the Classroom: Children's Responses to Gender Roles in Fairy-tales," *Gender and Education* 5, no. 3 (1993): 237–249.

24. Amy Siskind, "How Feminism Became the F-Word," The Daily Beast, January 11, 2009, http://www.thedailybeast.com/articles/2009/01/11/how-feminism-became -the-f-word.html.

25. For a study about how men and women come to embrace feminism, see Rebecca L. Warner, "Does the Sex of Your Child Matter? Support for Feminism Among Women and Men in the United States and Canada," *Journal of Marriage and Family* 5, no. 4 (1991): 1051–1056.

26. For a thoughtful, concise overview of different aspects of feminism, see Jarrah Hodge, "Feminisms 101," Gender Focus, November 13, 2010, http://www.gender-focus .com/tag/types-of-feminism/.

27. Martha Rampton, "The Three Waves of Feminism," *Pacific* 41, no. 2 (2008), http://www.pacificu.edu/magazine_archives/2008/fall/echoes/feminism.cfm.

28. Ibid.

29. Laura Mulvey, "Visual Pleasure and Narrative Cinema," *Screen* 16, no. 3 (1975): 6–18, http://imlportfolio.usc.edu/ctcs505/mulveyVisualPleasureNarrativeCinema .pdf.

30. For a thoughtful, accessible elaboration on this dynamic, see Susan J. Douglas, "Girls 'n' Spice: All Things Nice?" in *Mass Politics: The Politics of Popular Culture*, ed. Daniel M. Shea (New York: St. Martin's/Worth, 1999), 45–48.

31. For examples of work that highlights the gaps in second wave feminist thought, see, for instance, Patricia Hill Collins, "The Social Construction of Black

Feminist Thought," *Signs* 14, no. 4 (1989): 745–773; Patricia Hill Collins, *Black Feminist Thought: Knowledge, Consciousness, and the Politics of Empowerment* (New York: Routledge, 1999); Alma M. Garcia, ed., *Chicana Feminist Thought: The Basic Historical Writings* (New York: Routledge, 1997).

32. For example, black women are disproportionately underrepresented in corporate America. A recent study found that black women in that context face more criticism than do white women or black men: what the authors refer to as "double jeopardy." Ashleigh Shelby Rosette and Robert W. Livingston, "Failure Is Not an Option for Black Women: Effects of Organizational Performance on Leaders with Single Versus Dual-Subordinate Identities," *Journal of Experimental Social Psychology* 48, no. 5 (2012): 1162–1167.

33. American Association of University Women, "The Simple Truth About the Gender Pay Gap (Fall 2016)," http://www.aauw.org/research/the-simple-truth-about -the-gender-pay-gap/; Frank Bass and Jennifer Oldham, "Wage Gap for U.S. Women Endures Even as Jobs Increase," Bloomberg Businessweek, October 25, 2012, http:// www.businessweek.com/news/2012-10-25/wage-gap-for-u-dot-s-dot-women -endures-even-as-jobs-increase; Maloney and Schumer, "Women and the Economy 2010."

34. Susan Thistle, *From Marriage to the Market: The Transformation of Women's Lives and Work* (Berkeley: University of California Press, 2006).

35. Sylvia Allegretto and Devon Lynch, "The Composition of the Unemployed and Long-Term Unemployed in Tough Labor Markets," *Monthly Labor Review*, October 2010, http://www.bls.gov/opub/mlr/2010/10/art1full.pdf; US Bureau of Labor Statistics, "Civilian Labor Force Participation Rate by Age, Gender, Race, and Ethnicity," United States Department of Labor, December 8, 2015, http://www.bls .gov/emp/ep_table_303.htm.

36. Elizabeth Ty Wilde, Lily Batchelder, and David T. Ellwood, "The Mommy Track Divides: The Impact of Childbearing on Wages of Women of Differing Skill Levels," National Bureau of Economic Research Working Paper no. 16582, December 2010, http://www.nber.org/papers/w16582; Rebecca Korzec, "Working on the 'Mommy-Track': Motherhood and Women Lawyers," *Hastings Women's Law Journal* 8 (1997): 117–126; Mary C. Noonan and Mary E. Corcoran, "The Mommy Track and Partnership: Temporary Delay or Dead End?" *Annals of the American Academy of Political and Social Science* 596, no. 1 (2004): 130–150; E. Jeffrey Hill et al., "Beyond the Mommy Track: The Influence of New-Concept Part-Time Work for Professional Women on Work and Family," *Journal of Family and Economic Issues* 25, no. 1 (2004): 121–136; Paula England, "Gender Inequality in Labor Markets: The Role of Motherhood and Segregation," *Social Politics* 12, no. 2 (2005): 264–288.

37. Paternity leave is common in many European democracies, but not in the United States. Lisa Belkin, "Should Fathers Get Paid Paternity Leave?" *New York Times*, January 28, 2010, http://parenting.blogs.nytimes.com/2010/01/28/paid -paternity-leave-in-britain/; Jens Hansegard, "For Paternity Leave, Sweden Asks If Two Months Is Enough," *Wall Street Journal*, July 31, 2012, http://online.wsj.com /article/SB10000872396390444226904577561100020336384.html. Although the Family and Medical Leave Act of 1993 allows fathers to take up to twelve weeks away from work without being fired, that time is unpaid, and few families can afford to take

advantage of it. "Leave Benefits: Family & Medical Leave Act," US Department of Labor, http://www.dol.gov/dol/topic/benefits-leave/fmla.htm#.ULjwauOe8f8.

38. In 2013, Facebook chief operating officer Sheryl Sandberg wrote a best-selling book designed to encourage women and men to think differently about the oft repeated rallying cry of the second-wave feminist movement that women can "have it all" (at the office and at home). In *Lean In*, Sandberg describes the current state of women in corporate America and encourages both women and men to work together in both settings for greater gender equity.

39. See Kim V. L. England, "Suburban Pink Collar Ghettos: The Spatial Entrapment of Women?" *Annals of the Association of American Geographers* 83, no. 2 (2005): 225–242; Joseph H. Michalski, "Resource Structuralism and Gender Economic Inequality," *Michigan Sociological Review* 18 (2004): 23–63; England, "Gender Inequality in Labor Markets"; Tony Tam, "Sex Segregation and Occupational Gender Inequality in the United States: Devaluation or Specialized Training?" *American Journal of Sociology* 102, no. 6 (1997): 1652–1692.

40. U.S. Bureau of Labor Statistics, "Characteristics of Minimum Wage Workers, 2015," April 2016, http://www.bls.gov/opub/reports/minimum-wage/2015/pdf/home.pdf.

41. Olga Alonso-Villar and Coral del Rio Otero, "The Occupational Segregation of Black Women in the United States: A Look at Its Evolution from 1940 to 2010," ECINEQ, Society for the Study of Economic Inequality, Working Paper 304, 2015, http://econpapers.repec.org/paper/inqinqwps/ecineq2013-304.htm.

42. Ben Casselman, "Why Women Are No Longer Catching Up to Men on Pay," FiveThirtyEight.com, August 19, 2016, http://fivethirtyeight.com/features/why-women-are-no-longer-catching-up-to-men-on-pay/.

43. Johanna Brenner, "Feminist Political Discourses: Radical Versus Liberal Approaches to the Feminization of Poverty and Comparable Worth," *Gender & Society* 1, no. 4 (1987): 447–465; Martha E. Gimenez, "The Feminization of Poverty: Myth or Reality?" *Critical Sociology* 25, no. 2–3 (1999): 336–351.

44. Gene Falk, "Temporary Assistance for Needy Families (TANF): Size and Characteristics of the Cash Assistance Caseload," Congressional Research Service, January 29, 2016, https://fas.org/sgp/crs/misc/R43187.pdf.

45. Keiser Family Foundation, "Medicaid Enrollment by Gender: FY 2011," http://kff.org/medicaid/state-indicator/medicaid-enrollment-by-gender/?currentTimeframe=0.

46. National Women's Law Center, "National Snapshot: Poverty Among Women & Families, 2015," September 2016, https://nwlc.org/wp-content/uploads/2016/09/Poverty-Snapshot-Factsheet-2016.pdf.

47. Ibid.

48. Richard R. Peterson, *Women, Work, and Divorce* (Albany: State University of New York Press, 1989); Teresa A. Mauldin, "Economic Consequences of Divorce or Separation Among Women in Poverty," *Journal of Divorce and Remarriage* 14, no. 3–4 (1991): 163–178; James B. McLindon, "Separate but Unequal: The Economic Disaster of Divorce for Women and Children," *Family Law Quarterly* 21 (1987–1988): 351–409; Terry J. Arendell, "Women and the Economics of Divorce in the Contemporary United States," *Signs* 13, no. 1 (1987): 121–135.

49. National Women's Law Center, "National Snapshot: Poverty Among Women and Families, 2015."

50. US Social Security Administration, *Fast Facts & Figures About Social Security, 2015*, September 2015, 20, https://www.ssa.gov/policy/docs/chartbooks/fast_facts /2015/fast_facts15.pdf.

51. Cathleen D. Zick and Ken Smith, "Patterns of Economic Change Surrounding the Death of a Spouse," *Journal of Gerontology: Social Sciences* 46, no. 6 (1991): 310–320. For a concise review of the literature on this topic, see Youngae Lee and Jinkook Lee, "The Poverty of Widows: How Do They Become the Poor?" Ohio State University, http://paa2006.princeton.edu/papers/61592.

52. MacLeod, Darrell Montero, and Alan Speer, "America's Changing Attitudes Toward Welfare and Welfare Recipients, 1938–1995, *Journal of Sociology & Social Welfare* 26 no. 2 (1999): 175–186; "83% Favor Work Requirement for Welfare Recipients," Rasmussen Reports, July 18, 2012, http://www.rasmussen reports.com/public_content/business/jobs_employment/july_2012/83_favor_work _requirement_for_welfare_recipients.

53. See Beth Reingold and Adrienne R. Smith, "Welfare Policymaking and Intersections of Race, Ethnicity, and Gender in U.S. State Legislatures," *American Journal of Political Science* 56, no. 1 (2012): 131–147.

54. Valentina Zarya, "The Percentage of Female CEOs in the Fortune 500 Drops to 4%, Fortune, June 6, 2016, http://fortune.com/2016/06/06/women-ceos-fortune -500-2016/.

55. For example, see Christopher F. Karpowitz, Tali Mendelberg, and Lee Shaker, "Gender Inequality in Deliberative Participation," *American Political Science Review* 106, no. 3 (2012): 533–547; and Katty Kay and Claire Shipman, "The Confidence Gap," *Atlantic*, May 2014, http://www.theatlantic.com/magazine/archive/2014/05 /the-confidence-gap/359815/.

56. Margaret Wente, "Gender Parity Trumps Excellence in Science?"*(Toronto) Globe and Mail*, November 25, 2012, http://www.theglobeandmail.com/commentary /gender-parity-trumps-excellence-in-science/article5610999/. Consider, too, this recent report that pinpoints the college-level STEM gender gap to one course: Calculus I. The study showed that men and women lost confidence in their math skills equally in that course, but women were far more likely to be discouraged as a result. Jessica Ellis, Bailey K. Fosdick, and Chris Rasmussen, "Women 1.5 Times More Likely to Leave STEM Pipeline After Calculus Compared to Men: Lack of Mathematical Confidence a Potential Culprit," *PLOS One*, July 13, 2016, http://journals.plos.org /plosone/article?id=10.1371%2Fjournal.pone.0157447.

57. Andrea Pitzer, "U.S. Eugenics Legacy: Ruling on Buck Sterilization Still Stands," *USA Today*, June 24, 2009, http://usatoday30.usatoday.com/news/health/2009-06 -23-eugenics-carrie-buck_N.htm.

58. Martha Waggoner, "No Money for Forced Sterilization Victims in North Carolina," Huffington Post, June 20, 2012, http://www.huffingtonpost.com/2012 /06/27/no-money-for-forced-steri_n_1630417.html.

59. Melissa Schettini Kearney and Phillip B. Levine, "Why Is the Teen Birth Rate in the United States So High and Why Does It Matter?" National Bureau of Economic

Research Working Paper no. 17965, March 2012, http://www.nber.org/papers /w17965.

60. Napp Nazworth, "Wheaton College, Catholic University Jointly Sue over Birth Control Mandate," *Christian Post*, July 18, 2012, http://www.christianpost.com/news /wheaton-college-catholic-university-jointly-sue-over-birth-control-mandate-78491/.

61. At least in the Catholic case, there is ostensibly a double standard, as drugs such as Viagra that help men with impotence are considered acceptable for health insurers to provide. Church leaders note that such medicines, unlike contraceptives, do not violate Church doctrine because they can be used for procreation. Julie Rovner, "Why Catholic Groups' Health Plans Say No to Contraceptives, Yes to Viagra," National Public Radio, February 13, 2012, http://www.npr.org/blogs/health/2012/02/13/146822713/why -catholic-groups-health-plans-say-no-to-contraceptives-yes-to-viagra.

62. Megan Kelly Reid, "A Disaster on Top of a Disaster: How Gender, Race, and Class Shaped the Housing Experiences of Displaced Hurricane Katrina Survivors" (PhD diss., University of Texas, 2011), 58–59, http://repositories.lib.utexas.edu /bitstream/handle/2152/ETD-UT-2011-05-2926/REID-DISSERTATION.pdf.

63. Ibid., 51.

64. For a comprehensive overview of the statistics in this area, see Christianne Corbett, Catherine Hill, and Andresse St. Rose, *Where the Girls Are: The Facts About Gender Equity in Education* (Washington, DC: American Association of University Women, 2008), http://www.aauw.org/research/where-the-girls-are. For a thorough review of the scholarly literature, see Claudia Buchmann, Thomas A. DiPrete, and Anne McDaniel, "Gender Inequalities in Education," *Annual Review of Sociology* 34 (2008): 319–337. For a discussion of differentials with respect to science, technology, and mathematics, see Roland G. Fryer Jr. and Steven D. Levitt, "An Empirical Analysis of the Gender Gap in Mathematics," National Bureau of Economic Research Working Paper no. 15430, October 2009, http://www.nber.org /papers/w15430; Glenn Ellison and Ashley Swanson, "The Gender Gap in Secondary School Mathematics at High Achievement Levels: Evidence from the American Mathematics Competitions," National Bureau of Economic Research Working Paper no. 15238, August 2009; Ismael Ramos and Julia Lambating, "Risk Taking: Gender Differences and Educational Opportunity," *School Science and Mathematics* 96 no. 2 (1996): 94–98, http://www.nber.org/papers/w15238; Gijsbert Stoet and David C. Geary, "Can Stereotype Threat Explain the Gender Gap in Mathematics Performance and Achievement?" *Review of General Psychology* 16, no. 1 (2012): 93–102.

65. The biological element of this is not straightforward. The suggestion that biology is at work is not necessarily sexist. Such evidence of intrinsic skills does not suggest that one sex is "smarter" than the other but rather that there may be developmental differences that manifest in abilities being formed at different rates, particularly at very young ages. The way that we react to those tendencies can create environmental effects that will be important as children grow and develop cognitively. See Buchmann, DiPrete, and McDaniel, "Gender Inequalities in Education," 323–324, for a review.

66. Tamar Lewin, "Boys Are No Match for Girls in Completing High School," *New York Times*, April 19, 2006, http://www.nytimes.com/2006/04/19/education

/19graduation.html. However, as noted in Chapter 4, there are significant racial gaps in high school graduation rates.

67. Mark Hugo Lopez and Ana Gonzalez-Barrerra, "Women's College Enrollment Gains Leave Men Behind," Pew Research Center, March 6, 2014, http:// www.pewresearch.org/fact-tank/2014/03/06/womens-college-enrollment-gains -leave-men-behind/.

68. Buchmann, DiPrete, and McDaniel, "Gender Inequalities in Education."

69. Martha Groves, "SAT's Gender Gap Widening," *Los Angeles Times*, August 29, 2001, http://articles.latimes.com/2001/aug/29/news/mn-39684; American Physical Society, "Fighting the Gender Gap: Standardized Tests Are Poor Indicators of Ability in Physics," *AJPS News* 5, no. 5 (1996), http://www.aps.org/publications/ apsnews/199607/gender.cfm.

70. College Board, "2015 College-Bound Seniors: Total Group Profile Report," September 30, 2015, https://secure-media.collegeboard.org/digitalServices/pdf/sat /total-group-2015.pdf. This gap has persisted for decades, see Jonathan Wai et al., "Sex Differences in the Right Tail of Cognitive Abilities: A 30 Year Examination," *Intelligence* 38 (2010): 412–423. Recent work suggests that the gap may be attributable partly to test anxiety. See Brenda Hannon, "Test Anxiety and Performance-Avoidance Goals Explain Gender Differences in SAT-V, SAT-M, and Overall SAT Scores," *Personality and Individual Differences* 53, no. 7 (2012): 816–820.

71. For a concise review of this literature, see Akira Miyake et al., "Reducing the Gender Achievement Gap in College Science: A Classroom Study of Values Affirmation," *Science* 330, no. 6008 (2010): 1234–1237. One recent study suggests that there is some inertia related to this trend. Specifically, high-performing students in the sciences were more likely to take more science classes and pursue STEM majors in science classes early in their college careers. See Scott E. Carrell, Marianne E. Page, and James E. West, "Sex and Science: How Professor Gender Perpetuates the Gender Gap," *Quarterly Journal of Economics* 125, no. 3 (2010): 1101–1144.

72. Christianne Corbett and Catherine Hill, *Graduating to a Pay Gap* (Washington, DC: American Association of University Women, 2012), http://www.aauw.org /research/graduating-to-a-pay-gap/.

73. U.S. Census Bureau, "Women Now at the Head of the Class, Lead Men in College Attainment," October 7, 2015, http://blogs.census.gov/2015/10/07/women -now-at-the-head-of-the-class-lead-men-in-college-attainment/?cid=RS23.

74. Hironao Okahana, Keonna Feaster, and Jeff Allum, *Graduate Enrollment and Degrees: 2005 to 2010*, Council of Graduate Schools, September 2016, http://cgsnet .org/ckfinder/userfiles/files/Graduate%20Enrollment%20%20Degrees%20Fall%20 2015%20Final.pdf.

75. Leonard A. Sipes Jr., "Statistics on Women Offenders," Corrections.com, February 6, 2012, http://www.corrections.com/news/article/30166-statistics-on-women -offenders. Sipes bases his analysis on data from the US Bureau of Justice Statistics, http://bj`s.ojp.usdoj.gov/.

76. E. Ann Carson, "Prisoners in 2014," U.S. Department of Justice, Office of Justice Programs, Bureau of Justice Statistics, September 2015, http://www.bjs.gov/content /pub/pdf/p14.pdf.

77. The Sentencing Project, "Fact Sheet: Incarcerated Women and Girls," November 2015, http://www.sentencingproject.org/wp-content/uploads/2016/02/Incarcerated-Women-and-Girls.pdf.

78. Ibid.

79. National Resource Center on Children & Families of the Incarcerated, "Children and Families of the Incarcerated Fact Sheet," Rutgers University, n.d., https://nrccfi.camden.rutgers.edu/files/nrccfi-fact-sheet-2014.pdf.

80. Geneva Brown, "The Wind Cries Mary: The Intersectionality of Race, Gender, and Reentry: Challenges for African-American Women," *Journal of Civil Rights and Economic Development* 24, no. 4 (2010): 625–648. For a historical treatment of African American women in the criminal justice system, see Paula C. Johnson, "At the Intersection of Injustice: Experiences of African American Women in Crime and Sentencing," *Journal of Gender & the Law* 41, no. 1 (1995): 1–76. For an analysis of links between the broader prison industrial complex and race and gender, see Angela Y. Davis and Cassandra Shaylor, "Race, Gender, and the Prison Industrial Complex: California and Beyond," *Meridians* 2, no. 1 (2001): 1–25, http://www.jstor.org/stable/pdfplus/40338793.pdf. For a discussion of the relationship between motherhood and crime, see Dorothy E. Roberts, "Motherhood and Crime," *Social Text* 42 (1995): 99–123.

81. Quoted in Philip Cohen, "Single Moms Can't Be Scapegoated for the Murder Rate Anymore," *Atlantic*, November 26, 2012, http://www.theatlantic.com/sexes/archive/2012/11/single-moms-cant-be-scapegoated-for-the-murder-rate-anymore/265576/.

82. Ibid.

83. For a discussion of the importance of such factors, see Reuben M. Baron and David A. Kenny, "The Moderator-Mediator Variable Distinction in Social Psychological Research: Conceptual, Strategic, and Statistical Considerations," *Journal of Personality and Social Psychology* 51, no. 6 (1986): 1173–1182.

84. "October 16, 2012 Debate Transcript," Commission on Presidential Debates.

85. For a broad overview, see Ellen Annandale and Kate Hunt, eds., *Gender Inequalities in Health* (Philadelphia: Open University Press, 2000), http://www.mheducation.co.uk/openup/chapters/0335203647.pd.

86. *Roe v. Wade* (1973) 410 US 113, http://www.law.cornell.edu/supct/html/historics/USSC_CR_0410_0113_ZS.html.

87. Erik Eckholm, "Push for 'Personhood' Amendment Represents New Tack in Abortion Fight," *New York Times*, October 25, 2011, http://www.nytimes.com/2011/10/26/us/politics/personhood-amendments-would-ban-nearly-all-abortions.html.

88. Rachel Roth, *Making Women Pay: The Hidden Costs of Fetal Rights* (Ithaca, NY: Cornell University Press, 2003). In 2012 five Republican presidential hopefuls signed pledges to support the notion of fetal personhood. Keith Ashley, "Personhood Republican Presidential Candidate Page," Personhood USA, December 15, 2011, http://www.personhoodusa.com/blog/personhood-republican-presidential-candidate-pledge. A flurry of other legislative and judicial activity has swirled about in the past few years, as well. Laura Bassett, "On International Women's Day, Congress

Debates Measure to Limit Reproductive Rights," Huffington Post, March 8, 2012, http://www.huffingtonpost.com/2012/03/08/international-womens-day-congress -abortion_n_1332143.html; "Three Rulings Against Women's Rights," *New York Times*, July 31, 2012, http://www.nytimes.com/2012/08/01/opinion/three-rulings -against-womens-rights.html.

89. Fluke was nominated for *Time* magazine's Person of the Year Award in 2012. Kate Pickert, "Who Should Be TIME's Person of the Year 2012? The Candidates: Sandra Fluke, *Time*, November 26, 2012, http://www.time.com/time/specials /packages/article/0,28804,2128881_2128882_2129176,00.html. See also Leslie Marshall, "No Fluke that Sandra's on *Time's* List," *U.S. News & World Report*, November 28, 2012, http://www.usnews.com/opinion/blogs/leslie-marshall/2012/11/28/sandra -fluke-belongs-on-times-person-of-the-year-list.

90. Aaron Blake, "Todd Akin, GOP Senate Candidate: 'Legitimate Rape' Rarely Causes Pregnancy," *Washington Post*, August 19, 2012, http://www .washingtonpost.com/blogs/the-fix/wp/2012/08/19/todd-akin-gop-senate-candidate -legitimate-rape-rarely-causes-pregnancy/.

91. Michael R. Crittenden, "Mourdock's Rape Remark Sets Off Firestorm," *Wall Street Journal*, Washington Wire, October 24, 2012, http://blogs.wsj.com /washwire/2012/10/24/mourdocks-rape-remark-touches-off-firestorm/.

92. Valerie A. Earnshaw et al., "Maternal Experiences with Everyday Discrimination and Infant Birth Weight: A Test of Mediators and Moderators Among Young, Urban Women of Color," *Annals of Behavioral Medicine*, August 28, 2012, as reported by Christine Kearney, "Discrimination Can Lead to Low Birth Weight in Babies," Medical News Today, August 27, 2012, http://www.medicalnewstoday.com /articles/249507.php.

93. Jason L. Cummings and Pamela Braboy Jackson, "Race, Gender, and SES Disparities in Self-Assessed Health, 1974–2004," *Research on Aging* 30, no. 2 (2008): 137–168.

94. Laura Cohn, "The U.S. Made Zero Progress in Adding Women to Congress," *Forbes*, November 10, 2016, http://fortune.com/2016/11/10/election-results -women-in-congress/.

95. Jennifer E. Manning, "Membership in the 113th Congress: A Profile," Congressional Research Service, November 24, 2014, http://www.senate.gov/CRSpubs /0b699eff-adc5-43c4-927e-f63045bdce8e.pdf.

96. Karpowitz, Mendelberg, and Shaker, "Gender Inequality in Deliberative Participation"; see also Tali Mendelberg and Christopher F. Karpowitz, "More Women, but Not Nearly Enough," *New York Times*, November 8, 2012, http://campaignstops .blogs.nytimes.com/2012/11/08/more-women-but-not-nearly-enough/.

97. Patricia Scott Schroeder, "Women's Leadership: Perspectives from a Recovering Politician," in *The Difference "Difference" Makes: Women and Leadership*, ed. Deborah L. Rhode (Stanford, CA: Stanford University Press, 2003), 85.

98. "ERA: A Brief Overview," EqualRightsAmendment.org, http://www .equalrightsamendment.org/overview.htm.

99. "In the States," The Equal Rights Amendment: Unfinished Business for the Construction, http://www.equalrightsamendment.org/states.htm.

Chapter 9: Affirmative Action

1. John David Skrentny, *The Ironies of Affirmative Action: Politics, Culture, and Justice in America* (Chicago: University of Chicago Press, 1996).

2. Terry H. Anderson, *The Pursuit of Fairness: A History of Affirmative Action* (New York: Oxford University Press, 2004); Anderson, "The Strange Career of Affirmative Action," *South Central Review* 22, no. 2 (2005): 110–129; Carl E. Brody, "A Historical Review of Affirmative Action and the Interpretation of Its Legislative Intent by the Supreme Court," *Akron Law Review* 29 (1996): 291–337; Ira Katznelson, *When Affirmative Action Was White: An Untold History of Racial Inequality in Twentieth-Century America* (New York: Norton, 2005).

3. Brody, "Historical Review of Affirmative Action."

4. James W. Button and Barbara A. Rienzo, "The Impact of Affirmative Action: Black Employment in Six Southern Cities," *Social Science Quarterly* 84, no. 1 (2003): 1–14, as cited in Faye J. Crosby, Aarti Iyer, and Sirinda Sincharoen, "Understanding Affirmative Action," *Annual Review of Psychology* 57 (2006): 585–611.

5. For an in-depth study of affirmative action in higher education admission, see William Bowen and Derek Bok, *The Shape of the River: Long-Term Consequences of Considering Race in College and University Admissions* (Princeton: Princeton University Press, 2000).

6. Steven N. Durlauf, "Affirmative Action, Meritocracy, and Efficiency," *Politics, Philosophy, and Economics* 7, no. 2 (2008): 131–158; H. Roy Kaplan, "Racial Inequality and 'Meritocracy': A Closer Look," *Racism Review*, April 22, 2011, http://www.racismreview.com/blog/2011/04/22/racial-inequality-and-meritocracy-a-closer-look/.

7. 438 US 265, http://www.law.cornell.edu/supct/html/historics/USSC_CR_0438_0265_ZS.html.

8. US Commission on Civil Rights, "The Commission, Affirmative Action, and Current Challenges Facing Equal Opportunity in Education," March 2003, http://www.usccr.gov/aaction/ccraa.htm, n7.

9. 539 US 244, http://www.law.cornell.edu/supct/html/02-516.ZS.html.

10. 539 US 306, http://www.law.cornell.edu/supct/html/02-241.ZS.html.

11. The scale used for ranking was 150 points; a score of 100 was needed to guarantee admission. Twelve points were awarded to applicants who had a perfect score on the Scholastic Aptitude Test (SAT), three points for an outstanding essay, and twenty points for being a scholarship athlete. A perfect grade point average was worth eighty points. Walter E. Williams, "Affirmative Action or Racism," George Mason University, January 27, 2003, http://econfaculty.gmu.edu/wew/articles/03/aa.html.

12. Meredith Kolodner, "College Degree Gap Grows Wider Between Whites, Blacks and Latinos," The Hechinger Report, January 7, 2016, http://hechingerreport.org/25368-2/.

13. 570 US (2013), https://www.supremecourt.gov/opinions/12pdf/11-345_l5gm.pdf.

14. "New York, 13 Other States Back Affirmative Action Policy," *(Memphis) Commercial Appeal*, August 14, 2012, http://nydailyrecord.com/2012/08/14/ny-13-other-states-back-affirmative-action-policy/.

15. Richard Sander and Stuart Taylor Jr., "Why the Court Wants to Try Again," *Washington Post*, September 30, 2012, http://www.washingtonpost.com/opinions /supreme-court-wants-another-shot-at-affirmative-action/2012/09/30/82cd260 e-0b28-11e2-bb5e-492c0d30bff6_story.html.

16. 579 US (2016) https://www.supremecourt.gov/opinions/15pdf/14-981 _4g15.pdf.

17. In the wake of *Fisher*, some affirmative action advocates have shifted their attention to socioeconomic status and away from race as a direct consideration. Bill Keller, "Affirmative Reaction," *New York Times*, June 9, 2013, http://www.nytimes .com/2013/06/10/opinion/keller-affirmative-reaction.html. It is important to keep in mind, though, that considering income would have a different result than considering wealth. Using zip codes might achieve the desired result (given the robust economic and racial segregation in the United States) without violating constitutional principles relating to white students' civil rights. David Leonhardt, "The Liberals Against Affirmative Action," *New York Times*, March 9, 2013, http://www.nytimes .com/2013/03/10/sunday-review/the-liberals-against-affirmative-action.html.

18. Sam Barr, "Weighing In: Class-Based Affirmative Action Good, but Arguments Against Race-Based Affirmative Action Still Bad," *Harvard Political Review*, December 11, 2010, http://hpronline.org/hprgument/weighing-in-class-based -affirmative-action-good-but-arguments-against-race-based-affirmative-action-still -bad/.

19. Bowen and Bok, *Shape of the River*, chap. 2.

20. Faye J. Crosby et al., "Affirmative Action: Psychological Data and the Policy Debates," *American Psychologist* 58, no. 2 (2003): 93–115.

21. Barbara F. Reskin, *The Realities of Affirmative Action in Employment* (Washington, DC: American Sociological Association, 1998).

22. The full text of the bill as amended is available at http://www.eeoc.gov/laws /statutes/titlevii.cfm.

23. In this case, the Court ruled that ostensibly race-neutral policies (such as an IQ test and the requirement of holding a high school diploma at a time when far fewer African Americans than whites did so) that are not directly related to the job to be performed are unconstitutional if they cause a "disparate impact" on a protected class of citizens, according to Title VII of the Civil Rights Act of 1964. 401 US 424, http:// www.law.cornell.edu/supct/html/historics/USSC_CR_0401_0424_ZO.html.

24. In this case, twenty firefighters (nineteen of whom were white) who had passed a test for promotion sued the city of New Haven, Connecticut, for invalidating the results of the test because no African Americans qualified for promotion. The city claimed that it did so out of fear of a lawsuit by the black firefighters. The Court ruled, in a 5–4 decision, that the city violated Title VII of the Civil Rights Act of 1964 by denying promotions to the twenty firefighters who earned them by passing the test. 557 US. Available at https://www.law.cornell.edu/supct/cert/07-1428.

25. Crosby et al., "Affirmative Action," 94–95.

26. But see the recent final rule on affirmatively furthering fair housing from the U.S. Department of Housing and Urban Development, July 15, 2016, https://www .gpo.gov/fdsys/pkg/FR-2015-07-16/pdf/2015-17032.pdf.

27. National Public Radio, *Tell Me More*, "End of Fannie Mae, Freddie Mac Will Affect Minorities," February 15, 2011, http://www.npr.org/2011/02/15/133777142/End -Of-Fannie-Mae-Freddie-Mac-Will-Affect-Minorities.

28. PollingReport.com, "Race and Ethnicity," 2011, http://www.pollingreport.com /race.htm.

29. Frank Newport, "Most in U.S. Oppose Colleges Considering Race in Admissions," Gallup, July 8, 2016, http://www.gallup.com/poll/193508/oppose -colleges-considering-race-admissions.aspx.

30. David C. Wilson et al., "Affirmative Action Programs for Women and Minorities: Expressed Support Affected by Question Order," *Public Opinion Quarterly* 72, no. 3 (2008): 514–522.

31. Richard J. Hill, "Minorities, Women, and Institutional Change: Some Administrative Concerns," *Sociological Perspectives* 26, no. 1 (1983): 17–28; Tim Wise, "Is Sisterhood Conditional? White Women and the Rollback of Affirmative Action," *NWSA Journal* 10, no. 3 (1998): 1–26.

32. Lawrence Bobo, "Race, Interests, and Beliefs about Affirmative Action," *American Behavioral Scientist* 41, no. 7 (1998): 985–1003; David A. Kravitz and Judith Platania, "Attitudes and Beliefs About Affirmative Action: Effects of Target and of Respondent Sex and Ethnicity," *Journal of Applied Psychology* 78, no. 6 (1993): 928–938; Linda J. Sax and Marisol Arredondo, "Student Attitudes Toward Affirmative Action in College Admissions," *Research in Higher Education* 40, no. 4 (1999): 439–459; but see Dawn Michelle Baunach, "Attitudes Toward Gender-Based Affirmative Action," *Sociological Focus* 35, no. 4 (2002): 345–362.

33. Baunach, "Attitudes Toward Gender-Based Affirmative Action"; Sax and Arredond, "Student Attitudes Toward Affirmative Action in College Admissions"; Dara Z. Strolovitch, "Playing Favorites: Public Attitudes Toward Race-and Gender-Targeted Anti-discrimination Policy," *NWSA Journal* 10, no. 3 (1998): 27–53.

34. James R. Kluegel and Eliot R. Smith, "Affirmative Action Attitudes: Effects of Self-Interest, Racial Affect, and Stratification Beliefs on Whites' Views," *Social Forces* 61, no. 3 (1983): 797–824; Amy C. Steinbugler, Julie E. Press, and Janice Johnson Dias, "Gender, Race, and Affirmative Action: Operationalizing Intersectionality in Survey Research," *Gender & Society* 20, no. 6 (2006): 805–825; Steven A. Tuch and Michael Hughes, "Whites' Racial Policy Attitudes in the Twenty-First Century: The Continuing Significance of Racial Resentment," *Annals of the American Academy of Political and Social Science* 634 (2011): 134–152. Other demographic characteristics have also been found to affect attitudes about affirmative action. For instance, one study found that working women who have daughters are more likely to support affirmative action programs for women than do those who do not, though there was no such effect for men with daughters. Anastasia H. Prokos, Chardie L. Baird, and Jennifer Reid Keene, "Attitudes About Affirmative Action for Women: The Role of Children in Shaping Parents' Interests," *Sex Roles* 62 (2010): 347–360.

35. "Proposition 209: Text of Proposed Law," 1996, http://vigarchive.sos .ca.gov/1996/general/pamphlet/209text.htm.

36. Naomi Zevloff, "After Colorado Loss, Ward Connerly May Pull the Plug on Affirmative-Action Bans," *Colorado Independent*, November 7, 2008, http://

coloradoindependent.com/14617/ward-connerly-may-pull-the-plug. For an overview of plebiscite measures to eliminate affirmative action, see Jessica Larson and Stephen Menendian, "Anti-Affirmative Action Ballot Initiatives," Kirwan Institute for the Study of Race and Ethnicity, Ohio State University, 2008, http://www.kirwaninstitute. osu.edu/reports/2008/12_2008_AntiAffirmativeActionBallotInitiatives.pdf.

37. Justin Miller, "Ballot Wording Called Fair," *Michigan Daily*, January 9, 2006, http://www.michigandaily.com/content/ballot-wording-called-fair.

38. In *Gratz* v. *Bollinger* (the undergraduate program case), Jennifer Gratz and Patrick Hamacher brought suit; in *Grutter* v. *Bollinger* (the law school program case), Barbara Grutter brought suit. All three litigants are white, and two of the three (at least one in each case) are female.

39. Legal Information Institute, "Strict Scrutiny," 2010, http://www.law.cornell .edu/wex/strict_scrutiny.

40. For this reason, the Court's upholding of the University of Michigan Law School's policy is particularly noteworthy in *Grutter*.

41. Reverend Jackson has been a vocal supporter of affirmative action policies. He drafted a statement after attending oral arguments for the University of Michigan cases at the US Supreme Court in 2003, which can be read here: http://www .inmotionmagazine.com/opin/supreme.html.

42. Bowen and Bok, *Shape of the River*.

43. See, for instance, Cornel West, *Race Matters* (New York: Vintage, 1993).

44. James P. Sterba, *Affirmative Action for the Future* (Ithaca, NY: Cornell University Press, 2009).

Conclusion: The Space Between Power and Powerlessness

1. Steve Wyche, "Colin Kaepernick Explains Why He Sat During National Anthem," NFL.com, August 27, 2016, http://www.nfl.com/news/story/0ap3000000691077 /article/colin-kaepernick-explains-why-he-sat-during-national-anthem.

2. Josh Levin, "Colin Kaepernick's Protest Is Working," Slate.com, September 12, 2016, http://www.slate.com/articles/sports/sports_nut/2016/09/colin_kaepernick_s _protest_is_working.html.

3. Ibid.

4. For some examples of vulgar responses, see Nancy Armour, "How National Anthem Protests Bring Out Worst in People," *USA Today*, September 25, 2016, http://www.usatoday.com/story/sports/columnist/nancy-armour/2016/09/25/colin -kaepernick-anthem-protests-backlash-social-media-emails/91076216/.

5. Des Bieler, "Colin Kaepernick Responds to Justice Ruth Bader Ginsburg's Criticism of Anthem Protests," *Washington Post*, October 12, 2016, https://www .washingtonpost.com/news/early-lead/wp/2016/10/12/colin-kaepernick-responds -to-justice-ruth-bader-ginsburgs-criticism-of-anthem-protests/?utm_term =.d86f55be7c48.

6. Ariane de Vogue, "Ruth Bader Ginsburg Apologizes to Colin Kaepernick After Criticizing Anthem Protest," CNN.com, October 14, 2016, http://www.cnn .com/2016/10/14/politics/ruth-bader-ginsburg-apologizes-colin-kaepernick/.

7. George A. Lakoff, *The Political Mind: A Cognitive Scientist's Guide to Your Brain and Its Politics* (New York: Penguin, 2009); Drew Westen, *The Political Brain: The Role of Emotion in Deciding the Fate of the Nation* (New York: Public Affairs, 2007).

8. Dara Z. Strolovitch, "A More Level Playing Field or a New Mobilization of Bias? Interest Groups and Advocacy for the Disadvantaged," in *Interest Group Politics*, ed. Allan J. Cigler and Burdett A. Loomis, 7th ed. (Washington, DC: CQ Press, 2007), 101.

9. Andrew Darnton and Martin Kirk, *Finding Frames: New Ways to Engage the UK Public in Global Poverty*, UK Department for International Development, January 2011, http://www.findingframes.org/.

10. Child Labor Public Education Project, "Child Labor in U.S. History," http://www.continuetolearn.uiowa.edu/laborctr/child_labor/about/us_history.html.

11. Armstrong Williams, "Raising Minimum Wage Would Hurt U.S. Economy," July 14, 2006, http://archive.newsmax.com/archives/articles/2006/7/13/124958.shtml.

Index

boarding schools affecting Gender Roles?